Y0-BTM-021

Introduction to Agricultural Economic Analysis

INTRODUCTION TO

C. E. Bishop

Reynolds Professor of Agricultural Economics
North Carolina State College

W. D. Toussaint

Associate Professor of Agricultural Economics
North Carolina State College

Agricultural
Economic
Analysis

NEW YORK · JOHN WILEY & SONS, INC.
London · Chapman & Hall, Limited

To Dot and Eunice

Preface

This book provides an elementary statement of some of the analytical tools used in agricultural economics. The object of the book is to provide a theoretical foundation for use in analysis of agricultural economics problems. Emphasis is placed upon recognition of problems and solving them through the application of economic logic. Economic theory is presented in an elementary but rigorous form, and illustrations are developed to show the use of theoretical concepts in solving empirical problems. Examples have been drawn from studies of a wide range of problems and from many geographical areas. Individuals using the text will find it advantageous to draw upon local problems for further examples.

This book is written primarily for use by sophomores and juniors to equip them with principles used in more advanced courses. We believe that students can obtain greater benefits from studies in farm management, land economics, marketing, and other advanced courses if they have a good understanding of analytical principles prior to taking these courses. Also, the analytical principles developed in this book should be very useful as background material for courses in other sciences, such as agronomy, horticulture, animal industry, and poultry.

Many elementary texts in agricultural economics have attempted to survey the whole of economics as applied to agriculture. This book emphasizes those elements of economics directly affecting agriculture and the interrelationships between agriculture and the rest of the economy. Such important topics as money and banking and national income analysis are well treated in other elementary texts.

This book is divided into four sections. The first section emphasizes the reasons for economic organization, the functions of an economic system and the nature of decision-making in the operation of an economy. The significance of agriculture as a part of the economy of the United States also is considered.

The second section is concerned primarily with problems involved in making production decisions. Emphasis is placed upon the firm as a producing unit and the problems faced by producers. Principles of production economics pertaining to farms and to marketing firms are developed in the first part of this section. Production theory is then applied to particular problems. The theoretical principles are universal in application; results of the application, however, differ from one setting to another. The last part of the second section is concerned with aggregative supply of farm products. In this section, decisions of individual producing units are studied to determine their aggregate effects.

Section three is concerned with the forces affecting the demand for farm products. Emphasis is placed upon the principles of consumer behavior. The effects of changes in income and price upon consumption are discussed. The characteristics of demand for particular farm commodities and the importance of foreign trade to agriculture are also emphasized.

Section four is concerned with changes in economic conditions facing farmers over time. Emphasis is placed upon price movements and the factors contributing to these movements. Changes in the supply of agricultural commodities are analyzed from the standpoint of technological change in agricultural production. Changes in demand are studied from the standpoint of changes in numbers and composition of the population and from the growth and distribution of incomes among economic sectors.

The authors are indebted to their colleagues and students at North Carolina State College for numerous suggestions for improving the organization and content of this book. We are grateful to Miss Ruth Good for her help in proofing and indexing. The permission of authors of numerous publications to draw upon their research for examples used is greatly appreciated.

C. E. Bishop
W. D. Toussaint

Raleigh, N. C.
July, 1958

Contents

Part I   Introduction

1   ORGANIZATION IS NECESSARY TO PERFORM THE BASIC ECONOMIC
FUNCTIONS   3

The Role of Prices in a Free Enterprise Economic System   5

    Determining what to produce 5
    Organizing production 6
    Distributing the proceeds from the sale of products 8
    Providing for maintenance and progress 8
    Restricting consumption to the stock 9

The Modified Role of Prices in the United States Economy   10

2   AGRICULTURE IS AN INTEGRAL PART OF THE ECONOMY   12

Current Importance of Agriculture   12

Firms in Agriculture and Other Industries   15

3   THE FIRM IS A DECISION-MAKING UNIT   20

Producer Decisions   21

    What to produce 21
    What method of production to use 22
    How much to produce 22
    When to buy and sell 22
    Where to buy and sell 23

A Framework for Decision-Making   23

    The decision-maker 23
    Objectives of decisions 24
    The conditions facing decision-makers 25
    The "measuring stick" 26

Part II   Production and Supply

4 PRODUCT VARIES ACCORDING TO THE INPUTS USED   29

The Concept of a Production Function   30
Types of Production Functions   33
The Law of Diminishing Returns   35
Total, Average, and Marginal Product   36
Relationships between Total, Average, and Marginal Products   38
Three Regions of a Production Function   39
Examples of Irrational Production in Agriculture   41
Differences in Technology   42

5 A PRODUCER CHOOSES AMONG LEVELS OF PRODUCTION   44
Revenue Related to Production   44
Effects of Price Changes   48
   Linear production function 48
   Diminishing returns 49
   Inputs which must be applied in discrete units 50
Demand Curve for Inputs   51
Effects of Changes in Technology   51

6 SOME APPLICATIONS OF INPUT-OUTPUT ANALYSIS   53
Nitrogen Fertilization of Corn   53
Nitrogen Fertilization of Sudan Grass   55
Nitrogen Application for Fescue Seed   57
Feeding Dairy Cattle for Milk Production   58
Feeding for Egg Production   60
Feeding Broilers   62
Feeding Hogs for Pork   64

7 COST VARIES WITH PRODUCTION   68
Opportunity Return   69
Variable Cost and Fixed Cost   70
The Total Cost Function   71
Average and Marginal Cost   72
   Average fixed cost 73
   Average variable cost 75
   Average total cost 75
   Marginal cost 75
Net Revenue Is Related to Output   76
Effects of Price Changes   78
The Long-Run and Short-Run Time Periods   79

Contents

8   SOME APPLICATIONS OF COST FUNCTIONS IN PRODUCTION AND
    PROCESSING OF AGRICULTURAL PRODUCTS   82

    On-Farm Grain Drying and Storage   82

    Fryer Processing Plants   84

    Cotton Mechanization   86

    Peach Hydrocooling   88

9   COST CAN BE REDUCED BY CHANGING INPUTS   90

    Inputs Combine in Different Ways   93
        Fixed proportions 93
        Constant rate of substitution 94
        Varying rate of substitution 95

    Least-Cost Combination of Inputs   95

    Choosing the Optimum Level of Output   98

    Changes in Input Prices Affect Minimum Cost Combination of Inputs   98

    More Than Two Variable Inputs   99

10 SOME APPLICATIONS OF MINIMUM COST PRODUCTION   101

    Substitution of Grains in Feeding Beef   101

    Feeding Hay and Grain to Dairy Cows   103

    Producing Choice Beef from Hay and Grain   105

    Feeding Protein Supplement and Corn to Hogs   106

    Nitrogen and Phosphoric Acid Fertilization of Cotton   109

11 CHOICE OF PRODUCTS AFFECTS NET REVENUE   112

    Production Possibilities   113
        Joint products 115
        Competitive products 116
        Complementary products 118
        Supplementary products 120

    Choosing the Optimum Product Combination   121

    Optimum Combinations of Many Products   123

    Specialization and Diversification   125

    Type-of-Farming Areas   126

12 FARM ORGANIZATION AFFECTS FARM INCOME   129

    Enterprise Budgets   129

    Enterprise Combination   133

13 TIME AND UNCERTAINTY ARE IMPORTANT IN PRODUCTION DE-
    CISIONS   141

    Present Value of Future Income   142

    Future Value of Current Investment   143

    Valuation of an Input   145

    Depreciation   146

    Conservation of Resources   147

Major Types of Imperfect Knowledge   147
  Yield uncertainty 148
  Imperfect knowledge regarding conditions in product and input
    markets 148

Farmers Can Reduce Risk by Altering Production Plans   149
  Insurance 149
  Diversification 149
  Contract 150
  Flexibility 151
  Liquidity 152

14 LAND TENURE ARRANGEMENTS AFFECT USE OF INPUTS   153

Tenure Classes   154
  Owners 154
  Part-owners 154
  Tenants 155

Effects of Specified Leasing Practices   155
  Fixed rent 157
  Rent as a function of output 158

Length of Tenure and Capital Improvements   161

15 SUPPLY OF INDIVIDUAL FARM PRODUCTS VARIES   163

Changes in Supply from Firms   163

Changes in Total Supply   164

Optimum Output from the Standpoint of the Industry   166

Input Prices May Increase When Production Increases   167

Changes in the Supply of Particular Farm Commodities Over Time   168

Estimates of Supply of Farm Commodities   170

16 AGGREGATE SUPPLY OF FARM PRODUCTS ALSO VARIES   172

Aggregate Agricultural Production Is Highly Stable   173

Reasons for Low Elasticity of Supply of Agricultural Products in the
  Short Run   175

Part III   Consumption and Demand

17 CONSUMER DEMAND IS IMPORTANT TO FARMERS   181

Consumers Have Preferences Among Goods   181

Income and Price Changes Affect Consumption   185

18 MARKET DEMAND FOR FARM PRODUCTS AFFECTS FARM INCOMES   188

Price Elasticity Defined   188

Price Elasticity and Total Revenue   190

Examples of Price Elasticity of Demand   192

Changes in Demand   193

Income Elasticity of Demand   194

Long-Term Changes in per Capita Consumption   197

Contents   xiii

19 INTERNATIONAL TRADE INCREASES THE DEMAND FOR U. S. FARM
    PRODUCTS   199
    The Nature of Trade   199
    Trade Balance   200
    The Gains from Trade   201
    United States Exports and Imports of Major Commodities   205
    Outlook for Exports and Imports   207

20 OUR ECONOMY IS SUBJECT TO LARGE PRICE MOVEMENTS   209
    Long-Term Price Movements   209
    Cycles   210
    Seasonal Price Variation   211
    Other Factors Affecting Price Variation   213
        Grades 214
        Location 214
        Services 216
    Parity Prices   217

Part IV Economic Progress

21 TECHNOLOGICAL IMPROVEMENTS INCREASE FOOD AND FIBER
    SUPPLIES   225
    The Rate of Technological Change Greatly Affects the Rate of Economic
        Progress   225
    Technological Improvements Reduce Per-Unit Costs   226
    Technological Improvement in United States Agriculture   227
    Technological Improvements Have Greatly Increased Productivity per
        Unit of Livestock and Poultry   232
        Egg production 232
        Broiler production 232
        Milk production 234
    Gains from Technological Improvement in Agricultural Production Are
        Divided Between Producers and Consumers   234

22 OUR POPULATION IS CHANGING   237
    Population and Economic Growth   238
    The Demographic Transition   239
    Population Characteristics   243

23 ECONOMIC PROGRESS ALTERS THE LEVEL AND DISTRIBUTION OF
    INCOME   246
    The Concept of Poverty   246
    Measurement of Income   247
    Incomes of Farm and Nonfarm Families   248

The Geography of Low-Income Farm Families   251

Causes of Low-Income Areas in Agriculture   251

Adjustments of Farm Families to Raise Incomes   252

INDEX   255

Part **I**

INTRODUCTION

Organization is necessary to perform the basic economic functions

1

Producers, processors, and consumers of farm products face constantly changing economic conditions. The emphasis of this book is on the agricultural aspects of economics and how changes in economic conditions affect producers, processors, and consumers of agricultural products. Before examining these agricultural aspects in detail, however, we must first understand the workings of the whole economic system.

We recognize that virtually all the goods and services which people consume grow out of the operations of the economic system, and the quantity of these goods and services available for consumption depends upon the efficiency with which this economic system operates. The more efficiently the economy is organized, the greater will be the quantity of goods available for consumption.

In *any* economic system there are five basic functions which must be performed if the economy is to grow and develop. One of the functions of an economic system is to determine what goods and services are to be produced. In the production of goods and services, producers assume that their products will be consumed. To insure consumption of their products, the goods and services produced must be the ones desired with greatest intensity by consumers. This means that some method must be established whereby consumers may inform producers of their preferences concerning the kinds and quantities of goods which they would like to consume, and which they would like to have produced. That is, some method must be established for transmitting the desires of consumers to producers.

Another function of an economic system is to organize the production of goods and services to conform to the wishes of consumers. An economy is confronted with limited resources which can be used in producing goods and services. Since resources are limited, it is necessary to have some method of dividing available resources among producing units in a manner that permits these units to provide those goods and services which are in greatest demand by consumers. Unless the economic system is organized to perform this function efficiently, smaller amounts of the goods and services which are desired by consumers will be produced than would be possible under some other organization. That is, by transferring resources from one use to another, more goods and services could be produced.

A third function which an economic system must perform is to distribute the product. In a complex modern society, most producing units employ resources owned by many people. Incentives are provided resource owners to use their resources in producing those products desired by consumers. If the productive potential of an economy is to be realized, the rewards to owners of resources must be high enough to provide this incentive.

If an economy is to maintain or increase its production over time, it is necessary that provision be made for maintenance and expansion in plant and equipment. This is another function of an economic system. New and additional goods and services cannot be produced unless the economic system is organized in a manner which permits the introduction of these goods and services. Some incentive for research, invention, and innovation must be provided if new and improved goods and services are to be made available for consumption.

The other function of an economic system pertains only to a short time period. At any point in time, the amount of any commodity which is available for consumption is relatively fixed. Obviously, consumption cannot exceed the stock of commodity available. The economic system must be so organized that consumption at any point in time is restricted to the stock of goods and services available for consumption. This is the fifth function of an economic system. It is essentially a rationing function; it is concerned with adjusting consumption to the stock of goods on hand.

The first four functions which were discussed may be viewed as an expression of preferences on the part of consumers as to what they desire to have produced and an adjustment of production to conform to the desires of consumers. The fifth function takes the stock of goods and services as given and adjusts the amount consumed to the stock. All of these functions are necessary for economic progress and a smoothly functioning economy.

The Role of Prices in a Free Enterprise Economic System

The functions of an economic system which were discussed above must be performed by *any* economic system irrespective of its political organization. The manner in which these functions are performed, however, depends upon the way in which the economy is organized. In the remainder of this book we will be concerned with the manner in which a free enterprise exchange economy works. A *free enterprise exchange economy* is one in which the owners of resources, i.e., land, labor, and capital, are free to enter into the production of commodities or to sell the services of their resources to others who engage in the production of commodities for sale. In such an economy, owners are paid for the use of their resources and have the freedom to spend the money to buy products offered for sale.

Determining what to produce. If production is to be organized to produce those commodities in greatest demand by consumers, some means must be available for transmitting information to producers relative to consumer desires. In an exchange economy, prices provide the medium through which desires of consumers are transmitted to producers. Consumers register their preferences in the market place through their purchases. When consumers are given free choice, they purchase those commodities which are desired most in relation to other commodities. When sellers see that their stocks of a good are being depleted, they tend to raise the price of this good in order to increase profits. In turn, the higher price reduces the rate of disappearance of the commodity and encourages additional production of the good. By their purchases, consumers vote for the production of goods which they desire. The flow of goods through the market serves as a sort of barometer, with prices measuring the pressures or intensity of the desires of consumers for particular commodities.

Consumers may want fewer broilers than are being sent to the market, for example. Then it becomes necessary for merchants to reduce the price in order to dispose of supplies. This reduction in price provides information for broiler producers that more broilers are being produced than consumers are willing to purchase at the previous prices. On the other hand, when stocks of broilers are depleted, this provides information to producers that consumers are willing to purchase more broilers than are being supplied at existing prices. To increase their incomes, sellers who observe that their stocks are depleted increase their prices. In order to get more product, sellers increase prices paid to producers. Producers receive information about consumer demand through the movement of stocks of goods and through changes in product prices.

By expressing their wants in the market place, consumers cause prices of commodities to be changed and provide incentives for producers to produce desired commodities. Not all consumers, however, have equal weight in determining which commodities and in what quantities commodities will be produced. The influence of consumers in guiding production depends upon the amount of purchases which they make. The purchases of a consumer are limited by his wealth. Hence, the influence of a consumer on production also is limited by his wealth. For example, one person can go on a diet without influencing the production of whipped cream. It is likely, on the other hand, that a decision by a major automobile manufacturer to decrease production of automobiles will have a large effect on the quantity of steel purchased.

As consumers increase purchases of a commodity, two kinds of forces are set in motion. As prices of a commodity are increased relative to prices of other commodities in response to increased purchases by consumers, an incentive is provided for producers to expand their production of that commodity. On the other hand, when the price of a commodity is increased, an incentive is provided for consumers to reduce their purchases of that commodity and to increase their purchases of other similar commodities. That is, changes in commodity prices transmit information to consumers relative to changes in their consumption patterns which will increase their welfare. Changes in prices also transmit information to producers relative to changes which would be profitable for them.

Organizing production. If the desires of consumers are to be realized, production must be organized to yield goods and services which conform to these desires. Organization of production involves the division or allocation of resources among industries, among firms within an industry, and within each plant or firm. We shall speak of a *firm* as the decision-making or managerial unit. It is an organization set up to buy or sell products. A firm may be composed of one or more *plants*, which are physical units of production situated in one location.

There may be many firms producing the same commodity, and we shall include all the firms which are closely related in the production of similar products in an *industry*.

Some means must be established to allocate resources among and within firms. For example, steel must be divided among manufacturers of farm machinery in Illinois and manufacturers of automobiles in Michigan. Likewise, there must be some method of allocating tractors between cotton producers in Mississippi and cotton producers in Arizona. Also, there must be some method of choosing the combination of resources to be used in the production of cotton on particular farms in Mississippi.

High prices for some products in relation to their cost of production enable producers to pay high prices for resources and, thereby, to draw them away from industries whose products are less urgently desired. Allocation of resources among firms within industries is also accomplished largely through the pricing mechanism. Firms which are more efficient, that is, firms which can produce commodities for a relatively low cost, have an advantage over other firms. Either they can sell the commodities which they produce at a lower price, or they can pay a higher price for resources than other firms. When some firms reduce the price at which they are willing to sell their products and/or increase the price which they are willing to pay for resources, this tends to work to the disadvantage of other firms. These other firms find that they must take similar action or have their sales and profits reduced.

Within a firm, the desire for profit will lead to the substitution of resources which are low in price for those which are high in price. Thus, prices may also affect the techniques which are used in production. For example, if the price of labor increases, there will be a tendency for cotton producers to buy more mechanical cotton harvesters and to substitute machinery for labor in harvesting cotton.

Prices provide incentives to producers to produce those goods which are in greatest demand and to employ those resources which are most plentiful. When the prices of some commodities are increased, producers are motivated to produce those commodities. Producers of those commodities for which prices are increased also will obtain additional capital with which to purchase additional resources to expand production. The pricing system allocates resources to those uses in which they are in greatest demand. If prices are not permitted to perform this organizational role, some other mechanism must be established to perform it.

Distributing the proceeds from the sale of products. Owners employ their resources in the production of commodities for the market or sell their resources to others who are engaged in production. The price system directs resources to those uses where the returns for their employment are greatest. Returns from the sale of the product are distributed among resource owners through prices established for resource services. These payments for services have been given special names. Payments for labor services are called *wages.* Payments for the use of land are called *rent;* payments for the use of capital are called *interest;* and payments for management are called *profits.*

Producers prefer to use resources which are cheapest relative to what they can produce. On the other hand, prices provide an incentive to the owners of resources to get their resources transferred to the most productive uses. When it becomes profitable for a producer to expand production of a commodity, it may be necessary for him to increase the price that he is willing to pay for resource services. This motivates owners to transfer their resources from other uses to the production of his commodity.

Providing for maintenance and progress. If there is to be a continuous flow of goods and services, the potential returns to producers must be sufficiently large to provide an incentive for them to maintain their plant and equipment. When the receipts of a firm are less than its costs, there is a tendency to deplete plant and equipment. Maintenance must be provided if production is to continue. Also, if society desires to have new goods and services made available for consumption, incentives must be provided to get producers to assume the risk of producing these commodities. If it appears that production of a new commodity will not be profitable, it will not be developed.

In making decisions to produce a new commodity, a potential producer will survey his market to determine whether it would be profitable to produce that commodity. Whether, in fact, it would be profitable depends upon how many potential consumers he might have and what price they would be willing to pay for the commodity considered. His decision also would be influenced by the prices that he would have to pay for resources.

One resource price which is important in construction of new plants is the interest rate. Most producers find it necessary to borrow funds to engage in the production of new commodities or to expand existing facilities. The interest rate influences decisions to borrow funds. Hence, developments in the money market exert some influence on the allocation of resources and on the production of goods and services for consumption.

Restricting consumption to the stock. Prices serve as a means of rationing the consumption of goods and services. Since goods and services are limited, all of our wants cannot be satisfied. Therefore, some means of restricting our wants to the quantity of goods and services available for consumption is necessary. In an exchange economy, price performs this rationing role. At times, people are not satisfied with the way in which prices perform this role, and substitutes are developed. For example, in World War II, a second type of money, stamp money, was developed to change the rationing of goods and services so that purchases would not be proportional to the dollar wealth of consumers.

Purchases of any normal commodity can always be decreased by increasing its price. *There always exists a price which is sufficiently high to restrict the quantity of a good demanded to the amount that is available.* Similarly, when a given quantity of a good exists for consumption over a period of time, some future price always exists which would make it profitable to postpone sale of a good to a later date. For example, most of the wheat crop will not be consumed the first month after harvest. If it were, the prices later in the year would be very high. Instead, in the early part of the year, grain merchants and speculators will purchase wheat in anticipation of a future price rise, and their operation will serve to adjust the rate of consumption.

Figure 1 shows that all five of the functions performed in an eco-

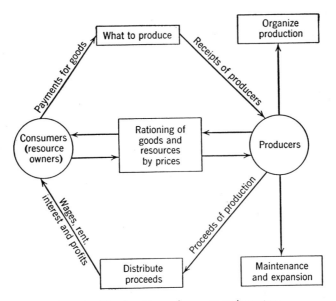

Figure 1. The functions of an economic system.

nomic system are interrelated. Through their purchases, consumers inform producers concerning what they would like to have produced. The payments of consumers for goods motivate producers to organize production in line with the wishes of consumers. Incentive is also provided to maintain and expand production of those goods desired by consumers. Then too, the payments for goods provide part of the capital needed in the production process.

In order to produce the goods desired by consumers, producers must obtain the resources needed to produce them. These resources are provided by the consumers in the form of labor, land, capital, and management. Producers pay for these resources in the form of wages, rent, interest, and profit. These payments become a part of consumer wealth and are then used to influence what is produced.

Both the resources available for production and the goods available for consumption are limited. Through prices (or an alternative rationing mechanism) the flow of resources to producers and of goods to consumers is restricted to the limited quantities available.

An exchange economy is indeed complex. The pricing system provides incentives to organize the economic system in a manner that makes it possible for consumers to obtain the maximum of goods and services consistent with their desires. Through the pricing system, the knowledge of relevant facts is dispersed among many people, and the separate actions of many different people are coordinated into a complex market economy. No member of the economy is able to study and analyze the whole economy. The market performs because individual decision-makers with their limited knowledge have information which sufficiently overlaps, so that, through many small markets, relevant information is transmitted to consumers and producers.

The Modified Role of Prices in the United States Economy

The pricing system does not operate in a manner which maintains perfect economic order at all times. Economic decisions are based on the knowledge of decision-makers. At any point in time, producers may not have accurate information pertaining to the kinds and quantities of goods desired by consumers. There are lags in the transmission of information from consumers to producers. Those producers who are in direct contact with the market are the first to become aware of changes in the demand for products. All producers are not in direct contact with the market, however. Obviously, producers cannot take into consideration changes in consumers' desires until notice of these changes has been transferred to them. Furthermore, even after information has been transmitted through the pricing mechanism relative to consumer desires, there are lags in organization of production to conform to these desires.

Another imperfection in the pricing system is that the transfer of resources from one use to another or the expansion of plant and equipment may be impeded by lack of capital. The capital market does not operate in a perfect manner. Risk is involved in investment, and lending agencies usually require collateral as a basis for making a loan. Hence, the availability of capital is limited by the wealth of the borrower. This limitation may cause inefficiency in the performance of the economic functions. To alleviate this difficulty, the government has entered into the credit field through such agencies as the Farmers' Home Administration, Federal Land Bank, and the Federal Housing Authority.

The ability of prices to perform their role is also influenced by the degree of control of individuals over the economic system. In some industries, a firm is able to control production and prohibit other firms from entering the industry. This creates an opportunity for what is called monopoly power in that such firms can establish the price at which their products will be sold. This monopoly power may impede the functioning of the pricing mechanism and create special advantages for owners of such firms. Government has taken steps to control monopoly power. In some cases, it has regulated the prices that firms charge for their products. An example of this is the regulation of rates charged by power and light companies.

In view of the imperfections in the transmission of information through the pricing system and a dissatisfaction with the results of payment for productive services through the pricing system, the government has taken steps to restrict the operation of the pricing mechanism. That is, other means are being used to aid the price system in allocating resources in line with desires of society as expressed through the political processes. For example, a progressive income tax has been used to redistribute income rather than to let individuals' incomes be determined strictly by the quantity of resources which they control and the prices they receive for resources used. Programs have been set up specifically to change the economic organization of agriculture in an effort to increase the share of the national income going to farmers. The Agricultural Adjustment Act of the 1930's and the Soil Bank Act of 1956 are examples of such special programs for agriculture. Nevertheless, within broad limits, prices serve as a guiding mechanism in allocating resources in the United States.

2 | Agriculture is an integral part of the economy

We have seen in Chapter 1 something of how an economic system functions. We examined the pricing mechanism as it operates through the market in guiding the organization of our economy. Agriculture is one sector of the total economy. In this chapter, we shall examine the importance of agriculture in the total economy and shall contrast firms in agriculture with those in other economic sectors. In the organization of the total economy, the pricing system provides incentives to transfer goods and services, not only within agriculture and other sectors of the economy but also between agriculture and other sectors.

Current Importance of Agriculture

Difficulties arise when we try to measure the importance of agriculture to our nation's economy. We all know that living would be impossible without agriculture, for we must eat. Also, agriculture is a source of fiber for much of the clothing we wear. Numerous statistics can be presented which suggest the importance of agriculture. But there is no one measure of the importance of agriculture's contribution to the total economy.

There are those who take the extreme position that the prosperity of the whole economy hinges upon the prosperity of agriculture, and

12

that depressed farm income leads to over-all depressed economic conditions. This is probably true in highly agrarian societies. As countries develop, however, the effect of agriculture on economic conditions of the total economy becomes less. Although many sectors of the United States economy have a substantial effect on the prosperity of the total economy, no one sector is solely responsible for prosperity.

The percentage of a nation's resources employed in agriculture depends to a large extent upon the efficiency with which agriculture is organized. As nations develop, the productivity of labor in agriculture increases, and labor is generally transferred from agriculture to other industries. In highly developed countries, therefore, the percentage of the labor force employed in agriculture is smaller than in less well-developed countries. For example, in Table 1, it is seen that, in 1951, 4.9 per cent of the labor force of the United Kingdom was employed in agriculture, forestry, hunting, and fishing compared with 70.6 per cent of the labor force of India.

TABLE 1. Percentage of the Labor Force in Agriculture, Forestry, Hunting, and Fishing, for Specified Countries and Years

Country	Year	Percentage of Labor Force Engaged in Agriculture, Forestry, Hunting, and Fisheries, per cent
United Kingdom	1951	4.9
United States	1950	12.2
Canada	1951	19.0
Argentina	1947	25.2
France	1946	36.0
Egypt	1947	53.6
India	1951	70.6

Source: United Nations, *Demographic Yearbook*, 1955.

The United States has been transformed from a highly agrarian society in the nineteenth century into the industrial country we know today. In the process of this transformation, the number of farm residents in the United States has been declining and continues to decline, as seen in Table 2. In 1956, only 13.2 per cent of the population lived on farms compared with 34.7 per cent in 1910. The movement from farms has continued at a rapid rate, until only 22.3 million people lived on farms in 1956.

The total number of employed persons engaged in agricultural production is probably a better measure of the magnitude of agriculture's position relative to the total economy than is farm population.

Many people living on farms gain their livelihood from nonfarm jobs. In 1954, 32.4 per cent of the farm operators reported that their income from agricultural products sold was less than their income from other sources. Actually, there were only about 8.5 million people, including family workers, employed on farms in 1956.

TABLE 2. Population on Farms, Per Cent of Population on Farms, and Percentage of National Income from Agriculture, United States

Year	Farm Population, millions	Population on Farms, per cent	Percentage of National Income from Agriculture, per cent
1910	32.1	34.7	16.3
1920	32.0	30.0	14.0
1930	30.5	24.8	8.4
1940	30.5	23.1	8.2
1950	25.0	16.5	8.1
1956	22.3	13.2	5.1

Source: USDA, AMS, *The Farm Income Situation,* July 1957, p. 23.

The fact that fewer people are engaged in agricultural pursuits to-day than was the case 50 years ago is deplored by many as being undesirable. Yet, it should be recognized that this shift of people out of agriculture has been partially responsible for the increased level-of-living which we enjoy today. People moving into urban communities have taken jobs in industry and commerce and have helped make available automobiles, television sets, health services, and other nonfarm goods and services.

The nature of agricultural production changes over time. For this reason, it is difficult to compare the importance of agriculture in different countries, or even in the same country, at two different time periods. Part of the reduction in farm population in the United States has been the result of shifting processing jobs formerly done on farms to nonfarm parts of the economy. In fact, many of the people who have migrated from farm to nonfarm residences work in the processing of farm products.

In comparing the number of farm and nonfarm workers over time, we must keep in mind that many people are engaged in the processing of farm products and in the production of items used in producing farm products. Although there are approximately 5 million farm firms in the United States, there also are about 100,000 processing plants, 90,000 wholesale establishments, and numerous retail outlets engaged primarily in the processing and marketing of goods having an agricultural origin. About 10 million people were engaged in the processing and marketing of agricultural products in 1956. One recent study concludes that in 1954 approximately 37 per cent of the civilian labor force in the United States was engaged in the production of items used in agriculture and in the production and marketing of food and fiber products.[1]

The share of national income going to agriculture also is often used as a measure of the importance of agriculture. In 1956, only 5.1 per cent of the national income originated in the agricultural sector. In the same year, however, expenditures for end products from food and fiber made up approximately 40 per cent of the total expenditures for personal consumption.[2]

Firms in Agriculture and Other Industries

The declining number of people on farms has been accompanied by an increase in size of farm. In the period from 1910 to 1954, average farm size increased from 138.1 acres to 242.2 acres. The major changes in farm size have been an increase in the number of farms of less than 10 acres and in those greater than 260 acres and a decrease in medium-sized farms, as can be seen in Table 3. The increase in

TABLE 3.   Size of Farms in the United States, 1900 and 1954

Size	1900	1954
Under 3 acres	41,882	99,896
3 to 9 acres	226,564	384,396
10 to 49 acres	1,664,797	1,212,922
50 to 99 acres	1,366,167	863,967
100 to 179 acres	1,422,328*	953,110
180 to 259 acres	490,104	463,986
260 to 499 acres	377,992	482,005
500 to 999 acres	102,547	191,648
1,000 acres and over	47,276	130,463
Total	5,739,657	4,782,393

Source: U. S. Census.

* Data for 1900 refer to size interval of 100 to 175 acres.

very small farms is a result of increased part-time farming operations, where people live on farms and work in industrial jobs. Indeed,

[1] J. H. Davis and R. A. Goldberg, *A Concept of Agribusiness,* Harvard University Press, Boston 1957, p. 11.

[2] *Ibid.,* p. 8.

many of these farms could more reasonably be thought of as rural residences rather than farms. Larger farms have increased in number as a result of the combination of units to take advantage of advances in mechanization.

Acreage, however, is not the only measure of farm size. We should ask if a 640-acre wheat farm in North Dakota is really larger than a 160-acre hog farm in Illinois. In acres, it is. In other respects, it may not be.

An alternative measure of farm size is the total value of all physical assets. This measure has the advantage of including the amounts of machinery and livestock held by farmers, as well as taking account of differences in land values. As seen in Table 4, total agricultural assets have increased greatly since 1940 if a constant price level is used to compute the value of assets. The per-farm increase in assets has been even greater because of the decrease in number of farms.

TABLE 4. Total Assets and Assets per Farm for U. S. Agriculture, Selected Years, 1940–1954*

Year	Total Physical Assets, billion dollars	Assets per Farm, dollars
1940	48.8	8,004
1945	50.7	8,653
1950	55.2	10,256
1954	59.4	12,420

Source: USDA, Agricultural Research Service, "The Balance Sheet of Agriculture, 1956," *Agriculture Information Bulletin No. 163*, Washington, D. C., November, 1956, p. 4.

* Using 1940 prices.

Probably a more useful measure of size is output. If we look at Table 5, it is evident that there is great diversity in farm size in the United States. The United States farm, however, is predominantly small. Although a few farms produced a large amount of products, about two-thirds of the commercial farms had sales of less than $5000 in 1950.

On the whole, farms have been increasing in size and decreasing in number. However, there are still a large number of farms in our economy. In fact. the large number of farms is one of the distinguishing features of our agriculture. Also, relative to other sectors of the economy, the average agricultural firm is small. The 1950 U. S. Census gives us some interesting information in this respect. Of the major

TABLE 5.   Size of Commercial Farms in United States
by Sales of Farm Products, 1954

Sales of Farm Products, dollars	Number of Farms, thousands
Over 25,000	134
10,000 to 24,999	449
5,000 to 9,999	707
2,500 to 4,999	811
1,200 to 2,499	763
250 to 1,199*	462

Source: U. S. Census.

* Provided there are less than 100 days off-farm work by the operator and that income of operator and his family from nonfarm sources is less than the value of all farm products sold.

industry groups, agriculture has by far the most firms and the smallest net income per firm, as seen in Table 6.   In 1950, there were about

TABLE 6.   Average Number of Business Firms and Income per Enterprise for Major Industry Groups, United States, 1950

Industry	Number of Firms, thousands	Income per Firm, dollars
Mining and quarrying	34	49,176
Manufacturing	303	83,148
Transportation, communication, and other public utilities	194	24,449
Wholesale trade	204	17,475
Finance, insurance, and real estate	347	11,403
Agriculture	5,382	2,521
Retail trade	1,685	7,846

Source: Bureau of the Census and Statistical Abstract of the United States, 1953, pp. 478, 483, 609.

5.4 million farms in the United States.   The average annual net income of farms in 1950 was $2521.   This is only about one-third the income received by the next lowest group, the retail trade.   Compare this income with that of one of our huge industrial giants, General Motors.   The payrolls of this organization amounted to $2771 million in 1954, and the total dollar sales were $9906 million in this same year.[1]   In 1954, the four largest manufacturers of automobiles ac-

[1] Harlow H. Curtice, "General Motors Policies and Practices," Testimony before U. S. Senate Committee on Banking and Currency, Washington, D. C., Mar. 1955.

counted for 75 per cent of all motor vehicles and parts shipped in that year.[1] The four largest primary aluminum producers accounted for 100 per cent of the aluminum shipped.

Many of the industries directly connected with agriculture also are composed of relatively large firms. For example, in 1954, the four largest meat packing firms accounted for 39 per cent of all shipments in this industry; for flour and meal products, 40 per cent was shipped by the four largest firms; and the four largest firms producing tractors shipped 73 per cent of all tractors.

The difference in firm size between farms and firms in other industries has a very important bearing on our economic analysis. Suppose that a firm like General Motors should wish to raise the price of its cars. It is likely that it could raise prices slightly and still sell about as many cars as it did at the lower price.

But what about the wheat farmer in Kansas? Suppose that wheat is selling for $2 per bushel but that the farmer decides to raise his price. If he would raise the price to $2.25 a bushel, how much wheat would he sell? Of course, he would not be able to sell any. Just what then is the difference between our farmer and General Motors? The answer is quite simple. There are not many other manufacturers of cars, and the other cars are somewhat different. But there are thousands of other wheat farmers, all producing essentially the same product. Since United States agriculture is composed primarily of small firms, no one firm can affect the price of the goods it sells or the resources it buys. This fact has important implications for the economic analysis in the remaining chapters.

One other major difference between farm and nonfarm firms is that a major proportion of nonfarm firms are operated as corporations, whereas farm firms are largely individual proprietorships. Only a small proportion of United States farms are operated as corporations.

The corporate form of business has a distinct advantage over individual proprietorship in that a corporation is a legal entity. As such, it has perpetual life. An individual proprietorship, on the other hand, is dissolved at the time of the death of the owner. In order to keep the business intact, it is necessary for someone to purchase the assets. Modern efficient farming requires relatively large amounts of capital. Younger farmers usually do not have the available capital to allow them to step right in as owners of large-scale, efficient farms. This

---

[1] U. S. Department of Commerce, *The Proportion of the Shipments (or Employees) of Each Industry, or the Shipments of Each Group of Products Accounted for by the Largest Companies as Reported in the 1954 Census of Manufactures,* July 1957.

is one of the major problems in transferring owner-operated farms from one generation to another.

Some farmers partially solve the problem of insufficient beginning capital by renting land until they can save enough money to buy farms. Others obtain farms through transfer from their fathers. Corporate ownership of farms tends to alleviate some of the difficulties associated with a turnover in ownership each generation. Yet corporate farming has not gained much favor in the United States, except possibly in a few specialized types of fruit and vegetable farms. The reasons for this are not known. Perhaps it is partly due to a feeling on the part of people that agriculture should be composed of individual operators on family farms because this method, in general, leads to a better society. Some states have in fact established laws against corporate ownership for this very reason. The Federal Government also has taken steps to encourage a family farm structure of American agriculture by establishing special farm credit legislation, making it easier to transfer owner-operated farms.

Up to this point, we have examined briefly the workings of an economic system. We have looked at the various segments of the United States economy in terms of relative size. Within agriculture, we have examined briefly some of the major characteristics of existing firms. We now want to study in more detail the behavior of firms as a first step in gaining an understanding of the economic position of agriculture in our economy.

3

The firm is a decision-making unit

In a business, factors of production called *inputs* or *resources* are transformed into goods and services called *outputs* or *products*. A farm is a particular business firm which combines resources in the production of agricultural products. On a farm, the farm manager combines producing units or enterprises, such as cows, hogs, chickens, corn, cotton, and tobacco, into an over-all business. Each enterprise, however, is a part of the farm firm. The firm is a decision-making unit or managerial unit of production.

Since the firm is a decision-making unit in the production of commodities, it is both a buyer and seller. The manager of the firm purchases inputs and transforms them into outputs or products which are sold. It is important to note that the amount of products which will be produced in the aggregate is determined by conditions confronted by individual producers. All adjustments in resource use must ultimately be made at the firm level.

There are two general types of information which may be gained from the study of the firm as an individual economic unit. First, by studying the firm and analyzing the conditions which confront producers, we may be able to indicate the courses of action profitable for producers to take. That is, by study of the firm, we may be able to provide the producer with information which would be useful in his decisions regarding the use of his resources. Thus, we may be able to indicate means by which individual firms can get greater returns for the use of resources which they control.

Another major reason for studying individual agricultural firms is to be able to predict the consequences of changes in economic conditions upon the production of the firm and, in turn, upon the aggregative amount of products which will be available for consumption. Hence, the firm is studied in order to point out or determine changes in resource use which might be profitable from the standpoint of the individual producers and to increase our knowledge of the effects of changes in economic conditions on the amount of production at the industry level. When individual firms increase production from a given amount of resources, society gains in that a greater quantity of product is available for distribution among the people.

Producer Decisions

Each owner has many alternative uses of his resources. Since he cannot employ his resources in all possible uses, he must choose among the many uses for them. For example, a person who has labor to sell must choose between using this labor in the production of commodities for sale or in the form of leisure. It may not be possible to have both leisure and money income from the use of the same labor. Also, the resource owner has to decide whether he will farm, whether he will enter some other business, or whether he will sell his labor to another producer.

As a producer, there are five major decisions that must be made. Producers must decide (1) what to produce; (2) what method of production to use; (3) how much of each commodity to produce; (4) when to buy and sell; and (5) where to buy and sell. The returns to a producer are affected by each of these decisions.

What to produce. There are many possible commodities that a firm can produce. Because resources are limited, the quantities of commodities which can be produced are limited. Therefore, a farmer must choose from among the many alternative commodities those which he will produce. Choices involving what products to produce often are made on an either/or basis; that is, frequently it is not possible to produce both *A* and *B* products. A choice must be made whether to produce *A* or *B*. For example, a farmer who has only 40 acres of cropland must decide whether to plant corn, soybeans, small grain, hay, or some combination of these. Some way must be determined, therefore, for choosing from among the many possibilities those which are preferable to the producer. Since farmers expect their products to be consumed, they must produce those products wanted by consumers. Also, the incomes of farmers are affected by their choice of products, and most farmers choose products on the basis of the income they expect these products to yield.

What method of production to use. Just as there are many possible products which might be produced, there are also many possible ways of producing them. A producer must have some way of evaluating the different possible methods of producing a commodity and of choosing between them. The method of production used affects cost of production. Most producers, therefore, seek to determine which method of production will result in least cost for producing the kinds and amounts of products in which they are interested.

Choice of products is not independent of the choice of methods of production. For example, if a farmer is seeking to choose that combination of products which maximizes his income, he cannot overlook the fact that the cost of production of the various commodities depends on the method of production used. On some farms, it may be cheaper to harvest cotton mechanically than to harvest it with manual labor. Also, it may be cheaper on some farms to apply nitrogen side dressing in liquid form than in solid form. Thus, whether it would pay a farmer to produce a particular commodity depends upon the method of production used.

How much to produce. We noted above that there are many possible commodities which can be produced by a firm, and that there are many ways of producing most commodities. Obviously there are also many possible levels of output for each commodity. Managers of businesses must decide for each commodity which they produce the quantity of product they will strive for. Businessmen do not produce more than they expect to sell for a profit. On the other hand, they tend to increase production when they expect to increase profits by doing so.

Again, the level of production which is most profitable for the producer to attain is not independent of the method of production used for the various commodities. A farm which is large enough to employ profitably a mechanical corn harvester, for example, may find that it is profitable to produce more corn than a farm which uses hand labor for harvesting. Producers must be able to compare the returns from different levels of output in making production decisions.

When to buy and sell. The prices that producers receive for their products often depend on when the products are bought and sold. In addition, the amount and quality of product which a producer has for sale vary over time. For example, hog prices change seasonally as a result of variations in hog marketings. A complication arises in that the weight of a hog increases as he is fed for a longer time period, and the price per pound decreases after the hog reaches a weight of about 220 pounds. The farmer must consider the effect of these things in determining when to sell his hogs.

Where to buy and sell. The producer has alternative markets for his products. Frequently, prices vary among these markets. Transportation costs to the markets also are different. The producer must determine whether the additional cost of transporting his products to a more distant market will be less than the additional return he expects to receive.

A Framework for Decision-Making

In making decisions it is unlikely that producers will proceed in a random manner. Rather, it is likely that they make choices in a consistent manner, or that they pursue what is called "rational action." In *rational action*, producers make decisions to obtain objectives; that is, they have some purpose in mind in making decisions. In view of the many possible decisions which must be made by producers, some means of evaluating and choosing from among the many possibilities is necessary if producers' objectives are to be realized.

We say that *an economic problem exists when persons who are seeking to maximize some goal have limited resources and must choose between alternative courses of action.* From an economic viewpoint, decisions are viewed as being pursued in such a way as to maximize some objective subject to the resources available to the person making choices. There are four basic elements involved in making economic decisions. These include (1) a decision-maker; (2) the objectives of the decision-maker; (3) the conditions under which decisions are made; and (4) a "measuring stick" for determining how well the objective is being attained.

The decision-maker. In making choices, someone must accept the responsibility for appraising the alternatives and choosing between them. In the case of a firm, this person is referred to as the manager or entrepreneur. He studies the alternative courses of action known to him, evaluates them, and decides which courses of action he will pursue. In the case of an owner-operated farm or business, the manager who makes the decisions must be prepared to accept directly the consequences of his choices. If particular courses of action which are chosen prove to be profitable, the owner-operator will find his choices to be rewarding. On the other hand, the decision-maker also accepts the risks involved in making unprofitable decisions. When choices that are made prove to be unprofitable, the decision-maker must be prepared to accept losses.

Objectives of decisions. There are many possible reasons why people enter a business or engage in farming. In the most general sense, people probably engage in business with a view of maximizing their satisfaction. This satisfaction may come from some combination of many objectives of lesser importance. For example, it is often contended that people engage in farming in order that they can be their "own boss," so that they can have freedom to work if and when they choose. Others contend that people enter a business for the purpose of obtaining net revenue. In the operation of a business, producers incur costs in purchasing inputs; they receive revenue from the sale of their products. The revenue left for the producer after he has paid all others for inputs used in production is called *net revenue*. It seems reasonable, therefore, that producers expect to obtain net revenue as a result of engaging in the production of goods and services.

Maximization of net revenue, however, must be considered as an objective which is of lower order than maximization of satisfaction. For example, suppose that we consider the production of cotton. What is the objective in producing cotton? The obvious answer is that cotton is produced for sale to obtain money income. In other words, obtaining money income is an objective which is of higher order than the objective of growing cotton as such. An objective which is of even greater importance, however, involves the use of the money which is obtained from the production and sale of cotton. Most people would not produce and sell cotton if they were not free, within limits, to use the proceeds from the sale of cotton in accordance with their desires. Hence, cotton is produced and sold so that people can obtain money to buy goods and services which ultimately give them satisfaction.

Firms in the United States probably have as their objective maximization of net revenue, subject to other considerations. However, we do not need to assume that net revenue maximization is the objective in order to make an economic analysis. Economic problems exist when an individual must make choices between alternatives with a view of maximizing any goal subject to the limited resources at his command. However, a logical as well as workable analytical approach is first to consider the firm as if it were trying to maximize net revenue. Economic analysis can be used to determine what action would be profitable to a producer. It must be kept in mind, however, that the organization of a firm which may bring about the greatest net revenue to the producer is not necessarily the organization which he will choose. Only the producer can decide which of the alternatives he prefers. His wants, likes, and dislikes all enter into his production and consumption decisions.

We should emphasize again that not all wants can be satisfied. All producers and families are limited in the amount of goods and services they can produce and in the amount they can purchase for consumption. The amount that can be produced or consumed depends on the conditions facing the particular decision-maker.

The conditions facing decision-makers. Each decision is made in a particular situation. Some of the existing conditions can be changed by the decision-maker, and some cannot. For example, a farmer has limited quantities of resources to use in the production of alternative farm products. Within the limits of his freedom, he can choose the uses to which he will put these resources. The problem with which he is confronted is to allocate or divide the resources over which he has control among the many possible uses for them in such a manner as to maximize the attainment of his objectives.

In making his decisions, however, the farmer must recognize that there are some conditions over which he has little control but which are likely to influence his choices. In this category are included such items as institutions, the weather, law, and other conditions which affect the range of choices open to the individual decision-maker. In fact, the production of some commodities is illegal. This restricts the range of alternatives open to the farmer.

Since there are many small farms, it is reasonable to assume that farmers as decision-makers are unable to exert much influence over the conditions of demand for products which they have for sale or the conditions of supply of inputs which they purchase. The amount of product that any one firm produces is so small relative to the total production of a commodity that a single farm firm is unlikely to be able to influence greatly the price received for its product. Likewise, any individual farmer purchases such a small proportion of the total amount of an input that he is unlikely to influence greatly the price he must pay for these inputs.

The knowledge a producer has of the conditions under which he makes decisions also influences the decisions he will make. In fact, the actual conditions under which decisions are made may not be as important as the producer's interpretation of the conditions. If a producer has imperfect knowledge of product prices or input prices, this will cause him to make decisions which will not coincide with those he would have made had he possessed correct knowledge. Even if all producers have the same objective, they will not necessarily pursue the same course of action in any particular situation unless they have the same interpretation of the conditions under which they make their decisions.

The "measuring stick." The fourth element of the decision-making framework pertains to the manner in which the resources that are controllable by the decision-maker are related to the objectives which he pursues. This "measuring stick" provides the guides or standards by which the decision-maker is able to appraise the different uses of his resources. Without some sort of "measuring stick," it would be impossible to tell whether the best decisions were being made.

In economic analysis, efficiency provides the "measuring stick" for evaluating choices. *Efficiency* in general refers to the ratio of valuable output to valuable input. One method of production is said to be more efficient than another when it yields a greater valuable output per unit of valuable input used. From an economic standpoint, efficiency is desirable. Hence, in evaluating choices, one course of action is regarded as preferable to another if it is more efficient. Most of the remainder of this book is concerned with a discussion of the problems involved in selecting the most efficient use of resources in making production and consumption decisions.

Part **II**

PRODUCTION AND SUPPLY

4 | Product varies according to the inputs used

Production is a process whereby some goods and services called inputs are transformed into other goods and services called outputs. Many types of activities are involved in the production process, including changes in form, location, and the time of use of products. Each of these changes involves the use of inputs to produce desired outputs. Changes in a product with respect to form, location, and time are often thought of as part of the marketing process. Actually, the use of marketing services to add value to a product involves production in the same sense as the use of resources on a farm to produce agricultural products. The principles of production are the same, irrespective of where production occurs. In the following chapters, examples used to illustrate production principles are drawn from the agricultural marketing sector of our economy as well as from the farm sector.

A North Dakota farmer combines his management, labor, land, and capital in organizing his farm to produce wheat. In effect, these resources are transformed into wheat. Production is not completed, however, when the wheat is harvested. The wheat must be transported from the farm to the elevator and then to the mill. Wheat in the elevator or at the mill is a different product from wheat on the North Dakota farm. Hence, production is involved in transferring the wheat to the mill. Likewise, production is involved in transforming

29

the wheat into flour, in storing the flour, in transferring the flour to bakers, and so on, until the wheat is ultimately consumed in the household.

The Concept of a Production Function

The firm's output of products depends upon the quantities of inputs used in production. This relationship between input and output can be characterized by a production function. The *production function* is a mathematical relationship describing the way in which the quantity of a particular product depends upon the quantities of particular inputs used. The kind of product and the amount of product which will be obtained depend upon (are functions of) the kind and quantity of inputs used. For example, a farmer might get a yield of 50 bushels of oats if he sows 1 bushel of seed on an acre of land. If he sows 1 1/2 bushels of seed on the same acre of land, the yield might be 60 bushels. These two inputs and outputs indicate how yields might vary as the seed input is varied.

A production function provides information concerning the quantity of output that may be expected when particular inputs are combined in a specified manner. The chemical, physical, and biological properties of inputs determine the kind and amount of outputs which will be received from particular combinations of inputs. There are many possible combinations of inputs. Obviously, not all production functions are known. It is the job of research and experimentation to discover the production functions which are chemically, physically, and biologically possible. Once these production functions have been discovered, they provide very useful information for making decisions by farmers and other producers. Note that producers do not control the production function.

Although an individual producer cannot alter a production function, he can choose between alternative functions. A producer must choose which of the many possible ways of producing particular products he will use. Economic considerations arise from the fact that a choice between alternative production functions must be made. If a producer is interested in maximizing net revenue from the use of his resources, he will wish to employ some production functions in preference to others.

One of the simplest production decisions involves questions concerning the effects of varying the quantity of one input on the amount of product or output produced. Consider the letter Y_1 to stand for the product which is produced and the letter f before the parenthesis to stand for the phrase "depends upon," i.e., "is a function of." Let the letter X_1 stand for an input used in the production of Y_1. The production function $Y_1 = f(X_1)$ tells decision-makers that the amount of product $Y_1 - Y_1$ depends upon, or is a function of, the amount of X_1 used in producing Y_1. For example, the amount of corn (Y_1) depends upon the amount of seed corn (X_1) used.

The symbolic expression, $Y_1 = f(X_1)$, however, does not explain the amount by which Y_1 changes as X_1 changes. In order to be most useful to decision-makers, information must be available concerning not only the kinds of inputs but also the quantities of inputs used to produce particular quantities of products.

A producer needs to know the quantitative relation between inputs and outputs. Suppose that a farmer is told that the amount of corn he can expect to harvest depends upon the amount of nitrogen he uses. The next question that we might expect the farmer to ask concerns the amount of nitrogen to apply in the production of corn. That is, he is concerned not only with the fact that nitrogen influences corn yield but he needs to know how much nitrogen to use and how much corn he can expect to receive from various quantities of nitrogen.

It is interesting for a farmer to know that corn can be produced by combining land, seed corn, nitrogen, phosphoric acid, potassium oxide, machinery, equipment and labor. This information, however, would not be very useful unless the farmer knew something about the manner in which these inputs must be combined in order to produce corn. That is, he must know how and when to prepare the land, apply the fertilizer, and sow the seed. Otherwise it is possible to combine these inputs without getting corn.

A cook without previous experience would be hopelessly lost if told that by combining baking powder, flour, eggs, milk, and sugar she could produce a cake. The kind and quantity of cake which can be produced with these ingredients depend upon the quantities used and the manner in which the cook combines them. Likewise, the kind and amount of product which a farmer produces depend upon the kind and quantities of inputs used in production and the way in which they are combined.

When a farmer is considering the question of how much nitrogen to use in corn production he may consider the other inputs as given or fixed in specified kinds and quantities. In this case, we say that $Y_1 = f(X_1 \mid X_2, X_3, \cdots, X_n)$; that is, the amount of Y_1 (corn) depends upon the amount of X_1 (nitrogen), given the amount of the

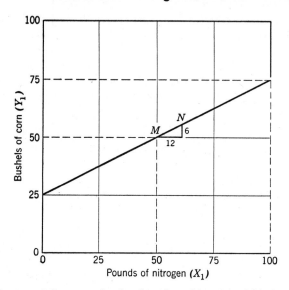

Figure 2. A linear production function with one variable input.

other inputs $(X_2, X_3, \cdots, X_n)$ which might be phosphoric acid, potassium oxide, land, seed corn, labor, rainfall, temperature, and cultivation.[1]

Now, the manner in which the amount of corn varies as the amount of nitrogen varies depends upon the amount of nitrogen used. It is possible that there is a constant relationship between application of nitrogen and the amount of corn produced. In this case the production function may be described by an equation of the form, $Y_1 = a + bX_1$. For example, it is sometimes indicated that farmers may expect 1 bushel of corn for each 2 pounds of nitrogen applied. This describes a linear relationship $Y_1 = a + 0.5X_1$, where the letter a indicates the yield of corn with no nitrogen applied, and the 0.5 indicates that Y_1 increases by 0.5 for every increase of 1 pound of nitrogen.

Suppose that a equals 25 bushels; that is, the farmer can expect 25 bushels of corn without applying nitrogen. The production function would then be $Y_1 = 25 + 0.5X_1$, and the relationship between corn and nitrogen would be as described in Figure 2. The pounds of nitrogen are shown on the horizontal axis and the bushels of corn on the vertical axis. The amount of corn increases 1 bushel for each 2 pounds of nitrogen applied. Thus, the yield of corn is increased 25 bushels by

[1] The vertical line in the equation indicates that the input X_1 is variable and that the others are fixed in quantity.

adding 50 pounds of nitrogen and 50 bushels by adding 100 pounds of nitrogen.

Once the manner in which the output varies in relation to the quantity of inputs has been determined, this relationship can be presented in tabular form. That is, a schedule can be constructed which shows the amount of product which we can expect from various quantities of the input. For example, the production function of Figure 2 is shown as a schedule in Table 7.

**TABLE 7.   Yield of Corn for Varying Levels of Nitrogen,
Linear Relationship**

Pounds of Nitrogen (X_1)	Bushels of Corn (Y_1)
0	25.0
25	37.5
50	50.0
75	62.5
100	75.0

In most production, the quantity of product forthcoming can be specified once the quality and quantity of inputs are known. For example, in automobile production, it is known that, when specified quantities of particular parts are combined in a certain manner, a given type of automobile will result. Even in the processing of some agricultural commodities, the output can be predicted with certainty. For example, the number of pork chops that can be obtained from a 200-pound market hog can be predicted quite accurately. In most agricultural production, however, the results of combining inputs over which the farmer has control are often affected adversely by the conditions over which he has little or no control. There may be considerable variation in the response a farmer gets from nitrogen when applied to corn, depending on what happens to the conditions over which he has little or no control. For example, a drought in one year may result in a smaller response from nitrogen when applied to corn than is obtained in a good year. An example of this is presented in Chapter 6. The uncertain nature of much of agricultural production leads to additional complications in making decisions. The effect of this uncertainty and risk on production and means of reducing risks are discussed in Chapter 8.

Types of Production Functions

There are three general types of relationships which can be observed in the production of a commodity when one input is varied and the quantities of all other inputs are fixed. First, it is possible that the amount of product increases by the same amount for each additional unit of input. This is the case in Figure 2. In this case, it is said that there are *constant returns* from the input being varied in the production of the particular commodity.

We can see that the production function of Figure 2 is a straight line; that is, it has the same slope throughout its entire range. *Slope* is a relatively simple concept which is of much use in economic analysis. It is defined as the Y or vertical distance divided by the X or horizontal distance. That is, slope is Y/X. We are going to be interested in the slope at particular points on a curve throughout this text. In working with slope, we will sometimes employ the Greek letter Δ (delta) which means "change in." For example, in going from M to N in Figure 2, the change in Y_1, ΔY_1, is 6, and the change in X_1, ΔX_1, is 12. Thus, the slope of the production function between M and N is 6/12 or 1/2. Since the production function is a straight line, the slope is 1/2 at any point on the curve, indicating that Y_1 increases one unit for each two-unit increase in X_1.

Another type of relationship which we observe is one in which each additional unit of input results in a larger increase in product than the preceding unit. Where this is true, we say that there are *increasing returns* from the input. Utilizing the concept of slope, the curve in Figure 3 illustrates a case of increasing returns. As inputs are added, ΔY_1, increases for any given ΔX_1. Thus, the slope of the curve be-

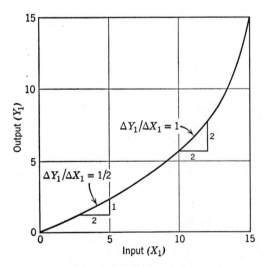

Figure 3. Increasing returns.

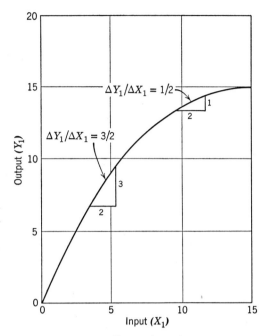

Figure 4. Decreasing returns.

comes steeper as inputs are added. Actual cases of increasing returns in agriculture are not common. When such cases are observed, they occur at relatively low levels of inputs.

The third type of relationship to be observed in production is one in which each additional unit of input results in a smaller increase in product than the preceding unit. This case is illustrated in Figure 4. The slope of the curve becomes smaller as more inputs are added. Thus, we say that this curve represents the case of decreasing or *diminishing returns*. This case is the one we would normally expect to find in the production of agricultural products. It is so important that a special section is devoted to discussion of it.

The Law of Diminishing Returns

A vast amount of experimental evidence down through the years has indicated that the relationship shown in Figure 4 inevitably occurs after a certain number of inputs is added. The fact that this phenomenon always comes about has led people to regard this as the *law of diminishing returns*, which may be stated as follows: *If successive units of one input are added to given quantities of other inputs, a point is eventually reached where the addition to product per additional unit of input will decline.*

Actually, the law of diminishing returns, as it is frequently called, refers to situations in which the proportions of the inputs are varied. Hence, it is useful to think of the law of diminishing returns as the *law of variable proportions.* Viewed in this way, we are concerned with the amount of product when inputs are combined in specified proportions as compared with the amount of product which results when inputs are combined in other proportions.

The law of variable proportions is a technological law describing a physical relationship between inputs and outputs. Since it is a technological law we cannot determine from the law of variable proportions or the production function itself, except in very special cases, the quantity of particular variable inputs which would yield the greatest net revenue from the production of a commodity. Price information is required along with knowledge of the physical relationships in order to determine the output which will yield maximum net revenue. This problem will be taken up in the next chapter.

Total, Average, and Marginal Product

By plotting the amount of product which results from different quantities of one variable input, we can obtain a total product curve. From this total product curve, two relationships which are useful in economic analysis, an average product and a marginal product curve, can be determined.

The *average product* (*AP*) of an input is defined as the ratio of the total product (*TP*) to the quantity of input used in producing that amount of product. In terms of the symbols which we have used, the average product is Y_1/X_1.

Examples of averages are frequently encountered. For example, a baseball player's batting average is one kind of an average. It tells us the number of hits (product) for a particular number of times at bat (inputs). In the same way, a student's average grade is similar to an average product. The total number of points in all examinations is divided by the number of examinations to obtain an average. For example, in Table 8, five units of input yield 30 units of product. This is an average of 30/5 or six units of product for each unit of input used. Thus, the average product is 6.

The *marginal product* (*MP*) is defined as the addition to product resulting from the addition of one unit of the input. As is the case with average product, the amount of other inputs used is held constant in

TABLE 8.   Units of Input and Corresponding Total,
Average, and Marginal Products

Inputs (X_1)	Total Product (Y_1)	Average Product (Y_1/X_1)	Marginal Product $(\Delta Y_1/\Delta X_1)$
0	0	—	
			5
1	5	5	
			9
2	14	7	
			7
3	21	7	
			5
4	26	6.5	
			4
5	30	6	
			3
6	33	5.5	
			2
7	35	5	
			1
8	36	4.5	
			0
9	36	4	
			−1
10	35	3.5	

computing marginal product. In terms of symbols, the marginal product is $\Delta Y_1/\Delta X_1$. Thus, the marginal product for a unit of input is the change in product divided by the change in input. Another way to look at the marginal product is that it is the rate of change in total product as the quantity of input increases.[1] In Table 8, the sixth input added increases the output by three units. Thus, the marginal product from this input is 3/1 or 3.

One point about marginal product is always troublesome. Strictly speaking, the marginal product represents the rate of change in product at particular levels of inputs. When the marginal product is computed over some range of inputs as $\Delta Y_1/\Delta X_1$, the result represents an average rate of change over the particular range. This is the case in Table 8. When plotting marginal product, therefore, the values of the marginal product are placed mid-way between the inputs for which the change in product is computed. Notice that we placed

[1] Mathematically, the marginal product is the first derivative of the total product function. It may be estimated by constructing a tangent to a total product curve and determining the slope of the tangent at the point in question.

the marginal product values mid-way between the inputs in Table 8 in order to emphasize the fact that the marginal concept represents an average rate of change between inputs.

Relationships between Total, Average, and Marginal Products

Since both average and marginal products are derived from the total product, the average and marginal product curves are related to the shape of the total product curve. These curves are shown in Figure 5 and correspond to the example in Table 8.

Since the marginal product is a measure of rate of change, the marginal product is positive when the total product is increasing. If the total product remains constant as an input is added, the marginal product is zero. In some cases, the total product actually may de-

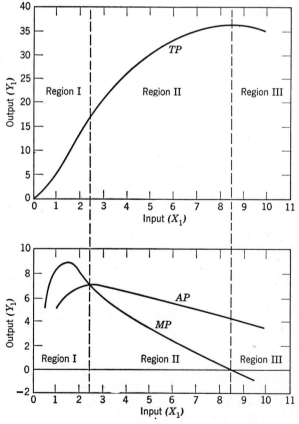

Figure 5. Total, average, and marginal product and the regions of production.

crease when additional inputs are added. When this is true, the product from additional units of input is negative. Thus, the marginal product is negative. When the total product is increasing at an increasing rate, the marginal product is increasing. On the other hand, when the total product is increasing, but at a decreasing rate, the marginal product is decreasing.

The average product is the amount of product obtained per unit of input at a particular level of production or level of input used. In order for the average product to increase as inputs are added, the addition to the product from an additional input must be greater than the average product from preceding inputs. Going back to our example of a student's grade, the student would have to have a higher grade on an exam than his previous average if he were to increase his overall average grade. Therefore, when the average product is increasing, the marginal product must be greater than the average product. On the other hand, when the average product is decreasing, the marginal product is less than the average product. In some instances, the average product does not change when additional inputs are used. When this is the case, the amount of product added by an additional unit of input is equal to the average product. That is, the average product is equal to the marginal product.

Because of these above-mentioned relationships, the marginal product and the average product can only be equal when the average product is at a maximum. For the marginal product to change from being greater to being less than the average product, the two curves must cross as in Figure 5. This is true because the average product increases when the marginal product is greater than the average product, and the average product decreases when the additional product is less than the average product. Thus, the two curves must be equal where the average product changes direction. This, of course, is where the average product is at a maximum.

For simplicity, the relationships between average product and marginal product can be summarized in the following way:

When $MP >$ (is greater than) AP, AP is increasing;
when $MP <$ (is less than) AP, AP is decreasing;
when $MP =$ (is equal to) AP, AP is at a maximum.

Three Regions of a Production Function

The input-output relations showing total, average, and marginal productivity can be divided into three regions in such a manner that we can isolate the portion of the production function in which production is most profitable.

As shown in Figure 5, Region I of the production function goes to the level of input at which the maximum average product is obtained. In this region, the average product is increasing. Hence, as we saw above, the marginal product must be greater than the average product. Now, if it is profitable to produce any output at all, it will always be profitable for the producer to continue to add inputs as long as the average product is increasing. In other words, if a producer is interested in maximizing net revenue and if production is ever profitable, it will always pay him to go at least to the point of highest average product in the application of inputs.

For example, suppose that we consider a situation in which one input, say land, is free and another input, say labor, is expensive and limited in quantity. Under these conditions it pays to limit the quantity of land used in relation to the quantity of labor used, even though land is free. This is, in fact, what we observe by studying the experiences of the early settlers of America. They did not make an attempt to cultivate the whole continent. Rather, they set about to clear such land as could be profitably combined with their labor, capital, and management. In doing so, they were inclined to operate with that combination of land and other inputs which gave a maximum return for these scarce inputs. Note that they permitted some land to remain idle rather than operate in a region of increasing average returns for labor, capital, and management.

The use of irrigation water in some parts of the West provides another example of this type of production problem. In some cases, farmers can use all of the water they wish without additional cost. Under these conditions, additional water essentially becomes a free good to the farmers. They, however, do not flood the land, but only use that amount of water which gives them a maximum return for their other inputs of land, labor, capital, and management.

In the third region of the production function, the total product is decreasing. Hence, in the third region, the marginal product or the amount of product added by additional units of input is negative. Since additional quantities of input reduce total output in the third region, we can say from the physical production function that it is not profitable to operate with a combination of resources existing in this region. The point at which marginal product becomes zero represents the maximum quantity of variable input which will ever be profitable to use in combination with other inputs. For example, if labor were free and land were expensive, it would be profitable to add labor up to the point where the return from land is at a maximum. At this point, the marginal product of an additional unit of labor is zero. If labor is added beyond this point, the marginal product is negative, and it does not pay to operate in this region.

We have seen from the preceding discussion that Region I and Region III set the limits to the region in which it is profitable to operate. Therefore, Region II is the region in which production is most profitable. In Region II, the total product is increasing; the marginal product is decreasing, is positive, and is less than the average product; and the average product is decreasing. This is the region of rational production. It is the region in which producers who seek to maximize net revenue will operate. It should be emphasized that this region of rational production is one of diminishing returns. Both average and marginal products are decreasing in this region.

From production function data alone, we have been able to isolate the region in which net revenue is at a maximum. However, the particular level of output or quantity of input most profitable to use in Region II cannot be determined from production data alone. The prices of the input and the product are necessary to determine that level of production which is most profitable. If the returns from using additional units of input exceed the additional cost, net revenue can be increased by using additional units. Thus, the particular level of input most profitable to employ is that at which the value of the additional product just equals the cost of the input. The principles underlying the choice of the most profitable level of input will be discussed in detail in Chapter 5.

Examples of Irrational Production in Agriculture

Producers do not have perfect knowledge of production relations. Because of this imperfect knowledge, it is possible to observe that producers combine resources in such proportions that they operate in Region I or Region III of the production function. For example, in the production of many crops, insufficient lime is used to reach Region II. Adding more lime would increase the average product from use of the lime.

On the other hand, evidence of production in Region III is often noted. For example, during the late summer and fall months, we frequently have evidence of too many cattle on a given quantity of pasture, resulting in overgrazing of pastures and less production than could have been obtained with fewer cattle. Also, we find evidence of overcrowding of broilers and layers in poultry houses.

Differences in Technology

In using a production function, we assume that inputs are combined in a particular way. Two production functions may be quite different even if the same input is used in producing one kind of output. The difference between functions is therefore due to a difference of technique in how the inputs are used in producing the output. For example, the application of nitrogen to grass as top dressing may give different results depending upon whether it is applied in October or in February. When the quantity of product which can be obtained from a particular quantity of inputs is increased, this is known as a technological improvement.

An example of an improvement in technology is shown in Figure 6. If techniques A and B require the same inputs, a producer can decide from the production data alone that technique B is superior to technique A. This is true because technique B yields a higher level of output for each level of input. In Figure 6, the amount OR of input X_1 yields OT of product Y_1 if technique B is used, and OS if technique A is used. Clearly, technique B is superior to technique A.

Data from North Carolina indicate the effects of time of application of nitrogen on the forage yield of tall fescue. The results, presented in Table 9, indicate that much higher yields can be obtained from 100 pounds of nitrogen if it is applied in February. Since higher yields can be obtained from the same quantity of input, application of nitrogen in February is the superior technique unless costs of applying nitrogen are higher in February than in other months. When no cost

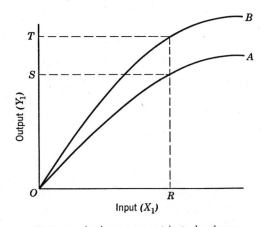

Figure 6. An improvement in technology.

differences are involved between techniques, a producer should choose the technique which gives the greater output for any given input level.

TABLE 9. Effect of Time of Application of 100 Pounds
of Nitrogen on the Forage Yield of Tall Fescue,
Wake County, North Carolina

Month	Pounds of Forage
May	3538
August	4322
October	3209
February	5639

Source: W. W. Woodhouse and D. S. Chamblee, "Nitrogen in Forage Production," North Carolina Agricultural Experiment Station, *Bulletin 383*, Raleigh, North Carolina, Sept. 1953.

5 | A producer chooses among levels of production

In the preceding chapter we learned that producers who seek to maximize net revenue will operate in Region II of the physical production function. Operation at any place in Region II is not sufficient, however, to attain maximum net revenue. In order to determine at what level in Region II a producer should operate to maximize net revenue, he must have information regarding the price of the product and the price of the input.

Revenue Related to Production

Once a physical production function has been derived, the amount of revenue which will be received from a particular production process can be determined by multiplying the quantity of product produced by the price of the product. In so doing, the production function is converted to a revenue function. If the producer does not produce enough of a commodity to affect the price which he receives, the revenue function has the same shape as the production function.

From the production function presented in Figure 5, a revenue function can be determined if the price of the product is known. For example, if P_{Y1} (the price of the product) is \$2, the total revenue (TR) received from particular levels of input is shown in Figure 7. Similarly, by multiplying the marginal product schedule by the price of the product, we can determine the amount by which the total revenue changes as inputs are added. The amount by which the total revenue changes when an additional unit of input is added is known as the *value of the marginal product* (*VMP*). In the same manner, by multiplying the average product by the price of the product, the *value of the average product* (*VAP*) can be determined for particular levels of input. Thus, *VAP* is the value of product per unit of input at any particular level of input.

If a producer knows the price of the input and the value of the marginal product schedule, he can determine the most profitable level

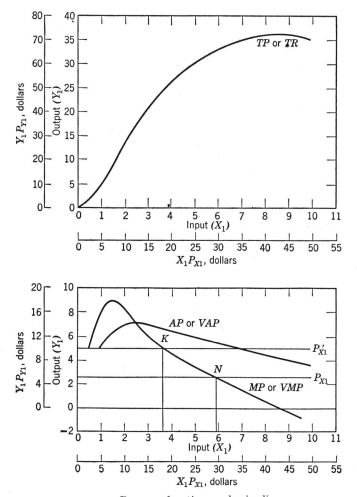

Figure 7. Revenue functions and price lines.

of input. If he can buy inputs at a stated price (P_{X1}), it pays him to add additional units of the input until the value of the marginal product is just equal to the price of the input.[1] At this point, the additional cost of an input is equal to the additional revenue which the input yields. As an example, if P_{X1} is \$5, the the total expenses for various levels of input can be seen in Table 10. Since the amount of the input the producer buys is insufficient to cause the price of the input to be raised, each additional unit costs him \$5. This is shown by the horizontal line P_{X1} in the lower part of Figure 7. We can see now that the most net revenue can be obtained when six units of X_1 are used. This is shown by point N in Figure 7. When six units of X_1 are used, the net revenue is \$36. If fewer units of the variable input are used, the value of the marginal product of the input exceeds the price of the input. This indicates that the return which the producer gets from the additional unit of input is greater than the cost. If the producer uses only five units of X_1, his net revenue is only \$35.

On the other hand, if inputs are added to the point where the price of the input exceeds the value of the marginal product, the added costs are greater than the added returns. This is the case when seven or more inputs are added. In Table 10, adding the seventh input brings an additional return of only \$4, but the input has a cost of \$5. Under these conditions, it does not pay the producer to add more than six units of X_1.

We see from the above that a condition for maximization of net revenue is that the price of the product times the marginal product shall equal the price of the input. This can be written as $P_{Y1}(\Delta Y_1/\Delta X_1)$ $= P_{X1}$. This says that the added return from the last input should equal the cost of adding that input. We can also write this condition for maximization of net revenue as $P_{Y1}\,\Delta Y_1 = P_{X1}\,\Delta X_1$, where $P_{Y1}\,\Delta Y_1$ is added revenue and $P_{X1}\,\Delta X_1$ is added cost. Another way of viewing this is that the ratio of the price of the input to the price of the product shall be equal to the marginal physical product of the input. This is written as $P_{X1}/P_{Y1} = \Delta Y_1/\Delta Y_1$.[2] It should be noted that this is a condition of maximization of net revenue from the application of a single variable X_1 to Y_1, with the level of other inputs unchanged.

[1] For the sake of simplicity, it is assumed that the cost of applying the input is included in the price of it, and that the price of the input does not change as additional units are used.

[2] It should be emphasized that all three algebraic expressions of the rule for maximizing net revenue are the same. Each form may be useful in demonstrating a particular point.

TABLE 10. Revenue, Cost, and Net Revenue Functions

Inputs (X₁)	Total Product (Y₁)	$P_{Y1} = \$2$			$P_{X1} = \$5$		$P_{X1} = \$10$	
		Total Revenue, dollars	Value of Average Product, dollars	Value of Marginal Product, dollars	Total Cost, dollars	Net Revenue, dollars	Total Cost, dollars	Net Revenue, dollars
0	0	0	—		0	0	0	0
				10				
1	5	10	10		5	5	10	0
				18				
2	14	28	14		10	18	20	8
				14				
3	21	42	14		15	27	30	<u>12</u>
				10				
4	26	52	13		20	32	40	<u>12</u>
				8				
5	30	60	12		25	35	50	10
				6				
6	33	66	11		30	<u>36</u>	60	6
				4				
7	35	70	10		35	35	70	0
				2				
8	36	72	9		40	32	80	−8
				0				
9	36	72	8		45	27	90	−18
				−2				
10	35	70	7		50	20	100	−30

47

From the condition for maximization of net revenue, we can see that there are three major factors that affect the most profitable level of an input. These are price of the product (P_{Y1}), price of the input (P_{X1}), and the physical production relationship as it affects the marginal product $(\Delta Y_1/\Delta X_1)$. An understanding of the manner in which changes in these three factors affect the most profitable input level is essential for a producer who wishes to maximize net revenue.

Effects of Price Changes

Input and output prices change frequently. Since the most profitable level of an input to use in the production of a commodity depends upon the price of the commodity and of the input, changes in prices of either of these affect the most profitable input level. The extent to which changes in prices affect the most profitable level of input depends upon the form of the production function.

Linear production function. If the production function is characterized by a linear relationship between input and output, the amount of input to use is one of two amounts. Either it does not pay to add any of the input, or an infinite amount should be used. If the production function is linear, the marginal product is constant, and the average product equals the marginal product. Under such conditions, if the value of the marginal product is greater than the price of the input, it pays to add the input in an infinite amount. On the other hand, if the price of the input is greater than the value of the marginal product, it does not pay to use any of the input.

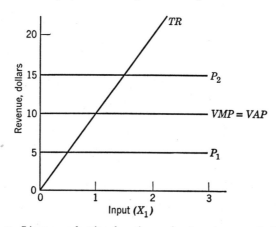

Figure 8. Linear production function and net revenue maximization.

In Figure 8, we have a linear revenue function; that is, it shows constant returns to the input X_1. In this illustration, the amount added to revenue by each additional input is $10. If each input costs $15 ($P_2$), a producer loses $5 for every unit of X_1 which he adds.

On the other hand, if the price of the input is $5 ($P_1$), the value of the marginal product is greater than the price of the input. Therefore, each unit of input added by the producer increases his net revenue by $5. We can see that, if the price of the input is less than $10 or the VMP, it pays to add as many inputs as possible. If P_{x1} is greater than $10, the producer should not produce at all. Of course, there is one other possibility. The price of the input might be equal to VMP. In this case, the producer neither loses nor gains by varying the amount of input used. His net revenue is zero regardless of the number of inputs of X_1 used in the production of Y_1.

We can see now that a linear production function is unlikely over a large range of inputs. If a production function for a commodity were linear throughout its entire range, we would expect to find producers using an infinite amount of input, if they used any at all in producing this commodity.

Diminishing returns. Under conditions of diminishing returns, the marginal product decreases as inputs are added. Therefore, the amount by which it pays a producer to change an input in response to price changes depends upon the manner in which the marginal product varies. If P_{x1} should increase, for example, the value of the ratio P_{x1}/P_{Y1} is increased. The marginal product is now less than the ratio of the price of the product to the new price of the input. In order to make the marginal product again equal to the ratio of the price of the input to the price of the product, the producer must alter the marginal product, P_{x1} or P_{Y1}. A producer ordinarily cannot change P_{x1} or P_{Y1}. Therefore, if he is to make $P_{x1}/P_{Y1} = \Delta Y_1/\Delta X_1$ again, he must increase $\Delta Y_1/\Delta X_1$. In order to increase the marginal product in a region of diminishing returns, it is necessary to decrease the quantity of the input used. Hence, if the price of the input (P_{x1}) increases relative to the price of the product (P_{Y1}), the amount of input which it pays to use and, consequently, the amount of Y_1 which it pays to produce decrease.

The effects of an increase in the price of an input are illustrated in Table 10. When P_{x1} is $5, the ratio P_{x1}/P_{Y1} is 5/2, or 2.5. If P_{x1} is increased to $10, the ratio is 10/2, or 5. The increased price of the input relative to the price of the product requires a reduction in the number of inputs used and in the amount of output produced if net revenue is to be maximized. With the new price ratio, a net revenue of $12 is the largest attainable. This net revenue can be obtained with either three or four inputs. In this case, both inputs yield the same net revenue because the revenue added by the fourth input is $10, and the cost of the input is $10. It is clear, in this example, that an increased price of an input necessitates a reduction in output to obtain maximum net revenue.

On the other hand, a decrease in P_{X1} decreases the ratio P_{X1}/P_{Y1}, and the marginal product becomes greater than the ratio of the price of the input to the price of the product. In this case, in the region of decreasing marginal returns, it pays to add additional units of the input and, consequently, to increase production of Y_1.

The effects of a change in the price of a commodity are comparable to those of a change in the price of an input. If there is an increase in P_{Y1}, the ratio P_{X1}/P_{Y1} decreases. If the marginal product of X_1 is to be brought into equality with the new price ratio, it is necessary to increase the amount of X_1. On the other hand, a decrease in P_{Y1} results in an increase in the ratio P_{X1}/P_{Y1}, and it is profitable to reduce the amount of X_1.

Changes in production brought about by price changes result from the fact that the ratio of the price of the input to the price of the product is altered. If the price of the input and the price of the product change in the same proportion, relative prices of the two do not change. If relative prices are not changed, the most profitable level of the input remains unchanged. Thus it can be seen that it is the ratio of prices which is important to the decision-maker in determining the most profitable level of input.

Inputs which must be applied in discrete units. The foregoing discussion of variable proportions has been based on the assumption that the variable input could be applied in continuous units. Many items used in farm production, however, must be applied in discrete or discontinuous units. For example, it is not possible to add a part of a tractor to a farm. Discontinuous inputs are still subject to increasing, constant, or decreasing returns, but the question of whether it would pay to add additional units refers to the discrete units for the input considered. That is, in the consideration of the addition of discrete units of inputs, the question is whether it would pay to add a whole unit or whether one would be better off by not adding the unit. This is an all-or-nothing proposition; either an additional unit will be added or no additional unit will be added. The method used to reach a decision, however, is the same as in the cases discussed above. If the additional revenue resulting from adding the input is greater than the cost of the input, it pays to add it.

Demand Curve for Inputs

Given information with respect to prices and the production function, a producer can determine how much of an input it pays him to use. We saw above that the amount of input which it pays to use changes as the price of the input changes, even though the price of the product remains constant. In the process of determining, for different input prices, the amount of an input at which net revenue is a maximum, a demand schedule for inputs is derived. *This demand schedule shows the maximum quantities of an input which it will pay to purchase at alternative prices of the input.* In Figure 7, we saw that the intersection of the price line and the value of the marginal product curve determined the most profitable level of input. Thus, the value of marginal product curve is, in itself, the demand curve for an input in the production of one commodity. This is shown in Figure 9.

Effects of Changes in Technology

The effects of a change in technology on the most profitable level of production depend upon the manner in which the change in technology affects the shape of the total product curve. If the change in technology is such that the marginal product for a given level of

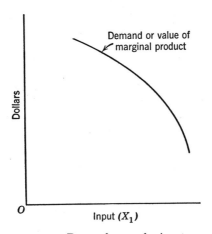

Figure 9. Demand curve for inputs.

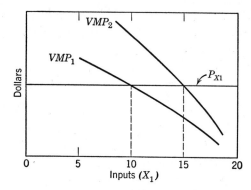

Figure 10. Technological change and the maximization of net revenue.

input is increased, it is profitable to expand the quantity of input used. For example, in Figure 10 the marginal product at each level of input has been increased by a change in technology. Hence, the value of the marginal product has been increased, and, as a result of the change in technology, it pays the producer to increase the amount of X_1 used from 10 to 15 units.

On the other hand, it is possible that a technological change may increase the total product for some levels of input but will not increase the marginal product at these levels. The marginal product of the twentieth unit of input, for example, may be the same for both methods of production. Yet, the total production may be greater if one method were used instead of the other. If this is the case, the value of the marginal product remains the same for both methods of production, and the level of input at which the value of the marginal product equals price is unchanged. Although it is profitable to expand production of the commodity, it is not profitable to expand the quantity of input used.

6 | Some applications of input-output analysis

Economic decisions by farmers frequently fall in the category of problems concerning the most profitable level of application of one input, given the level of others inputs, in the production of one commodity. In order that we can see how economic principles discussed in Chapters 4 and 5 can be used in solving such problems, examples of such decisions are discussed in this chapter.

Nitrogen Fertilization of Corn

Under many soil and climatic conditions, the amount of corn a farmer can expect to obtain depends on the amount of nitrogen used per acre of land. Nitrogen is often applied to corn as a side dressing and, hence, is applied after other fertilizers have been used. In determining how much nitrogen to apply, the farmer must compare the added revenue which would be received from the application of nitrogen with the additional cost of applying nitrogen. He estimates the additional revenue he expects to receive by multiplying the additional amount of corn expected to be harvested by the price he might reasonably expect to receive for his corn. Additional costs include expenditures for additional nitrogen, expenses involved in the application of the nitrogen, and expenses involved in harvesting and marketing the additional corn. If the farmer is to make decisions consistent

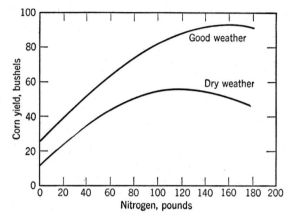

Figure 11. Response of corn to nitrogen, coastal plain, North Carolina.

with maximization of net revenue, it is necessary for him to know how each of these items varies with the level of application of nitrogen.

Research studies in North Carolina show production functions for corn as related to nitrogen inputs on soils found in the Coastal Plain Area.[1] In this experiment the amount of nitrogen was varied on different fields while the amounts of other inputs were held constant. Results of this experiment are shown in Figure 11.

First, we should note that the response of corn to nitrogen is affected by weather conditions. Under both dry weather and wet weather conditions, diminishing returns are in evidence. Notice that the difference in dry weather yield and good weather yield increases as the level of nitrogen increases. Furthermore, the total yield of corn under dry weather conditions actually decreases after about 120 pounds of nitrogen are used.

Weather conditions are important in determining the increase in yield resulting from the application of nitrogen. We know, however, that farmers cannot control weather conditions. They take weather conditions as they occur and adjust themselves to them. However, nitrogen frequently is applied at the time of the last cultivation. Farmers may some day be able to use long-range weather predictions as a basis for selecting between good weather and dry weather responses in choosing the appropriate level of nitrogen.

The quantity of an input most profitable to use in the production

[1] B. A. Krantz and W. V. Chandler, "Fertilize Corn for Higher Yields," North Carolina Agricultural Experiment Station, *Bulletin 366,* Revised, Mar. 1954; Paul R. Johnson, "Alternative Functions for Analyzing a Fertilizer-Yield Relationship," *Journal of Farm Economics,* vol. 35, Nov. 1953, pp. 519–529.

of a commodity is expected to change as the price of the input and/or the price of the commodity changes. We learned this in Chapter 5. The extent to which the most profitable level of application of an input varies depends on the shape of the production function and on the price of the input in relation to the price of the product. For example, the optimum level of application of nitrogen to corn on Coastal Plain soils in North Carolina is shown in Table 11 for the good weather production function and for various prices of nitrogen and corn.

TABLE 11. Effects of Changes in Price of Nitrogen and of Corn on the Optimum Amount of Nitrogen*

Price of Corn per Bushel, dollars	Price of Nitrogen per Pound		
	$0.075	$0.150	$0.225
0.85	161	139	118
1.35	168	155	142
1.60	170	159	148
1.85	172	162	153

* Good weather conditions.

We note that the amount of nitrogen most profitable to use increases as the price of corn increases relative to the price of nitrogen. However, rather large changes in the price of corn or in the price of nitrogen are necessary to cause significant changes in the most profitable level of nitrogen fertilization.

Nitrogen Fertilization of Sudan Grass

Sweet sudan grass is frequently used for mid-summer pastures in parts of the South when many of the perennial grasses are in a dormant period. One of the questions confronting farmers who plant sudan grass is the determination of the optimum level of nitrogen fertilization. Data obtained in North Carolina indicate the response of sudan grass to nitrogen, as shown in Table 12.

These data indicate that there is a range of increasing returns to nitrogen on sudan grass under the soil and weather conditions in which this experiment was conducted. The marginal product per pound of nitrogen, in the range from 25 to 50 pounds, was 33.6 compared to 18.1 in the range from 0 to 25 pounds of nitrogen. On the basis of these data, the farmer can say that, if it pays to add any nitrogen, it pays him to add at least 50 pounds.

TABLE 12.   The Response of Sudan Grass to Nitrogen Applications,
Norfolk Sandy Loam Soils, North Carolina

Pounds of Nitrogen Applied per Acre on June 15 (X_1)	Pounds of Dry Forage per Acre on September 1 (Y_1)	Marginal Product per Pound of Nitrogen ($\Delta Y_1/\Delta X_1$)
0	599	
		18.1
25	1051	
		33.6
50	1893	
		3.6
100	2073	

Source: W. W. Woodhouse, Jr. and D. S. Chamblee, "Nitrogen in Forage Production," North Carolina Agricultural Experiment Station, *Bulletin 383,* Sept. 1953.

The actual level of nitrogen application which will be most profitable for the farmer cannot be easily determined in the production of sudan grass. In this case, the product is not readily sold. Most farmers do not rent their pastures or sell sudan forage. Rather, the sudan grass is sold through livestock in the form of livestock products. As a result, there is seldom a market price which can be attached to sudan. This means that, in order to answer the question of how much nitrogen it would pay him to use in production of sudan grass, a farmer must have information concerning the relationships between sudan grass and livestock products as well as those for nitrogen and sudan grass. Given information about the conversion rate of sudan to beef and the price of livestock products, a farmer could estimate the value of the sudan grass. With a price established for the sudan, it would then be possible to determine how much nitrogen to use.

Suppose a farmer decides that, for purposes of feeding his cattle, sudan has a value of $20 per ton or 1 cent per pound. If nitrogen costs 15 cents per pound applied, we can determine quite readily the most profitable nitrogen level to use. We know first that the most profitable level of input always lies in an area of decreasing returns. As we have seen, this means that at least 50 pounds should be used. If we put on 100 pounds of nitrogen, the marginal product is only 3.6 pounds of sudan per pound of nitrogen. Since sudan has a value of only 1 cent per pound, the value of the marginal product is only 3.6 cents. Nitrogen, however, costs 15 cents per pound. Thus, an average loss of 11.4 (15 − 3.6) cents would be received for each pound of the additional 50 pounds of nitrogen. That is, the use of 100 pounds of nitrogen is $5.70 less profitable than 50 pounds. Thus, if any amount of nitrogen is profitable, it must be 50 pounds. We can check on this by seeing how much forage production is increased by adding 50 pounds of nitrogen. This increase is 1294 (1893 − 599) pounds of sudan. On a per-pound-of-nitrogen basis, this is 25.9 pounds of sudan for each pound of nitrogen, up to 50 pounds. Application of 50 pounds of nitrogen is, of course, profitable in this case because a return of 25.9 cents is received for each 15 cents spent.

We accept the 50-pound level, but we also know that it is possible that 60 pounds might be better. Since we do not have the necessary information on other levels of nitrogen, however, we take the most profitable level about which we have the data. In other words, we do not have the data for a nice smooth curve showing the relationship between all possible inputs and outputs. What we really have are data for various discrete points from what would be a curve if we had all the information. The fact that we do not have complete information should not bother us too much, however. By using the data we do have, we can increase profit over what would be the case without any information.

Nitrogen Application for Fescue Seed

Thus far we have considered a case of nitrogen application to a crop where diminishing returns were involved and a case where in-

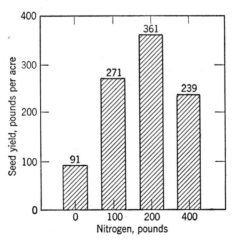

Figure 12. Effect of rate of nitrogen application on seed yield of tall fescue. (*Source:* W. W. Woodhouse, Jr., and D. S. Chamblee, "Nitrogen in Forage Production," North Carolina Agricultural Experiment Station, *Bulletin 383*, Sept. 1953.)

creasing returns were involved. It is also possible to get the level of nitrogen so high that total production actually decreases. This is particularly true in the case of seed crops. Data from North Carolina, as shown in Figure 12, indicated that, when nitrogen is applied to a pure stand of tall fescue on Cecil sandy loam soils, 400 pounds of nitrogen produce a smaller total yield of fescue seed per acre than 200 pounds of nitrogen.

In the case of nitrogen fertilization of fescue for seed, we can see from the production data alone that it would not pay to apply as much as 400 pounds of nitrogen since the yield of seed with 400 pounds of nitrogen is actually less than that from 100 pounds. Thus, an application of 400 pounds is in Region III of the production function.

In order to determine the particular level of nitrogen which would yield maximum net revenue, the procedure to follow is the same as that used in the application of nitrogen in corn production. The necessary information includes an estimate of the change in seed production corresponding to changes in the level of nitrogen, the cost of application of additional nitrogen, the cost of harvesting and marketing of the additional crop, and the price expected for seed. Given this information, a farmer can determine the level of nitrogen which would be most profitable.

Feeding Dairy Cattle for Milk Production

One of the problems faced by dairymen is to determine how much to feed their cows. Most feeding standards and feeding recommendations assume that a cow needs some minimum quantity of feed for body maintenance, and that, thereafter, milk production increases proportionately to the increase in total digestible nutrients fed the cow until a limit in milk production is reached. This limit, it is assumed, is determined by the productive capacity of the cow. According to Morrison,[1] about 3285 pounds of TDN per year are needed for maintenance for an 1150-pound cow. Morrison also indicates that 0.31 pound of TDN is required per pound of 4 per cent milk in the range where the cow is converting feed to milk.

A large experiment was conducted by ten agricultural experiment stations in the late 1930's to determine the nature of the production function for milk as related to pounds of TDN consumed. The results of this experiment are shown in Table 13. The results obtained from experimental feeding of cows are compared with the feeding

[1] Frank B. Morrison, *Feeds and Feeding*, 21st edition, The Morrison Publishing Company, Ithaca, New York, 1949, p. 1147.

TABLE 13. Estimated Quantities of Milk Associated
with Different Levels of Feed

Level of Feeding from Lowest to Highest	Total Hay Equivalent Fed in a Year, pounds	Grain Fed in a Year, pounds	Adjusted Total Digestible Nutrients, pounds	Estimated Quantities of Milk These Feeds Would Produce, pounds	Live Weight, pounds
1	11,338	0	5,102	6,438	1,080
2	11,048	450	5,376	7,020	1,090
3	10,751	900	5,642	7,517	1,100
4	10,447	1,350	5,901	7,947	1,110
5	10,136	1,800	6,154	8,317	1,120
6	9,817	2,250	6,400	8,639	1,130
7	9,492	2,700	6,638	8,915	1,140
8	9,159	3,150	6,868	9,156	1,150
9	8,818	3,600	7,091	9,366	1,160
10	8,471	4,050	7,307	9,550	1,170
11	8,116	4,500	7,514	9,708	1,180
12	7,754	4,950	7,713	9,847	1,190
13	7,385	5,400	7,905	9,971	1,200

Source: Einar Jensen et al., "Input-Output Relationships in Milk Production," *USDA Technical Bulletin No. 815*, May 1942.

standard recommendations in Figure 13. More milk is received per pound of grain fed in the lower ranges than would be expected on the basis of feeding standards. On the other hand, less milk is received per pound of grain fed in the upper ranges.

It should be noted that the cow produces some milk on the less than maintenance ration. She does this by drawing on her body fat and converting it into milk. Also, at the heavy feeding rates, the cow gains weight as the feed is increased. In determining the level of feeding which would maximize net revenue, a farmer cannot ignore the effects of changes in the ration on the weight of the cow and its relation to the future productive capacity of the cow, as well as on current milk production.

The above experiment was conducted in terms of TDN. This, however, is not the sole consideration in feeding dairy cattle. One cannot overlook the protein content since milk production is affected by the amount of digestible protein in the ration. Also questions arise as to the most economical source of nutrients. It may be profitable,

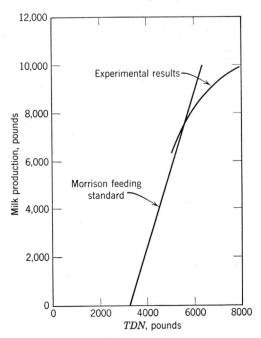

Figure 13. Milk Production and pounds of TDN.

for example, to substitute one kind of hay for another or one kind of concentrate for another. Rations based on TDN usually assume that TDN from one source is a perfect substitute for TDN from another source. If this is not true, we shall see in Chapter 9 that the cost of milk production may be reduced by varying the proportions in which the feeds are used.

Another problem of concern to dairymen is that the response of dairy cattle to feed may vary with the lactation. Cows in the earlier part of the lactation are likely to transform a larger proportion of their feed into milk than cows in later stages of the lactation. On the other hand, cows in the later stages of the lactation are likely to transform a larger part of their feed into body fat. Hence, the response of milk production to feed depends in part upon the stage of the lactation. A farmer must consider this, therefore, in determining an optimum ration for his cows.

Feeding for Egg Production

Chickens consume a large proportion of the grain produced in the United States, and eggs are a major source of income to many farmers. One of the decisions of a poultryman is to determine how much to feed his chickens. Some breeds of chickens have been bred for relatively high levels of egg production. Other breeds have been bred for meat as well as egg production. Limited data are available on the relation of feed consumption to egg production. Perhaps the most extensive research which has been conducted in an effort to define the relation of feed to egg production was reported in a study by Hansen.[1] This study was designed to determine the effects of limited feeding on egg production. The results are suggestive of the production function, at least through a part of the relevant range.

In this feeding experiment, White Leghorn pullets were used. All of the pullets were of the same strain and of approximately the same weight. The first of three groups of pullets was given free access to an all-mash ration, and thus received all they would eat. The second group was given only 87.5 per cent of that eaten by the first group, and the third group was given only 75 per cent of the quantity eaten by the first group. The results of the experiment are shown in Table 14.

TABLE 14. Effect of Reduced Feed Intake on Egg Production

Percentage of Level 1

Level of Feeding	Rate of Feeding, per cent	Eggs per Layer, per cent
1	100	100
2	87.5	68.2
3	75.0	47.5

The results of this feeding experiment show an increasing return from feed as the layers were fed more nearly the full quantity they would eat. This suggests that the laying capacity of the White Leghorn hen is limited by her ability to assimilate feed. This capacity of the layers to utilize feed for production of eggs was so low that even in the upper levels of production the relationship between feed inputs and eggs still did not reach the zone of rational production. From these data, it appears that it would pay farmers to self-feed layers so as to get the maximum egg production. As noted in Chapter 4, it pays to continue to add inputs when the average product is increasing. The average product in this case is increasing since the percentage increase in egg production is greater than the percentage increase in feed.

[1] P. L. Hansen, "Input-Output Relationships in Egg Production," *Journal of Farm Economics*, Vol. XXXI, Nov. 1949.

Even though diminishing returns did not exist when feeding layers, this does not mean that egg producers have no economic problems. Rather, egg producers may be able to increase the profitability of egg production by varying the combination of feeds and the breed or strain of chicks used.

Feeding Broilers

Technological improvements have occurred in recent years which have greatly changed the costs of producing broilers. Changes in rations have been developed which give high efficiency in the conversion of feed into meat. Ten to 15 years ago, 3 to 3.5 pounds of feed per pound of meat were required for a 3-pound broiler. Today many producers are producing a 3-pound broiler with 2.2 to 2.6 pounds of feed per pound of meat. The changes in the rate of conversion have been brought about by increasing the fats and oils, by decreasing the fiber content of the ration, and by adding antibiotics. These changes in feeds and feeding methods also have reduced substantially the time involved in producing 3-pound broilers.

One of the most comprehensive studies to determine input-output relationships in broiler production was recently conducted in Connecticut. The study was conducted by feeding chicks a standardized ration containing antibiotics. The original weight of the chicks was 0.13 pound. The amount of feed consumed and weight of the broilers are given by weeks in Table 15. We notice that the gain from additional pounds of feed decreases substantially as the size of the bird increases. This is of particular importance to broiler producers. A broiler producer needs to give consideration to the amount of feed required to add more weight if he is to maximize net revenue.

The marginal product and value of marginal product per pound of feed are shown in Table 15. During the fifth week, the chick gains 0.29 pound and consumes 0.70 pound of feed. The marginal product per pound of feed is 0.29/0.70 or 0.41 pound. We have assumed a broiler price of 18 cents per pound in estimating the value of marginal product. The value of the marginal product tells the broiler producer the amount of additional revenue he will obtain from an additional pound of feed. The broiler producer also needs to consider the feed price in determining the weight at which he should sell his birds in order to maximize net revenue. If feed is 5 cents per pound, for example, the birds should be sold at the end of ten weeks. During the eleventh week, 1 pound of additional feed costs 5 cents and returns only 4.7 cents. Thus, the producer loses 0.3 cent for each pound of feed fed during the eleventh week.

TABLE 15. Broiler Meat Produced and Feed Consumed per Bird for Straight-Run Chicks, Other Inputs Constant, Heavy Breeds, Connecticut, 1952

Week	Total Gain in Weight, pounds	Total Input of Feed, pounds	Marginal Product per Pound of Feed, pound	Value of Marginal Product, cents*
1	0.13	0.29		
			0.45	8.1
2	0.26	0.58		
			0.44	7.9
3	0.43	0.97		
			0.42	7.6
4	0.61	1.40		
			0.41	7.4
5	0.90	2.10		
			0.39	7.0
6	1.29	3.10		
			0.37	6.7
7	1.66	4.09		
			0.35	6.3
8	2.04	5.19		
			0.32	5.8
9	2.46	6.50		
			0.29	5.2
10	2.89	7.98		
			0.26	4.7
11	3.31	9.59		
			0.22	4.0
12	3.71	11.40		
			0.18	3.2
13	4.03	13.16		
			0.14	2.5
14	4.28	14.96		
			0.10	1.8
15	4.48	16.92		

Source: G. G. Judge and I. F. Fellows, "Economic Interpretations of Broiler Production Problems," Storrs Agricultural Experiment Station, *Bulletin 302*, July 1953.

* Assumes a broiler price of 18 cents per pound.

If the price of broilers changes relative to the price of feed, the most profitable weight of the bird will change. In our example, if feed were 4.5 cents per pound and broilers still sold at 18 cents per pound, the broiler producer would maximize net revenue by feeding the broilers for 11 weeks. During the eleventh week, a pound of feed costs 4.5 cents but returns an additional 4.7 cents.

Many broiler producers are financed by feed dealers, hatcherymen and broiler processors. Information concerning the additional amount of feed required to add weight to the broiler is of value to these people as well as to the producers. If the hatcherymen, feed dealers, and processors expect the producers to remain in business, they should be concerned about the net revenue of the producer from each batch of birds produced. They are interested in the fact that, as the weight of the bird increases, the amount of feed required to add an additional unit of weight increases. Under these conditions, as we learned in Chapter 5, if the price of broilers increases relative to the price of feed, it pays the producer to market his broilers at a heavier weight.

Another factor must be considered, however, in determining the weight at which broilers will be marketed. The price processors are willing to pay for broilers depends on the weight of the broiler. Hence, producers may not be justified in using the same price for all weights of broilers. Both small and large broilers may be discounted in price. Total revenue will be affected by an increase in weight when birds are fed to a heavier weight. It will also be affected by a decrease in the price of the birds per pound. Hence, both of these things must be considered in determining the most profitable weight to which to feed broilers. The change in total revenue can then be compared with the change in cost of feeding an additional amount of feed to see if net revenue will be increased. The manner in which the most profitable weight can be determined when the price of the product varies with the weight is shown in the next example.

Another problem which complicates determining how much feed is profitable to feed broilers is the fact that the number of batches of broilers which can be produced in a year depends upon the length of the feeding period for each lot raised. The producer must give consideration, therefore, to the effects of length of the feeding period on the number of lots he will be able to produce in a particular period of time.

Feeding Hogs for Pork

Two recent studies describe production functions in feeding hogs.[1] In both cases, the primary purpose was to describe the relationship

---

[1] E. O. Heady et al., "New Procedures in Estimating Feed Substitution Rates and in Determining Economic Efficiency in Pork Production," Iowa Agricultural Experiment Station, *Research Bulletin 409*, May 1954; L. J. Atkinson, "Feed Consumption and the Production of Pork and Lard," *USDA Technical Bulletin 917*, June 1946.

between inputs of feed of a standardized ration and outputs of pork. This information is useful in deciding whether to produce hogs, and, for farmers who are feeding hogs, the information is helpful in determining the weight to which the hogs should be fed. The relation between inputs of feed and total gain of hogs above a 34-pound shoat when the hog is fed a ration containing 16 per cent protein are shown in Table 16.

TABLE 16. Gain Beyond Weaning for Different Feed Levels per Pig with a 16 Per Cent Protein Ration Containing Aureomycin

Pounds of Feed*	Total Weight, pounds†	Total Revenue, dollars‡	Total Feed Cost, dollars§	Net Revenue, dollars
50	56.1	11.22	2.15	9.07
100	73.5	14.70	4.30	10.40
150	89.4	17.88	6.45	11.43
200	104.4	20.88	8.60	12.28
250	118.9	23.78	10.75	13.03
300	132.8	26.56	12.90	13.66
350	146.4	29.28	15.05	14.23
400	159.7	31.94	17.20	14.74
450	172.7	34.54	19.35	15.19
500	185.4	37.08	21.50	15.58
550	198.0	39.60	23.65	15.95
600	210.3	42.06	25.80	16.26
650	222.5	41.16	27.95	13.21
700	234.6	43.40	30.10	13.30
750	246.5	45.60	32.25	13.35
800	258.2	47.77	34.40	13.37

Source: Based in part upon E. O. Heady et al., "New Procedures in Estimating Feed Substitution Rates and in Determining Economic Efficiency in Pork Production," Iowa Agricultural Experiment Station, *Research Bulletin 409*, May 1954, p. 939.

* Pounds fed after weaning.
† Includes weight of hog (34 pounds) at the beginning of the experiment.
‡ Assumes a price of $20 per cwt up to 220 pounds and a price of $18.50 per cwt for hogs larger than 220 pounds.
§ Assumes a feed price of $4.30 per cwt.

Under conditions where the price for hogs does not vary with their weight, we would determine the weight at which net revenue would be maximum exactly as we did in Chapter 5. However, there is a further complicating problem in the production of pork in that the percentage of fat in the carcass increases as the weight of the hog increases. Since the market discriminates against hogs of heavy weight, a change in price as well as a change in the weight of the hog must be considered in determining the most profitable level of feeding. The hog feeder must compare the cost of adding additional weight with the added value of additional weight. The expected additional revenue is found by comparing the present weight of the hog times the present price per pound and the weight of the hog times the expected price at heavier weights. The additional cost is found by multiplying the quantity of the inputs times the prices of the inputs necessary to obtain the additional weight. By comparing the added costs and added returns the farmer can decide whether it would be profitable for him to feed his hogs to a heavier weight.

The effect of a changing price for hogs at larger weights can be shown in reference to Table 16. If feed were $4.30 per hundred weight (cwt) and hogs were $20 per cwt, it would pay to feed hogs to a weight of at least 258 pounds, using 800 pounds of feed. It takes 50 pounds of feed to add 11.7 pounds of weight to a 246-pound hog. This additional weight would result in an increase in revenue of $2.34 if the price did not change as weight increased, compared to an added cost of $2.15 for the 50 pounds of feed. But we have assumed in Table 16 that the price drops to $18.50 for hogs larger than 220 pounds. The net revenue received from sale of a 224-pound hog is actually less than that received for a 210-pound hog. The lower price applies not only to the last pound of gain but also to the first 220 pounds. When the price changes for different weights, we cannot simply arrive at the optimum weight by finding the point where added revenue equals added cost. We must actually determine net revenue at various output levels. In this example, the maximum net revenue is $16.26 for a 210-pound hog.

For different combinations of feed and hog prices, different results may be obtained. If the price decrease is relatively small as hog weight increases, it may pay to feed to larger weights. In Table 17, the necessary selling price to permit the feeder to break even in putting 25 pounds of additional weight on hogs weighing 175 pounds is shown for various prices of feed and prices of hogs.

Another factor which must be considered in the case of hogs is that there are seasonal changes in prices due to changes in supply and demand. Expected prices must be the basis for determining whether it would be profitable to feed hogs to heavier weights. After all, it is the price of the hogs on the day they are sold that determines the revenue received for them. If keeping the hogs another month involves selling them at a time when supplies are increasing and prices

TABLE 17. Necessary Selling Price to Permit the Feeder to Break Even in Putting 25 Pounds Additional Weight on Hogs Weighing 175 Pounds

Present Feed Price, dollars per 100 pounds of ration	Current Price of Hogs per 100 Pounds, dollars					
	14.00	16.00	18.00	20.00	22.00	24.00
	For a 16 Per Cent Protein Ration					
5.00	15.00	16.75	18.50	20.25	22.00	23.75
4.80	14.89	16.64	18.39	20.14	21.89	23.64
4.60	14.78	16.53	18.28	20.03	21.78	23.53
4.40	14.67	16.42	18.17	19.92	21.67	23.42
4.20	14.56	16.31	18.06	19.81	21.56	23.31
4.00	14.45	16.20	17.95	19.70	21.45	23.20
3.80	14.34	16.09	17.84	19.59	21.34	23.09
3.60	14.23	15.98	17.73	19.48	21.23	22.98
3.40	14.12	15.87	17.62	19.37	21.12	22.87
3.20	14.01	15.76	17.51	19.26	21.01	22.76
3.00	13.90	15.65	17.40	19.15	20.90	22.65

Source: E. O. Heady et al., "New Procedures in Estimating Feed Substitution Rates and in Determining Economic Efficiency in Pork Production," Iowa Agricultural Experiment Station, *Research Bulletin 409*, May 1954, pp. 960–961.

are lower, the farmer should take this into consideration in determining the most profitable time to market his hogs. Feed constitutes the largest proportion of the inputs involved in feeding hogs to heavier weights. The significance of price changes over time, however, may offset or outweigh the significance of changes in feed cost.

7 | Cost varies with production

Most producers probably view production decisions from the standpoint of costs of production. In Chapters 5 and 6 emphasis has been placed upon the cost of using additional units of an input. In this chapter emphasis is placed upon the cost of producing additional units of output. Costs are related to volume of output in the same manner as production expenses were related to output in Chapter 5. Cost analyses are applicable to situations where more than one input is variable. In this chapter, we illustrate the construction of cost relations, using the same production function used in Chapters 4 and 5. In subsequent chapters we develop cost relations where more than one input is variable.

Frequently we read about cost of production of commodities relative to their prices. In fact, cost of production often becomes a policy issue when producers complain that the prices they receive for their products do not cover the cost of production. When spoken of in this way, cost of production generally refers to the expenses involved per unit of output produced. That is, reference is made to the average cost of producing a given amount of product.

When we speak of cost of producing a product, we refer to the expenses incurred in producing a *particular amount of product* in a *particular time period*. Without specifying the amount and the time period, any reference to cost is meaningless. A problem of major economic importance concerns the price which is relevant for the inputs. Many inputs, such as fertilizer, hybrid seed, gasoline, and weed spray, are purchased. It is easy for a farmer to price these items. Other inputs, such as land and family labor, are not actually paid a price, and some price must be assigned to these inputs if a farmer is to make a rational choice among alternatives. The establishment of such a price can be a thorny problem.

Opportunity Return

The price which should be used for any input is *the return which must be given up* due to the fact that the input is taken from the best alternative use. This is the concept of *opportunity return* or, as it is commonly called, opportunity cost. Opportunity return applies not only to those resources for which no price is available but also to purchased inputs. A producer's funds are limited. Ordinarily he is not able to buy all of the inputs he desires. If a farmer must pay $3 per cwt for 8–8–8 fertilizer, for example, he may not use this price in determining whether application of the fertilizer in production of corn is profitable. If the $3 which he pays for fertilizer would have given a net return of $10 if used to buy insecticide, and if funds are not available to buy both fertilizer and insecticide, the farmer in effect pays an opportunity return of $10 for use of the fertilizer on corn.

Opportunity return for an input may take several values depending on the viewpoint taken. When considering the farm as a whole, the opportunity return for family labor is the return which the family could get for its labor in other employment. Where no alternatives are open to the family, the value of its labor in nonfarm uses is zero. On the other hand, in determining the opportunity return for labor for an individual farm enterprise, the relevant family labor charge is the amount of income foregone by removing this labor from another enterprise. The opportunity return for labor in this case would likely be greater than zero.

Opportunity return is an extremely important concept. It serves as a general guide in the purchase and use of inputs. Then too, we shall see that this concept helps to tie together the rules of profit maximization in Chapter 5 with those of this chapter and Chapters 9 and 11.

Variable Cost and Fixed Cost

In economics, we often find it useful to think of planning periods as being short-run or long-run periods. By the *short run* is meant a period of time which is long enough to permit desired changes in output without altering the size of the plant. The *long run* is generally considered to be that period which is sufficiently long for output to be altered by varying either the size of the plant or by making a more intensive or a less intensive utilization of the existing plant.[1] For example, during the short run, it may be possible to increase the number of broilers processed by varying the amount of labor used. Two or even three shifts of labor can be used to increase production. In the long run, the number of broilers processed can be varied either by increasing the size of the plant or by increasing the number of workers. Thus, the number of ways in which production can be varied depends upon the length of the time period (the planning period) under consideration.

In line with these two lengths of planning periods, there are two major categories of costs; namely fixed costs and variable costs. Costs which would be incurred even if no output were produced are referred to as fixed costs. These are sunk costs. It should be emphasized that costs do not become fixed until they have been incurred. But after costs have been incurred, they do not vary with changes in output and can have no bearing upon decisions regarding an increase or decrease in production. In the short run, some costs are fixed, and others can be varied. After the long run, however, all costs become variable, and costs which were fixed in the short run influence decisions to cease production or to alter the level of output.

Variable costs are the costs of adding the variable inputs. These costs will be incurred only if production is carried on, and the amount of these costs will depend on the kinds and quantities of inputs used. In making production decisions as to the quantities of variable inputs to use to maximize net revenue, therefore, the variable costs are the relevant costs.

Fixed costs plus variable costs equal total costs. Total costs are necessary in computing net revenue, since net revenue is equal to total revenue less total costs. Over the long run, if total revenue is not greater than total costs, producers will not stay in production.

Whether a particular cost item will be considered as a fixed cost

[1] J. Viner, "Cost Curves and Supply Curves," *Zeitschrift für Nationalökonomie*, III, 1932, pp. 32–46.

or as a variable cost depends upon whether the input concerned is fixed or variable for the problem under consideration. During the long-run planning period, all inputs are considered variable. Thus, for the long-run period, there are no fixed costs. There are, however, various lengths of planning periods depending upon the questions under consideration. A farmer contemplating to enter the dairy business, for example, thinks of the costs of buildings, pastures, cows, and feed as variable costs. A farmer already operating a dairy, and therefore having cows and buildings, will, in choosing a ration for his cows, consider the costs of buildings and cows as fixed; costs of pasture and feed will be variable. For the extreme short-run period, the farmer probably will consider all costs fixed, with the possible exception of purchased feed. The costs which are relevant for a particular decision, therefore, depend upon the nature of the decision.

The Total Cost Function

The shape of the total cost curve is determined by the production function, provided that the price which the producer pays for inputs does not vary as the quantity of inputs purchased varies. Just how the production function and the total cost curve are related can be seen in Figures 14 and 15. The curve TP in Figure 14 shows the relationship between output and cost of the input. Since each unit of input costs the same amount, this curve is identical to the production function in which Y_1 is a function of the variable input X_1 in physical terms.

There are also fixed costs involved in the production of Y_1. Now,

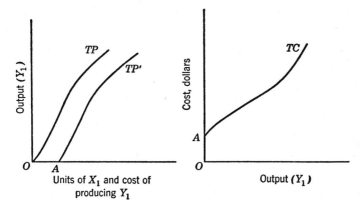

Figure 14. Relation of cost of production to the production function.

Figure 15. Relation of cost of production to level of output.

fixed costs can be shown by moving the production function to the right by a distance equal to the fixed costs. In this case, the amount of fixed cost is represented by the distance *OA*. Notice that the fixed costs do not change the shape of the curve; only the position is affected.

For most purposes, cost is thought of as related to output rather than inputs. For this reason, cost curves are portrayed with cost on the vertical axis and output on the horizontal axis as in Figure 15. The total cost curve in Figure 15 is the same curve as *TP'* in Figure 14; only the graph is turned sideways and backwards.

There are logical reasons for expecting the total cost curve to have the general form shown in Figure 15. Since each additional unit of input has a cost, we would expect the total cost curve to rise throughout its entire range. Only if the variable input were free would the total cost curve be horizontal, that is, would cost be independent of output. Certainly, we would not expect total cost to fall as output increases. Under such conditions, it would cost less to produce more, and, consequently, the rational producer would continue to expand his production indefinitely and throw away that quantity of product which he could not sell at the market price. In so doing, he would continuously increase his net revenue.

Likewise, we would not expect to find people operating in a region in which total cost increased as production decreased. This would happen in Region III of the production function, but, as we have already learned, producers seeking to maximize net revenue will not operate in Region III. Hence, from the viewpoint of the firm, we would expect the total cost curve to lie between the limits of a horizontal and a vertical line as does the total cost curve in Figure 15.

The total cost curve would not be expected to increase proportionately to the increase in the quantity of the variable inputs throughout the entire range of production. This situation would imply a linear production function as shown in Figure 8, and, as was shown in Chapter 5, this is not a realistic situation throughout the entire range of production. If total cost increased proportionately to the increase in variable inputs throughout the entire range of production, it would be profitable to produce an infinite amount of product if any is produced.

Average and Marginal Cost

The same relationships hold among the various cost curves as for the product curves. However, with cost curves, there is the added

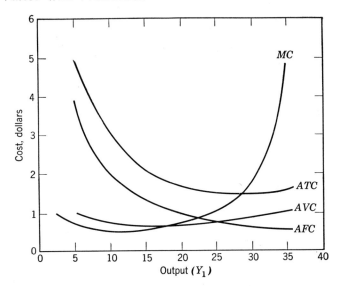

Figure 16. Average costs and marginal cost.

complication of having variable and fixed cost curves as well as a total cost curve. That is, when speaking of average cost, the type of cost—variable, fixed, or total—must be specified. With marginal cost, however, there is only one curve, since the marginal effect is caused only by the variable input.

A firm having a total cost structure as that shown in Figure 15 would be faced with a set of average and marginal cost curves similar to those in Figure 16, where these curves are based on the example in Figure 7. These cost curves have a definite relation to the total cost curve and to their corresponding marginal product and average product curves.

Average fixed cost. Average fixed cost is the fixed cost per unit of output. One characteristic of the *AFC* curve is important. *As more output is produced, the average fixed cost will fall continually,* but at a decreasing rate as shown in Table 18. This follows from the fact that a fixed amount of cost is divided by increasingly large numbers as output increases. Thus, one effect of increasing output is always the decrease of the fixed cost per unit of product. For example, a broiler processor can reduce the per unit fixed costs of interest, depreciation, insurance, and taxes for a processing plant by increasing the number of broilers processed per unit of time. Since these costs are independent of output, an increase in output will decrease fixed costs per unit of output.

TABLE 18. Cost Relationships for a Hypothetical Firm*

Output (Y_1)	Variable Cost ($P_{X1}X_1$), dollars	Fixed Cost, dollars	Total Cost ($VC+FC$), dollars	Average Variable Cost (VC/Y_1), dollars	Average Fixed Cost (FC/Y_1), dollars	Average Total Cost (TC/Y_1), dollars	Change in Output (ΔY_1)	Change in Cost (ΔVC), dollars	Marginal Cost ($\Delta VC/\Delta Y_1$), dollars
0	0	20	20	—	—	—	5	5	1.00
5	5	20	25	1.00	4.00	5.00	9	5	0.56
14	10	20	30	0.71	1.43	2.14	7	5	0.71
21	15	20	35	0.71	0.95	1.67	5	5	1.00
26	20	20	40	0.77	0.77	1.54	4	5	1.25
30	25	20	45	0.83	0.67	1.50	3	5	1.67
33	30	20	50	0.91	0.61	1.52	2	5	2.50
35	35	20	55	1.00	0.57	1.57	1	5	5.00
36	40	20	60	1.11	0.56	1.67			

* Costs are based on the physical data in Table 8, a fixed cost of $20 and a cost of $5 per input.

Average variable cost. The firm's AVC curve is directly related to the AP curve for the variable input. The way in which AVC and AP are related can be easily seen by a little arithmetic. Consider the case where $Y_1 = f(X_1)$. Then

$$AVC = VC/Y_1$$

but

$$VC = P_{X_1}X_1$$

Therefore,

$$AVC = P_{X_1}(X_1/Y_1)$$

and inverting,

$$AVC = \frac{P_{X_1}}{Y_1/X_1}$$

But

$$Y_1/X_1 = AP$$

Thus,

$$AVC = P_{X_1}/AP$$

Thus, we see that there is an inverse relationship between AP and AVC; when AP is increasing, AVC is decreasing; when AP is decreasing, AVC is rising. From this presentation, one other point should also be obvious. *When AP is at a maximum, AVC must be at its lowest point.* This low point is $0.71 per unit of output at 14 and 21 units of output in Table 18. Note that in Table 8, the highest AP was 7, also at 14 and 21 units of output.

Average total cost. Average total cost refers to the average of all costs per unit of output. Since total cost is the sum of fixed and variable costs, it is also true that ATC is the sum of AVC and AFC. This curve will also reach a low point but at a greater output than the low point of the AVC curve. For example, the lowest ATC in Table 18 is $1.50 per unit of output at an output level of 30 units. The average total cost falls over a greater range of output than the average variable cost because of the lowering influence of average fixed cost. For a range beyond the low point of the AVC curve, AFC falls at a faster rate than AVC increases. This causes ATC to continue to fall beyond the low point on the AVC curve; the ATC curve only starts to rise when the rate of decrease of the AFC curve is less than the rate of increase of the AVC curve.

Marginal cost. Marginal cost is the change in cost associated with an increase of one unit in output. Marginal cost is related to marginal product in the same manner that AVC is related to AP.

$$MC = \Delta \text{Cost}/\Delta Y_1$$

but

$$\Delta \text{Cost} = P_{X_1} \Delta X_1$$

Therefore,

$$MC = P_{X_1}(\Delta X_1/\Delta Y_1)$$

and inverting, $$MC = \frac{P_{X1}}{\Delta Y_1/\Delta X_1}$$

But $$\Delta Y_1/\Delta X_1 = MP$$

Thus, $$MC = P_{X1}/MP$$

It is seen that there is an inverse relationship between MP and MC. *When MP is at a maximum, MC is at a low point.* In Table 18, this low point is $0.56 per unit and is between 5 and 14 units of output. Likewise, the highest MP in Table 8 is 9 and is between the same units of output.

Marginal cost also has a definite relationship to the two average curves, ATC and AVC. Using the same reasoning as when comparing MP and AP, it will be seen that the AVC and ATC curves will fall as long as the MC curve is below them. Conversely, AVC and ATC will rise when MC is greater than the average curves. It also must follow that *MC is equal to AVC and ATC at the low points of these two curves.* These characteristics of the curves can be seen in Figure 16. Note that MC and AFC are in no way related. Fixed costs have no bearing on the additional cost as more output is produced.

Net Revenue is Related to Output

If the price of a commodity does not vary with the quantity a producer sells, total revenue increases in proportion to increases in output. Thus, his total revenue schedule relative to output is a straight line, the slope of which is the price of the commodity. Using our previous

TABLE 19. Net Revenue for Two Different Output Prices, Price of Input Constant

	$P_{X1} = \$5$	$P_{Y1} = \$2$		$P_{Y1} = \$1.50$	
Output (Y_1)	Total Cost (TC), dollars	Total Revenue (TR), dollars	Net Revenue ($TR - TC$), dollars	Total Revenue (TR), dollars	Net Revenue ($TR - TC$), dollars
0	20	0	−20	0	−20.0
5	25	10	−15	7.5	−17.5
14	30	28	−2	21.0	−9.0
21	35	42	7	31.5	−3.5
26	40	52	12	39.0	−1.0
30	45	60	15	45.0	0
33	50	66	16	49.5	−0.5
35	55	70	15	52.5	−2.5
36	60	72	12	54.0	−6.0

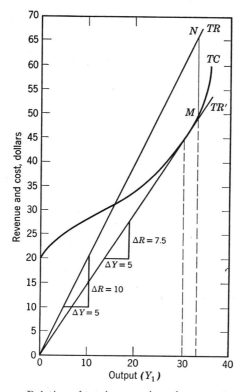

Figure 17. Relation of total cost and total revenue to output.

example, the TR and TC curves for a firm are depicted in Figure 17. Notice that the slope of the TR curve is $\Delta R/\Delta Y_1 = 10/5 = 2$, the price of the product which was assumed in the example in Chapter 5.

The producer who seeks to maximize net revenue will try to produce that level of output at which the difference between TR and TC is greatest. With P_{X1} at \$5 and P_{Y1} at \$2, this difference is greatest at an output of 33 units; the net revenue is equal to \$16 or the distance MN in Figure 17. This can also be shown as in Table 19 where total revenue and total cost are computed. From these total revenues and total costs, a series of net revenues for all outputs is obtained.

At an output of 33 units, the rate of change of both TR and TC is equal. This, of course, says that MC is equal to the price of the product. The relation of marginal cost and price to net revenue is shown in Figure 18. Net revenue is at a maximum at 33 units of output where MC is equal to the price of \$2. If more units of output are produced, the added cost will be greater than the added returns. If fewer units of output are produced, some net revenue will be foregone since the additional revenue from increased output exceeds the additional cost.

One condition for maximum net revenue is that *MC must equal price of the product*. An additional requirement also is necessary; *MC must be rising*. If this were not true and $MC = P_{Y1}$ where MC was falling, the producer would be operating under conditions of maximum loss. Fulfilling these two conditions assures a producer of operating so as to obtain maximum net revenue or a minimum loss; it does not mean that net revenue is positive.

A third condition for determining whether or not production should be carried on is that *total revenue must be greater than total variable cost*. In terms of the average relationships, this condition is that P_{Y1} *must be greater than average variable cost* if a positive NR is to be obtained. All three conditions are fulfilled when $P_{Y1} = \$2$, $P_{X1} = \$5$, and 33 units of output are produced, yielding a maximum, positive net revenue of \$16.

Effects of Price Changes

It is logical to expect changes in the optimum output if either P_{Y1} or P_{X1} changes. A decrease in product price means a lowering of the price line. Hence, the marginal revenue is decreased for each level of output. For example, if P_{Y1} were \$1.50, as shown in Figure 18, the

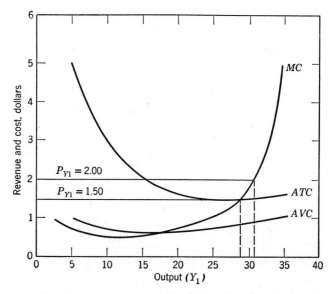

Figure 18. Relation of average cost, marginal cost, and revenue to output.

total revenue curve would be TR' in Figure 17. It is seen that a reduction in price of the product causes the optimum output to be reduced. Also, this is shown in Table 19, where the best the producer can do is to break even at an output of 30 units. On the other hand, a rise in product price increases the marginal revenue and usually increases the most profitable output.

Changes in input prices cause changes in production in the opposite direction from those brought about by changes in product prices. An increase in the price of the variable input causes the cost curves to move upward. The intersection of MC with P_{Y1} will be at a lower output, and production should be reduced to maximize NR. If the price of the input decreases, the cost of producing any given level of output decreases, and the most profitable level of production increases.

As was pointed out above, the fact that MC equals MR does not mean that a producer receives a positive net revenue. At a product price of $1.10, the optimum output would be 26 units. At this output, total costs exceed total revenue. Under such a situation, would the producer be wise to operate at all? The answer, as we shall see, depends on the time period involved.

The Long-Run and Short-Run Time Periods

The fixed costs, amounting to $20 in our example, cannot be altered in the short run. As long as the producer can make enough money to cover his variable costs, he will continue to operate. Thus, *operation is profitable in the short run if $P_{Y1} > AVC$*. At an output of 26 units, AVC is only $0.77. The producer would be wise to produce even though he knows that his earnings will not cover his fixed plus variable costs. That is, by producing this amount of output, the producer loses less than if he does not produce at all. This is true because the producer has to pay the fixed costs, whether he produces or not.

This situation of operating when price is greater than average variable cost but less than average total cost is common in agriculture. The Montana farmer with wheat ready for combining, for example, does not calculate costs of preparing land, seeding, and fertilizing in order to decide whether it would pay to harvest the wheat. At the time of harvest, his concern is that the costs of harvesting and marketing must be less than the returns from the wheat. He may lose money on the year's wheat operation, but he would lose more money if he does not harvest wheat when harvesting costs are less than revenue. For any given period of time, the relevant question for the farmer is whether the added costs will be more or less than the added returns.

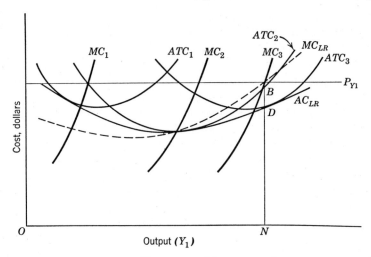

Figure 19. Short-run and long-run costs.

A supply curve can be developed by observing the effect of a change in the product price on a firm's optimum output. A *supply curve* shows the maximum quantities offered for sale per unit of time at alternative prices. As shown in Figure 18, an increase in product price makes it profitable to increase output. The MC curve actually shows the amounts which will be supplied at various product prices. At a price less than the lowest point on the AVC curve, nothing will be offered since variable costs cannot be covered. From this, it can be seen that in the short run the supply curve of a firm for any product is that portion of the MC curve which is above the AVC curve.

It might be anticipated that the firm's long-run supply curve would be the MC curve above the ATC curve. But this is not so. Each ATC curve, such as those in Figure 18, is representative of only one particular size of plant. These curves may be quite different for some other size of operation. The fixed costs for a 200-acre farm will be higher than the fixed costs for a 25-acre farm of comparable type. The average cost curves show cost per unit of output. These average costs for the 200-acre farm may be greater, smaller, or the same as average costs for the 25-acre farm.

A situation like that in Figure 19 is one possibility. The three ATC curves represent the average total costs for three different sizes of plant. For each output, there is some plant which gives a minimum average cost. For example, suppose that a producer is anticipating building a plant and going into production of Y_1. He wants to know how much output to produce and what size of plant to construct.

In the long-run planning situation, the producer is faced with a long-run marginal cost curve such as MC_{LR} in Figure 19. This curve shows the added costs of producing one more unit of output when all inputs can be varied.

If the producer expects an average price of P_{Y1} for his product, he will maximize net revenue by producing ON units of output. This is the amount of product at which the long-run marginal cost curve equals the expected product price. The producer can obtain ON units of output in either plant 2 or plant 3. The average cost per unit of output is NB if he builds plant 2, but it is only ND if he builds plant 3. From this we see that plant 3 is of the most efficient size for this level of output. We can see then that the plant which is most efficient in size depends upon the output at which the producer expects to operate.

In the long run, the size of plant is variable. The long-run cost curve for such a firm will be like AC_{LR}, where this curve is composed of the low costs of producing all possible outputs. The region where the long-run average cost curve falls is commonly thought of as the region of increasing returns to scale or, as we prefer, *increasing returns to size*. *Decreasing returns to size* is illustrated by that portion of the long-run cost curve where average cost is increasing.

It is now apparent that the long-run supply curve of a firm is not any portion of the MC curve for a plant of given size. The long-run marginal cost curve is shown by the curve MC_{LR}. The portion of this curve above the AC_{LR} curve is the long-run supply curve for the firm. The long-run supply curve is flatter than the supply curve for the short period. We see that, as the period of time increases, the number of inputs which can be varied increases. Thus, the response of production to changes in price is greater the longer the period of time considered.

8

Some applications of cost functions in production and processing of agricultural products

Cost analyses are often helpful to farmers and processors in making decisions. Among other uses, cost analyses can be used to determine whether an enterprise is profitable, what size of plant should be constructed, and what level of output is necessary before it pays to purchase some machine. Examples of such analyses are given in this chapter.

On-Farm Grain Drying and Storage

The low price of grain at harvest and the higher price later provide an incentive for grain producers to consider the possibility of increasing their net revenue by storing grain for sale at the later date. Costs are associated with storage of grain, however. It may even be necessary to dry the grain artificially before it can be safely stored. We know that all of the increase in price associated with storage is not net revenue. To make a rational decision concerning storage, the farmer must have knowledge of additional costs and returns resulting from the storage.

A Texas study was made to investigate the factors pertaining to the problem of drying and storing rice.[1] Rice needs to be harvested when

[1] R. J. Hildreth and J. W. Sorenson, Jr., "Profits and Losses from On-Farm Drying and Storage of Rice in Texas," Texas Agricultural Experiment Station, *Bulletin 865,* College Station, Texas, July 1957.

the moisture content is between 18 and 25 per cent in order to maintain milling quality, but it must not have a moisture content greater than 12 or 13 per cent for safe storage. Thus, rice must be dried artificially, and it is logical to investigate drying and storage as a single process.

It was found that for 1954–1956 the average variable costs of drying and storing rice amounted to about 38.3 cents per barrel; this did not appear to change as volume increased. Included in these average variable costs were costs of cleaning bins, labor, hauling to bins, electricity, insect control, fuel for grain moving equipment, grain insurance, and loss in weight or shrinkage during storage.

For a farmer already owning storage bins and drying equipment, net returns expected from the drying and storage operation need only be greater than variable costs for drying and storage to be profitable. That is, if an added return of more than 38.3 cents per barrel is expected, the rice should be dried and stored. For the period of 1945–1955, the average price rise per barrel was $1.67. The least rise in any one year was $0.54 per barrel for the 1945–1946 crop. This indicates that storage of rice would have been profitable every year for the farmer who already owned the drier and granary.

A farmer contemplating storage, and who does not already own storage facilities, must consider all costs which include the costs of adding such facilities. To this farmer, all costs of storage are variable. He must include as variable costs the cost of interest on investment, property taxes, annual repairs, insurance, and depreciation. It was estimated that these costs amounted to $3124 per year for a 7700-barrel capacity drier and a storage bin with an installed auger. This cost of $3124 per year does not change with volume, but the average cost is lower as the amount stored increases. In Figure 20, this situation is presented graphically.

The volume of rice which is dried and stored has a large effect on the total costs per bushel of storing grain. Therefore, the volume stored affects the farmer's decision as to whether to build drying and storage facilities and store grain on his farm or to sell at time of harvest. For example, suppose that a $1.00 per barrel rise in price from harvest to a period about 8 or 9 months later is anticipated on the average. Under these conditions, a farmer must have slightly over 5000 barrels per year if he is to buy a drier and bin and break even on his venture. If he expects to obtain an average seasonal price increase of $1.50 per barrel, he will increase his net revenue by buying a drier and bin if he has more than about 2800 barrels to store each year.

Farmers in many areas, particularly in the Great Plains, have an

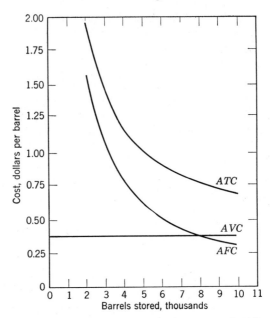

Figure 20. Costs of on-farm drying and storage of rice in a building with installed auger.

additional alternative in storing grain. They can store grain in commercial facilities. Where this is possible, a farmer may find that commercial storage is most profitable for small volumes, whereas on-farm storage results in more net revenue if the farmer has larger volumes to store. A farmer may find that commercial storage is cheaper than on-farm storage for any volume stored unless on-farm facilities are already available. If a farmer owns a granary, the variable costs may be less than the costs of storing commercially. In any case, all available alternatives must be weighed by a farmer before making his decision.

Fryer Processing Plants

A Washington State College bulletin distinguishes between short-run and long-run cost relationships in the fryer processing industry.[1] Five model plants were considered, and costs of operation were estimated from observations of processing plants in Washington. The five plants represent different sizes of operation or daily capacities.

[1] E. L. Baum, J. E. Faris, and H. G. Walkup, "Economies of Scale in the Operation of Fryer Processing Plants," Washington State College, *Technical Bulletin No. 7,* Aug. 1952.

Two effects are shown by this study. Given the size of plant, the effect on average cost of changing the volume of fryers shows what can be considered the short-run cost behavior. Varying the size of plant gives an indication of the long-run effects on average cost. Both effects can be seen in Table 20. Changing the number of fryers processed for any plant shows that there are increasing returns from the variable inputs involved. In plant A, for example, average costs decrease from $0.194 to $0.166 per bird when the percentage of plant capacity used is increased from 40 per cent capacity to full capacity. Full capacity is the maximum number of fryers which can be processed in one eight-hour day given the existing plant equipment.

TABLE 20. Costs of Processing a Fryer for Five Model Fryer Processing Plants Operating at 100 Per Cent, 70 Per Cent, and 40 Per Cent of Plant Capacity, March 1951

| | Plant | | | | |
	A	B	C	D	E
Daily Capacity of Fryers	500	1600	3100	4500	9000
Cost in dollars at					
100 per cent of capacity	0.166	0.148	0.135	0.128	0.118
70 per cent of capacity	0.174	0.153	0.140	0.134	0.123
40 per cent of capacity	0.194	0.166	0.153	0.147	0.136

Source: E. L. Baum, J. E. Faris, and H. G. Walkup, "Economies of Scale in the Operation of Fryer Processing Plants," Washington State College, *Technical Bulletin No. 7*, Aug. 1952.

Increasing returns to size of plant is shown by the fact that processing cost per fryer decreases as plant size increases. At 100 per cent of capacity, processing in the largest plant can be accomplished about 5 cents per bird cheaper than in the smallest plant. Increasing the rate of production with a given capacity and increasing plant size bring about a decrease in the processing cost per bird. No range of decreasing returns is noted, as can be seen in Figure 21. Another study of broiler processing plants shows that the average total cost decreases very little beyond an output of 9600 and up to 38,400 birds per day.[1]

[1] James R. Donald and C. E. Bishop, "Broiler Processing Costs—A Study of Economies of Scale in the Processing of Broilers," *A. E. Information Series No. 59*, Department of Agricultural Economics, North Carolina State College, June 1957.

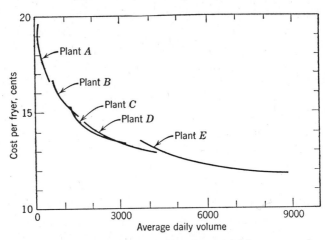

Figure 21. Short-run average cost curves for five model fryer processing plants.

Cost analyses, such as that of Baum and associates are very useful to the prospective processor. For example, a processor expecting a daily volume of 1600 birds might wish to build a plant with a daily capacity of 3100 birds. The per-unit cost would be about the same in either case, and the plant operator would have flexibility to increase his output as the need arose. With expansion in the fryer industry continuing, it may be wise to build with a view to the future. The information in this study indicates that there is an incentive for plants to increase size. As plants become larger, the larger plants can sell at lower prices. Under these conditions, smaller plants will find it increasingly difficult to stay in business.

Cotton Mechanization

The introduction of new machinery often involves the problem of comparing machine costs with labor costs. This is the case with the mechanical cotton picker. A research study in North Carolina gives a comparison of hand and machine methods of harvesting cotton.[1]

Labor is usually hired for hand picking of cotton on the basis of a price per 100 pounds of seed cotton picked. Hence, the average cost curve for hand picking cotton is linear and horizontal. The investment in a mechanical cotton picker means that average costs are high for smaller quantities and decrease as quantity increases. Whether

[1] J. Gwyn Sutherland and H. B. James, "Cotton Mechanization in North Carolina," North Carolina Agricultural Experiment Station, *Technical Bulletin No. 104,* Jan. 1954.

mechanical picking is more profitable than hand picking depends on the prices paid for the two kinds of picking and on the yield and acres picked.

The relationship between the costs of these two methods is shown in Figure 22. Costs are plotted against acres harvested, which is the same as bales of cotton since production of a bale an acre is assumed. The costs of picking include the costs of operating the machine plus the fixed costs of depreciation and interest on investment. Other cost factors also enter into the picture. The picker leaves more cotton in the field than does hand picking, and this is a cost attributed to the mechanical picker. There is also a reduction in grade and some additional ginning charges for mechanically picked cotton because of the additional trash.

The costs of operation and the costs due to field loss of cotton, added ginning charges, and loss in grade are constant per acre. The fixed costs give the picker cost curve its shape. As seen in Figure 22, if labor can be hired to pick cotton at $3 per 100 pounds, picking can be done cheaper by hand than by machine, even if 200 acres of cotton are being harvested. If labor is $4 per 100 pounds, mechanical picking is cheaper than hand labor if more than 75 acres are being harvested.

If the farmer owns a mechanical picker, only the variable costs are relevant in determining whether to use the machine or to use hand-harvesting methods. As long as the costs of hand harvesting are

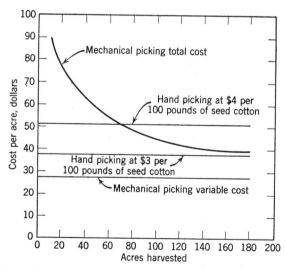

Figure 22. Comparison of total costs per acre for harvesting cotton yielding one bale of lint per acre, by method of harvest.

greater than the variable costs of operating the machine, the farmer should use the machine. We see in Figure 22 that the farmer who owns a mechanical picker will find it profitable to use the picker even if hand-picking rates are as low as $3.00 per cwt.

This study shows quite well one effect of an expansion in industrial employment. As alternative employment opportunities become available to farm laborers, wages for farm labor rise, and it becomes relatively more profitable to mechanize production. This, of course, is what has been happening in much of the Cotton Belt in the period since World War II.

Peach Hydrocooling

Precooling peaches is thought to reduce bruising and rotting during transit and to increase the period of time that peaches can be kept in stores without spoiling. Hydrocooling is a process of precooling by the use of ice water sprayed over the material to be cooled. The results of a study on this process are presented in a North Carolina Agricultural Experiment Station study.[1]

Hydrocooling peaches actually produces a different product. The peach packer wishes to compare the costs of cooling peaches with the added returns that he can expect for his peaches if cooled. The market determines the price; the packer must calculate the costs.

The costs of ice to cool the water in the hydrocooler make up a large portion of the total costs of hydrocooling. Ice costs have been separated from the other variable costs in Table 21. Neither the ice costs nor the other variable costs need be incurred unless some output is produced. However, the average variable costs of labor, electricity, and the fungicide are constant regardless of output. The ice costs per bushel decrease with output. Thus, the peach packer is faced with average variable costs which decrease as volume increases. This affects his day-to-day decisions as to whether peaches should be cooled or sold without cooling.

The average ice cost curve decreases because it takes a given amount of ice to cool the water before packing begins. For each bushel cooled, the amount of ice needed is constant. This fact has important implications. The packer can afford to cool other growers' peaches on a custom basis at a cost which is lower than average total costs or even average ice costs at small volumes. He can do this

---

[1] W. D. Toussaint, T. T. Hatton, and George Abshier, "Hydrocooling Peaches in the North Carolina Sandhills, 1954," North Carolina State College, *A.E. Information Series No. 39,* February 1955.

TABLE 21. Estimated Per-Bushel Costs of Hydrocooling
Peaches with a 25-Foot Cooler

Annual Volume Packed	Fixed Cost per Bushel, dollars*	Ice Cost per Bushel, dollars†	Other Variable Cost per Bushel, dollars‡	Total Cost per Bushel, dollars
1,000	0.930	0.309	0.015	1.254
2,000	0.465	0.192	0.015	0.672
3,000	0.310	0.153	0.015	0.478
5,000	0.186	0.121	0.015	0.322
10,000	0.093	0.098	0.015	0.206
15,000	0.063	0.090	0.015	0.167
20,000	0.047	0.086	0.015	0.148
30,000	0.031	0.082	0.015	0.128

Source: W. D. Toussaint, T. T. Hatton, and George Abshier, "Hydrocooling Peaches in the North Carolina Sandhills, 1954," North Carolina State College, *A.E. Information Series No. 39*, Feb. 1955, p. 29.

* Includes depreciation, taxes, insurance, and interest on investment.
† Based on cooling peaches 35°F and packing 30 days per year.
‡ Includes labor, hypochlorite, and electricity.

because the water is already cool, and additional costs to him are only the other variable costs plus the added ice necessary to cool the peaches.

From the long-run standpoint of buying a hydrocooler, the packer must compare expected additional returns and costs. With the total cost information in Table 21, the packer can make such a decision if he knows the added returns and the volume to be cooled. If he receives 20 cents per bushel premium for hydrocooled peaches, the packer cannot afford to buy a cooler unless he will process over 10,000 bushels per year. Such cost data as this can be used by packers to enable them to choose between joint ownership of machines, cooperatives, or individual ownership. The advantages of larger operation can be weighed against any disadvantages of multiple ownership.

9 | Cost can be reduced by changing inputs

In the preceding chapters, production decisions were considered in situations which involved varying one input, but many production problems show variation of two or more inputs. A producer must choose the particular combination of inputs which would be most profitable to use. For example, a farmer must choose the amounts of hay and grain to be used in feeding dairy cows or the amounts of potash, phosphate, and nitrogen to be used in growing wheat.

To start with the simplest case of this type, we will consider a situation of two variable inputs. It can be written $Y_1 = f(X_1, X_2 \mid X_3, X_4, \cdots, X_n)$. That is, production depends on the amounts of X_1 and X_2 used while the other inputs are held constant at particular levels. The problem is to determine the amounts of X_1 and X_2 to use in the production of Y_1.

The box diagram of Figure 23 shows the amounts of product which can be obtained with different amounts of X_1 and X_2, all other inputs being held constant at given levels. As more of the two inputs are used, the general result is to get greater quantities of product. Because some inputs are held constant, however, production will increase at a decreasing rate after some point and will eventually decrease. That is, diminishing returns from the application of the variable inputs will be encountered.

It should be noted that this box diagram is simply an accumulation of single-variable production functions. Reading along any row or up any column shows the relationship between output and one input, all other inputs held constant. We can see now that in Chapter 4 we discussed a special production function. We varied only one input and estimated the effects on output. We are now making our analysis more general by varying two inputs and determining the effects on output.

In the production of most commodities the same output can be obtained by various combinations of inputs. When this is possible, the producer may be able to reduce the cost of obtaining a particular level of output by changing the combination of inputs used. The

X_2 \ X_1	0	5	10	15	20	25	30	35	40	45	50
100	24	25	27	30	32	33	32	31	30	29	26
90	23	24	26	29	31	32	33	32	31	30	29
80	20	23	25	27	29	31	32	33	32	31	31
70	15	21	23	25	27	29	31	32	33	33	33
60	10	18	21	24	26	28	29	30	32	32	33
50	7	14	19	22	24	26	27	28	30	31	32
40	5	10	16	19	22	24	25	26	28	29	30
30	3	7	13	16	19	21	22	24	26	27	28
20	2	4	9	12	15	17	19	21	23	24	25
10	1	2	5	7	11	13	16	18	20	21	22
0	0	1	2	4	6	8	10	13	17	19	20

$Y_1 = 30$ $Y_1 = 5$ $Y_1 = 10$ $Y_1 = 20$

Figure 23. Output of Y_1 for different amounts of two variable inputs, X_1 and X_2.

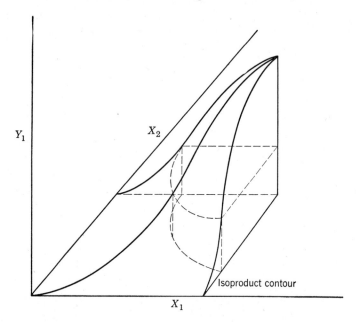

Y_1

X_2

Isoproduct contour

X_1

Figure 24. A production function with two variable inputs.

curved lines in Figure 23 join all combinations of X_1 and X_2 which result in an equal amount of product. These lines are called *iso-product* or equal product contours; they will be useful, as we shall see below, in choosing the combination of inputs which will yield a given amount of product at a minimum cost.

A production function having two variable inputs can be shown graphically. However, this is no longer a problem which can be represented directly by a two-dimensional graph. There are now three variables to consider. As the quantities of X_1 and X_2 are increased and all other inputs are held constant, a production surface is formed as in Figure 24. The height of the surface is the yield, and the inputs are measured horizontally. The shape of the surface will vary for different types of production.

The three-dimensional diagram of Figure 24 is difficult to visualize and to analyze. The analysis can be simplified by reducing the surface to a series of isoproduct curves as shown by the dotted line in Figure 24, which represents all combinations of X_1 and X_2 which will yield the same quantity of Y_1. These isoproduct contours are analogous to contour lines on a map, where each line represents a combination of points, all of the same height. Isoproduct curves can be constructed for each level of output. A map of isoproduct curves shows the amounts of inputs necessary to get any particular level of output in the same manner that a topographic map indicates how far we would have to travel to reach a specified altitude on a mountain.

Inputs Combine in Different Ways

The shapes of the production surface and the isoproduct contour lines are determined by the manner in which the variable inputs combine. The ways in which inputs combine can be classified into three groups: (1) Inputs which combine in fixed proportions; (2) inputs which may be substituted in a constant ratio; and (3) inputs for which the rate of substitution varies according to the combination of the two inputs used.

Fixed proportions. Inputs which combine in fixed proportions in the production of any commodity present no economic problem insofar as choosing the optimum proportion of inputs is concerned. There is only one way of combining inputs which will yield the product under consideration. A common example is the case of water. To obtain a molecule of water, two atoms of hydrogen are combined with one atom of oxygen. Three atoms of hydrogen and one oxygen atom will still yield only one water molecule. That is, such inputs are said to combine in a fixed ratio. The case of fixed proportions is illustrated in Figure 25. The contour lines are simply points, the points farther out from the origin representing higher levels of output.

Pure examples of fixed proportions are not too easy to find in agriculture. A tractor and a man fit the situation quite well, however. To add another tractor will be of little use unless a man is added to drive the tractor. This statement, of course, is not always true. One farmer may wish to have two tractors of different size and capability

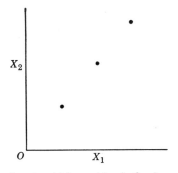

Figure 25. Inputs which combine in fixed proportions.

to perform different tasks. Where this situation is true, the fixed proportion analogy does not hold.

Constant rate of substitution. The two inputs in Figure 26 substitute at a constant rate. That is, the rate at which these two inputs can be exchanged in the production of a particular level of output is constant regardless of the ratio of the two inputs used. This rate of substitution indicates the amount by which X_2 must be changed to offset a change in the amount of X_1 in order to maintain production at a particular level. It is commonly called the *marginal rate of substitution* between inputs and is denoted by $\Delta X_2/\Delta X_1$, which is the slope of the product contour at any point.

For inputs which can be exchanged at a constant rate, the slope of the product contours is constant. Examples of inputs which can be exchanged at a constant rate can be found in agriculture. In the feeding of some types of livestock, oats and barley or sorghum grain and corn are very nearly in this class. For example, one bushel of corn has a definite relationship to a given quantity of sorghum grain in terms of feeding value. This relationship is constant or nearly so regardless of the ratio of feeds used in the ration.

The labor inputs of two workers often can be exchanged at a constant rate. If the laborers do not perform equivalent amounts of work in the same time, at least one will perform a constant amount of work relative to the other laborer, possibly twice as much or half as much. If two laborers will perform the same amount of work and one wishes a higher wage, the choice which an employer will make is clear. He will hire the laborer who is willing to work for the lower wage. If

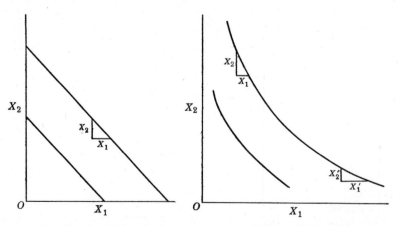

Figure 26. Inputs which substitute at constant rates.   **Figure 27.** Inputs which substitute at varying rates.

one laborer does twice as much work but only asks for a 10 per cent higher wage, the employer will hire this man in order to reduce cost. Thus, when inputs can be exchanged at a constant rate, only one should be used. The one to use depends upon the relative prices and the rate at which the inputs can be exchanged.

Varying rate of substitution. This case is illustrated in Figure 27. The marginal rate of substitution varies over the product contour. The amount of X_1 required to offset the loss of one unit of X_2 and to maintain production constant increases as the amount of X_1 used increases. That is, $\Delta X_2/\Delta X_1$ is greater than $\Delta X_2'/\Delta X_1'$. The slope of this isoproduct curve becomes less steep as more X_1 is used relative to X_2. The case of varying rates of substitution is encountered with many inputs.

Agriculture holds many examples of inputs which substitute at varying rates. Hay and grain substitute in this manner in the production of milk. A cow fed entirely on hay would produce the same quantity of milk with a small addition of grain and a relatively large decrease in hay. As more and more grain is added, however, the additional grain replaces less and less hay. It is more difficult to select the minimum cost combination of inputs in this case than in the others.

Least-Cost Combination of Inputs

The marginal rate of substitution referred to above is a physical phenomenon. It shows how much of one input can be removed with the output remaining at the same level if one unit of the other input is added. The concept is two-directional. That is, $\Delta X_2/\Delta X_1$ can be thought of as showing what happens when X_1 is added or taken away or what happens when X_2 is taken away or added. Since the concept is strictly physical, it alone cannot tell a producer the combination of inputs which will minimize cost in the production of a given quantity of output.

To determine the quantities of the variable inputs which would give him a certain amount of product at a minimum cost, a producer must know the rates at which the inputs can be exchanged in the market in addition to the rates at which they can be exchanged in production. When the prices of inputs which farmers buy do not change as the quantity purchased increases, the rate of substitution of two inputs in the market is the ratio of the prices of the two inputs. If the price of corn is $1.50 per bushel and the price of oats is $0.75 per bushel, the rate of substitution of oats for corn is 2 to 1. Two bushels of oats can be purchased for the same amount as one bushel of corn. Thus, P_{X1}/P_{X2} is the rate of substitution in the market. It is this ratio, compared with the physical substitution ratio, $\Delta X_2/\Delta X_1$, which tells the farmer how to choose his optimum input combination.

The combination of inputs which will yield a given quantity of output at *least cost* is where $\Delta X_2/\Delta X_1 = P_{X1}/P_{X2}$. This statement of the condition which gives a least-cost combination of inputs can also be written as $P_{X2} \Delta X_2 = P_{X1} \Delta X_1$. This is the same as saying that the cost of adding X_2 is equal to the reduction in cost from using less of X_1. If $P_{X2} \Delta X_2 > P_{X1} \Delta X_1$, adding X_1 and decreasing X_2 will decrease cost. If, on the other hand, $P_{X2} \Delta X_2 < P_{X1} \Delta X_1$, adding X_2 and decreasing X_1 will decrease cost in producing a given quantity of product. Unless $\Delta X_2/\Delta X_1 = P_{X1}/P_{X2}$, it is possible either to increase output with the same cost or to decrease the cost of obtaining a given level of output.

An isoproduct contour which represents all combinations of X_1 and X_2 producing 10 units of output is shown in Figure 28. This product contour is one of those shown in Figure 23. The problem is to choose the combination of X_1 and X_2 which will produce 10 units of product at least cost.

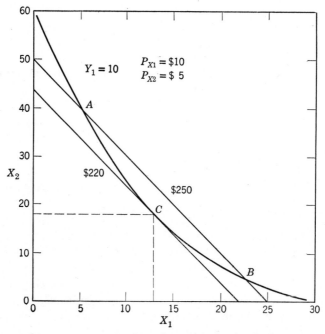

Figure 28. Minimum cost production of a particular level of output using two variable inputs.

If the prices of the two inputs are known, all combinations of X_1 and X_2 which can be purchased for a given amount of money can be determined. For example, if P_{X1} is \$10 and P_{X2} is \$5, \$250 will buy 50 units of X_2, 25 units of X_1, or any combination of the two inputs as shown by the \$250 cost line in Figure 28. Since P_{X1} and P_{X2} are constant regardless of the amount purchased, the equal cost or *isocost* line will be a straight line, and the slope of the line is P_{X1}/P_{X2}.

The \$250 isocost curve intersects the 10-unit isoproduct contour at point A and point B. That is, either 40 X_2 and 5 X_1 or 5 X_2 and 22.5 X_1 can be used to produce the 10 units of output. In either case, the cost is \$250. The same output can be produced at a lower cost, however. At C, 18 units of X_2 and 13 units of X_1 yield 10 units of product at a cost of only \$220. At point C, the slope of the product contour or $\Delta X_2/\Delta X_1$ is equal to P_{X1}/P_{X2} which is the slope of the isocost curve. This is the least-cost combination of X_1 and X_2 producing 10 units of product. Ten units of product cannot be produced at less cost because no combination of X_1 and X_2 below the \$220 isocost curve will yield 10 units of product.

The same results can be seen in Table 22. The combinations of X_1 and X_2 for 10 units of product are the same combinations as those which define the product contour in Figure 28. In the table, there are two different combinations of inputs that can be used to produce either 5 or 10 units of product at least cost. The figures in Table 22

TABLE 22.   Combinations of Inputs to Obtain Equal Amounts
of Product, Hypothetical Data

	$Y_1 = 5$				$Y_1 = 10$		
X_1	X_2	$\Delta X_2/\Delta X_1$	Cost, dollars*	X_1	X_2	$\Delta X_2/\Delta X_1$	Cost, dollars*
0	40	—	200	0	60	—	300
3	28	4	170	5	40	4	250
6	19	3	155	10	25	3	225
9	12	7/3	150	15	15	2	225
12	6	2	150	20	7	8/5	235
15	2	4/3	160	25	3	4/5	265
18	0	2/3	180	30	0	3/5	300

* P_{X1} = \$10 and P_{X2} = \$5.

do not include all possible combinations of inputs. The least-cost combination which was determined graphically lies between the underlined costs in the table. This happens because large units of measurement are used. If every possible combination of inputs were shown in the table, the graphic and tabular solutions would be identical.

The existence of two least-cost combinations in Table 22 can be easily explained. To go from the combination of 10 X_1 and 25 X_2 to 15 X_1 and 15 X_2 in the production of 10 units of output, $\Delta X_2/\Delta X_1$ or the marginal rate of substitution is 2. This says that two units of X_2 can be replaced by one unit of X_1 in this range, and output will not change. But X_1 costs twice as much as X_2. Since X_1 costs twice as much as X_2 for each unit, and two units of X_2 will replace one unit of X_1 when moving to another input combination, the cost of either input combination must be the same.

Choosing the Optimum Level of Output

Finding the least-cost input combination in producing a given amount of product is helpful to the producer. But he also wishes to know the amount of product which he should produce. To solve this problem, an additional analytical step is required.

A revenue and a cost are associated with each least-cost input combination. The producer wishes to find the level of output where total revenue minus total cost is greatest. An example is provided in Table 22. The least-cost combinations for either five or ten units of product are shown. It costs $150 to produce five units and $225 to produce ten units. If the product price is $40, the revenues from the production of five units and ten units are $200 and $400 respectively. The net revenues for producing five units and ten units of product at the least-cost input combinations are $50 and $175 respectively. In this case, the producer would receive more net revenue from producing ten units than five units of the product. To choose the amount of product which would yield the greatest net revenue, he would proceed in the same manner to compare the net revenues for other levels of output, each produced with minimum cost.

Changes in Input Prices Affect Minimum Cost Combination of Inputs

Since the least-cost combination of inputs is obtained when $\Delta X_2/ \Delta X_1$ equals P_{X1}/P_{X2}, a change in the relative prices of X_1 and X_2 changes the least-cost combination of inputs used to produce a particular level of output. If a producer is to produce at minimum cost in a situation in which prices are changing, it is necessary for him to change the combination of inputs used. The rates at which inputs can be substituted in production are determined by the production function. By changing the amount of an input in relation to another, a producer can find a combination of inputs where the rate of substitution in production is equal to the new price ratio of the inputs.

More than Two Variable Inputs

In many production decisions, all inputs may be variable, i.e., $Y_1 = f(X_1, X_2, \cdots, X_n)$. When more than two variable inputs are considered, the analysis is quite complex. A graphic presentation is impossible since at least four dimensions are required. However, the condition for the least-cost combination of three or more inputs can be shown in mathematical terms.

It has been shown above that the optimum combination of inputs X_1 and X_2 is where $P_{X1} \Delta X_1 = P_{X2} \Delta X_2$. It must also be true that $P_{X1} \Delta X_1 = P_{X3} \Delta X_3$ for the least-cost combination of inputs X_1 and X_3. Thus, for any number of variable inputs, the optimum combination of inputs is where $P_{X1} \Delta X_1 = P_{X2} \Delta X_2 = \cdots = P_{Xn} \Delta X_n$. That is, the optimum combination of inputs is attained when inputs are combined in such proportions that the reduction in costs from reducing the amount of one input is equal to the cost of adding another input in sufficient amount to maintain output.

This condition for least-cost production can be stated in another way. It was shown in Chapter 5 that the condition for maximizing net revenue with one variable input was that $VMP = P_{X1}$, or $P_{Y1}(\Delta Y_1/\Delta X_1) = P_{X1}$. Likewise $P_{Y1}(\Delta Y_1/\Delta X_2) = P_{X2}$ at the optimum level of use of X_2. From these two equations, it can be seen that $[P_{Y1}(\Delta Y_1/\Delta X_1)]/P_{X1} = 1$ and $[P_{Y1}(\Delta Y_1/\Delta X_2)]/P_{X2} = 1$. Since both equations equal 1, they are equal to each other, and $[P_{Y1}(\Delta Y_1/\Delta X_1)]/P_{X1} = [P_{Y1}(\Delta Y_1/\Delta X_2)]/P_{X2}$ when both X_1 and X_2 are used to produce Y_1. Dividing both sides by P_{Y1} and extending to n variables, we see that $(\Delta Y_1/\Delta X_1)/P_{X1} = (\Delta Y_1/\Delta X_2)/P_{X2} = \cdots = (\Delta Y_1/\Delta X_n)/P_{Xn}$ when $X_1, X_2, \cdots, X_n$ are used in the production of Y_1. This equation tells us that a product is produced at least cost only if the marginal products of the inputs are proportional to the prices of the inputs. If all inputs had the same price, but some inputs were more productive than others, it is obvious that it would be profitable to purchase the more productive inputs. As additional units of those inputs with high marginal products in relation to their prices are used, the marginal products will decrease until the ratios of the marginal products to input prices are the same for all inputs.

Equality of the ratios of the marginal products of the variable inputs to their respective prices is a condition for minimum cost of producing a particular quantity of a product using n variable inputs. However, the minimization of cost of producing a particular level of output of a product does not necessarily mean that the most profitable level of output is being produced. To determine the most profitable level of output, the producer compares costs and revenues for various levels of output, all of which are produced at least cost. A condition of profit maximization is that marginal cost equal the product price, P_{Y1}.

We saw in Chapter 7 that $MC = P_{X1}/(\Delta Y_1/\Delta X_1)$; therefore $(\Delta Y_1/\Delta X_1)/P_{X1}$ must be the same as $1/MC$. Hence, output would be expanded until

$$\frac{\Delta Y_1/\Delta X_1}{P_{X1}} \frac{\Delta Y_1/\Delta X_2}{P_{X2}} = \cdots = \frac{\Delta Y_n/\Delta X_n}{P_{Xn}} = \frac{1}{MC} = \frac{1}{P_{Y1}}$$

10 | Some applications of minimum cost production

Some of the problems faced by producers in choosing the kinds and quantities of inputs to use in their production process are relatively simple; some are quite complex. This chapter contains examples of the types of problems encountered and indicates how economic logic can be used in solving the problems.

Substitution of Grains in Feeding Beef

In some types of feeding, several grains may be exchanged for each other at a constant rate. Corn, oats, barley, and sorghum grain are reported in one study to be of equal feeding value per pound for wintering beef cattle.[1] Where this is true, only one of the grains should be fed; the one to feed depends upon the prices. Using corn for comparative purposes, the relative value of other grains can be seen in Table 23 for those cases where the feeds can be exchanged at a constant rate.

We can derive the prices in this table by comparing the relative weights per bushel of corn with the other grains. The ratio of weights per bushel multiplied by the price of corn gives us the equivalent price for the other grains. Barley weighs 48 pounds per bushel, and

[1] R. D. Jennings, "Consumption of Feed by Livestock, 1909–47, Relation between Feed, Livestock, and Feed at the National Level," *USDA Circular No. 836,* Washington, D. C., Dec. 1949, p. 53.

TABLE 23.　Relative Values of Barley, Oats, and Sorghum Grain
for Different Prices of Corn for Wintering Beef Cattle

Price Farmer Can Pay for Other Grains

Price of Corn, dollars per bushel	Barley, dollars per bushel	Oats, dollars per bushel	Sorghum Grain, dollars per cwt
1.00	0.86	0.57	1.79
1.10	0.94	0.63	1.96
1.20	1.03	0.69	2.14
1.30	1.11	0.74	2.32
1.40	1.20	0.80	2.50
1.50	1.29	0.86	2.68
1.60	1.37	0.91	2.86
1.70	1.46	0.97	3.04
1.80	1.54	1.03	3.21
1.90	1.63	1.09	3.39
2.00	1.71	1.14	3.57

Source: R. D. Jennings, "Consumption of Feed by Livestock, 1909–47, Relation between Feed, Livestock, and Feed at the National Level," *USDA Circular No. 836*, Washington, D. C., Dec. 1949.

corn weighs 56 pounds per bushel. That is, each bushel of barley has 48/56 or 0.857 as many pounds of feed as corn. The study showed that the feeds were of equal feeding value, pound for pound. If we now multiply 0.857 times the price of corn, we obtain the price of barley at which corn and barley are equally good buys. When corn is $1.20 per bushel, the equivalent price for barley is $1.20 × 0.857 or $1.03 per bushel. Equivalent prices can be established for any of these grains relative to grains other than corn. Oats, for example, has 32 pounds per bushel. Thus, the price of barley equivalent to the price of oats is 1.5 times the price of oats.

Prices of grains vary seasonally. Farmers can take advantage of constant rates of substitution in production by purchasing the feed which is relatively cheapest at a given time. For example, corn prices are generally lowest in the fall; oats and barley prices are lowest in the summer. Furthermore, a particularly large crop of any one grain in any year may depress the price of that grain a good deal and make it a profitable buy from the feeding standpoint. The information in Table 23 can be used to determine which grain should be purchased. With a corn price of $1.50, for example, it would be more profitable to buy barley if the price is less than $1.29, oats if the price is less than $0.86, and sorghum grain if the price is less than $2.68.

Feeding Hay and Grain to Dairy Cows

Another example is drawn from a study in North Carolina to determine the extent to which hay could be substituted for corn in the production of milk by Holstein cows.[1] The data in Table 24 are the

TABLE 24. Feed Combinations in Producing 23 Pounds
of 4 Per Cent Fat-Corrected Milk per Day

Combination	Alfalfa (X_1), pounds	Corn (X_2), pounds	Marginal Rate of Substitution $(\Delta X_2/\Delta X_1)$, pounds
1	8	13.0	—
2	10	9.4	1.80
3	12	7.1	1.15
4	14	5.7	0.70
5	16	4.7	0.50
6	18	3.9	0.40
7	20	3.4	0.25
8	22	2.9	0.25
9	24	2.6	0.15
10	26	2.3	0.15
11	28	2.0	0.15
12	30	1.8	0.10

combinations of these two feeds which produce, on the average, 23 pounds of 4 per cent fat-corrected milk per day.

The relative prices of alfalfa and corn change considerably over time. One year may be a good corn year and a poor hay year; another year, the situation may be entirely reversed. The dairy farmer must change his ration under such conditions if he is to obtain maximum net revenue. If alfalfa were $60 per ton (3 cents per pound) and corn $1.12 per bushel (2 cents per pound), for example, the price ratio of a pound of alfalfa to a pound of corn is 3/2 or 1.5.

Moving from combination 2 to combination 3 requires the addition of 2 pounds of alfalfa to replace 2.3 pounds of corn. That is, one pound of alfalfa replaces 1.15 pounds of corn while the amount of milk produced remains constant. But, a pound of alfalfa costs 1.5 times as much as a pound of corn. Thus, combination 2 must be

[1] W. C. McArthur, "An Economic Analysis of Feed Utilization for Milk Production," unpublished Ph.D. dissertation, North Carolina State College, Aug. 1956.

cheaper than combination 3. Combination 2 includes 10 pounds of hay at 3 cents per pound plus 9.4 pounds of grain at 2 cents per pound which gives a total cost of 48.8 cents per cow for one day. Combination 3 costs 12 times 3 plus 7.1 times 2, or 50.2 cents per cow for one day.

Using the formula $P_{X1} \Delta X_1 = P_{X2} \Delta X_2$, it also can be seen that combination 2 is the least-cost combination. To go from combination 1 to combination 2, $P_{X1} \Delta X_1$ is 3×2 or a 6-cent increase; $P_{X2} \Delta X_2$ is 2×3.6, or a 7.2-cent decrease in cost. The decrease in cost is greater than the increase, so combination 2 is 1.2 cents per cow cheaper than combination 1. To go from combination 2 to 3, $P_{X1} \Delta X_1$ is 3×2, or a 6-cent increase; $P_{X2} \Delta X_2$ is 2×2.3 or a 4.6-cent decrease. The amount paid for the additional hay exceeds the cost of the grain saved, and this would result in an increase in cost and decrease in net revenue. With these prices, combination 2 will produce 23 pounds of milk at a minimum feed cost of 48.8 cents.

Under other conditions, the least-cost combination is different. With alfalfa at $20 per ton (1 cent per pound) and corn at $1.68 per bushel (3 cents per pound), for example, the price ratio is 0.33, and the optimum combination is number 6 at a cost of 29.7 cents per cow.

The dollar importance of changing input combinations to conform with price ratio changes can be illustrated by the following example. Suppose that the farmer is feeding combination 2 and does not change when the prices change to $20 for alfalfa and $1.68 for corn. At the new prices, combination 2 costs 38.2 cents or 8.5 cents per cow more than combination 6. This is shown in Table 25. If the farmer has a

TABLE 25. Relative Costs of Two Feed Combinations in Production
of 23 Pounds of 4 Per Cent Fat-Corrected Milk per Day
for Given Prices of Alfalfa and Corn*

	Combination Number	
Item	2	6
Amount of alfalfa, pounds	10.0	18.0
Amount of corn, pounds	9.4	3.9
Cost of alfalfa at 1 cent per pound, cents	10.0	18.0
Cost of corn at 3 cents per pound, cents	28.2	11.7
Total cost, cents	38.2	29.7†

* Input combination from Table 24 and assumed prices of $20 per ton for alfalfa and $1.68 per bushel for corn.

† The least-cost combination for the prices assumed.

50-cow herd, he loses 50 × 0.085, or $4.25 a day by failing to change rations. Over a 300-day lactation period, the loss would be $1275, a fairly substantial amount.

Producing Choice Beef from Hay and Grain

Grain and hay are also used in feeding beef cattle. Brome-alfalfa hay and pasture were used in conjunction with grain in the feeding of choice yearling steers in another study. The data in Table 26 are combinations of hay and grain needed to produce 100 pounds of choice beef.

TABLE 26. Substitution Relationships in the Production
of 100 Pounds of Choice Beef on Yearling Steers

Hay (X_1), pounds	Grain (X_2), pounds	Marginal Rate of Substitution ($\Delta X_2/\Delta X_1$), pounds
400	953.4	—
600	882.7	0.35
800	817.5	0.33
1000	757.9	0.30
1200	703.7	0.27
1400	654.0	0.25
1600	611.8	0.21
1800	574.0	0.19
2000	541.8	0.16
2200	515.1	0.13
2400	493.8	0.11
2600	478.0	0.08

Source: Earl O. Heady and Russell O. Olson, "Substitution Relationships, Resource Requirements and Income Variability in the Utilization of Forage Crops," Iowa Agricultural Experiment Station, *Research Bulletin 390*, Ames, Iowa, Sept. 1952.

It is of interest to compare the rates of substitution of hay and grain in the production of milk and beef. The rate of substitution is much lower in beef production than in milk production. Hay does not replace as much grain at comparable combinations of the two feeds in producing beef. This, of course, follows everyday observations. In the cattle-feeding area of the Corn Belt, we find many feeder cattle fed almost exclusively on grain in feeding for choice and prime beef, but dairy cattle generally are fed generous portions of hay.

Hogs, sheep, and chickens eat hay as well as grain. Hay and grain can be exchanged at different rates for different kinds of livestock. For example, the rate at which hay replaces grain would be lower for hogs than for beef cattle. Hogs utilize hay but are not ruminants. Thus, they do not utilize it as efficiently as cattle or sheep.

Feeding Protein Supplement and Corn to Hogs

Although hogs can be fattened with hay and grain, the most common ration in hog feeding is grain, usually corn, and a protein supplement. As another example of an input substitution study, data are presented from an Iowa experiment in which hogs were fed various

TABLE 27. Feed Combinations to Produce 100 Pounds of Gain and Feed Replacement Rates with Aureomycin for 60-Pound and 110-Pound Hogs

SBOM (X_1), pounds	Corn (X_2), pounds	Marginal Substitution Rate $(\Delta X_2/\Delta X_1)$*	SBOM (X_1), pounds	Corn (X_2), pounds	Marginal Substitution Rate $(\Delta X_2/\Delta X_1)$*
\multicolumn{3}{60-Pound Hogs}			\multicolumn{3}{110-Pound Hogs}		
10	421.7	—	10	356.8	—
15	336.5	17.04	15	336.3	4.10
20	286.7	9.96	20	319.0	3.46
25	253.1	6.72	25	306.0	2.60
30	228.7	4.88	30	295.0	2.20
35	209.8	3.78	35	287.5	1.50
40	194.8	3.00	40	280.6	1.38
45	182.4	2.48	45	274.6	1.20
50	172.0	2.08	50	269.2	1.08
55	163.1	1.78	55	264.4	0.96
60	155.4	1.54	60	260.2	0.84
65	148.6	1.36	65	256.4	0.76
70	142.6	1.20	70	252.9	0.70
75	137.2	1.08	—	—	—

Source: Earl O. Heady, Roger Woodworth, Damon V. Catron, and Gordon Ashton, "New Procedures in Estimating Feed Substitution Rates and in Determining Economic Efficiency in Pork Production," Iowa Agricultural Experiment Station, *Research Bulletin 409*, Ames, Iowa, May 1954, p. 944.

* Pounds of corn replaced by 1 pound of SBOM.

combinations of soybean oil meal (SBOM) and corn in a ration which included aureomycin.[1] Feed combinations to produce 100 pounds of pork on hogs with beginning weights of 60 pounds and 110 pounds are shown in Table 27.

In this hog study, data are presented showing the least-cost combination of producing 100 pounds of pork for different price ratios of soybean oil meal to corn. Some of these data are shown in Table 28 for two beginning hog weights, 60 pounds and 110 pounds. At low

TABLE 28. Least-Cost Ration and Feed Quantities for Stated Price Ratios for 60-Pound and 110-Pound Hogs*

Price Ratio (Pounds of SBOM to Pounds of Corn)	60-Pound Pig (34 to 75 Pounds)			110-Pound Pig (75 to 150 Pounds)		
	Corn	SBOM	Protein, per cent	Corn	SBOM	Protein, per cent
1.0	136.3	75.9	21.0	269.3	49.9	13.9
1.2	145.5	67.5	19.6	277.1	42.8	13.1
1.4	153.7	61.2	18.4	283.9	37.6	12.5
1.6	161.3	56.2	17.5	289.9	33.6	12.0
1.8	168.1	52.0	16.7	295.1	30.4	11.6
2.0	174.7	48.7	16.0	300.1	27.8	11.3
2.2	180.7	45.8	15.5	304.6	25.7	11.1
2.4	186.4	43.3	15.0	308.8	23.8	10.9
2.6	191.9	41.1	14.6	312.7	22.3	10.7
2.8	197.0	39.2	14.2	316.3	20.9	10.5
3.0	201.9	37.5	13.9	319.8	19.7	10.4
3.2	206.6	36.0	13.6	323.0	18.7	10.3
3.5	213.4	34.0	13.2	327.5	17.3	10.1
4.0	223.8	31.2	12.7	334.5	15.5	10.0

Source: Earl O. Heady, Roger Woodworth, Damon V. Catron, and Gordon Ashton, "New Procedures in Estimating Feed Substitution Rates and in Determining Economic Efficiency in Pork Production," Iowa Agricultural Experiment Station, *Research Bulletin 409*, Ames, Iowa, May 1954, p. 948.

* Pounds feed per 100 pounds gain.

rates of soybean oil meal, the amount of corn replaced by one pound of protein supplement, the marginal rate of substitution, is much higher for 60-pound hogs than for the 110-pound hogs. For example, in going from combinations containing only 10 pounds of soybean

[1] Earl O. Heady, Roger Woodworth, Damon V. Catron, and Gordon Ashton, "New Procedures in Estimating Feed Substitution Rates and in Determining Economic Efficiency in Pork Production," Iowa Agricultural Experiment Station, *Research Bulletin 409*, Ames, Iowa, May 1954.

oil meal to combinations containing 15 pounds of meal, one pound of meal will replace 17 pounds of corn for the 60-pound hogs but only 4 pounds of corn for the larger, 110-pound hogs. The least-cost combination for any price ratio always includes a higher percentage of protein for the smaller hog. This would be expected, of course, since protein is needed for growth, and nutritionists have for some time recommended higher protein rations for younger hogs.

A table like this is useful to the hog feeder. He only has to check prices of protein supplement and corn and calculate the price ratio to determine the ration which will give him least-cost production. If corn is priced at $1.68 per bushel or 3 cents a pound, and soybean oil meal is $4.50 per cwt, the ratio of price of meal to price of corn is 1.5. The farmer then looks at Table 28 and finds that a ration containing about 18 per cent protein would be best for younger hogs, and a ration of slightly over 12 per cent protein will produce his gains for least cost if the hogs weigh about 110 pounds.

We should emphasize again that the production function describes a physical relationship. It does not change when prices change. As the price ratio changes, however, the farmer adjusts his feeding to alter the marginal rate of substitution of the feeds to make it equal the new price ratio. By paying close attention to market conditions, hog feeders can reduce costs and increase net revenue by changing feeding rations in response to changes in feed prices.

The combination of feeds used affects the time needed to put a

TABLE 29.   Days Required to Feed Hog from Weaning to Market for Different Percentages of Protein in the Ration

Protein in Ration, per cent	Days to Gain 191 Pounds Over 34-to 225-Pound Weight Interval
10	150
12	120
14	110
16	108
18	112
20	122

Source: Earl O. Heady, Roger Woodworth, Damon V. Catron, and Gordon Ashton, "New Procedures in Estimating Feed Substitution Rates and in Determining Economic Efficiency in Pork Production," Iowa Agricultural Experiment Station, *Research Bulletin 409*, Ames, Iowa, May 1954, p. 955.

given amount of weight on a hog. The experiment gives evidence, as shown in Table 29, that the time required to raise hogs to market weight is least for rations containing from 14 to 18 per cent protein. Time of feeding is greater for percentages of protein which are smaller or larger than this range.

The hog farmer must consider the time factor in his plans since hog prices change seasonally, and his labor may have other profitable uses. In a sense, protein substitutes for both corn and time. Both factors must be considered when making plans concerning date of farrowing and in the choice of feed combination.

Nitrogen and Phosphoric Acid Fertilization of Cotton

A research project recently conducted in Mississippi provides information pertaining to the rates of substitution of nitrogen and phosphoric acid in the production of cotton.[1] The results of the study present evidence that the yield of cotton depends upon the amount of both nitrogen and phosphoric acid used. Estimated yields in Table 30 show how cotton yield varies as the amounts of both N and P_2O_5

TABLE 30. Predicted Total Yields of Seed Cotton for Specified Nutrient Combinations

Nitrogen per Acre, pounds	P_2O_5 per Acre, Pounds								
	0	20	40	60	80	100	120	140	160
0	634	714	779	832	870	895	905	903	886
20	879	962	1031	1086	1128	1156	1170	1171	1157
40	1075	1161	1233	1292	1337	1369	1386	1390	1380
60	1222	1312	1388	1450	1498	1533	1554	1561	1554
80	1321	1414	1493	1559	1610	1648	1673	1683	1680
100	1372	1468	1550	1619	1674	1715	1743	1757	1757
120	1373	1473	1559	1631	1689	1734	1765	1782	1786
140	1327	1430	1519	1594	1656	1704	1738	1759	1766

are increased. Diminishing returns for either fertilizer element alone or for both used together are in evidence.

Isoproduct contours were constructed from these data as shown in Figure 29. From these contours, we can see that the amount of N which is necessary to offset the reduction of P_2O_5 by one unit increases

---

[1] Unpublished information obtained from research conducted by the Department of Agricultural Economics, Mississippi State College, State College, Mississippi, 1957.

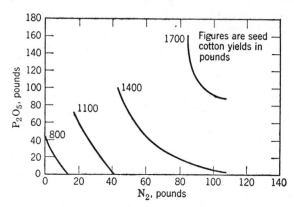

Figure 29. Isoproduct contours in producing seed cotton

as the amount of N used increases. It is evident that, if the ratio of the prices of N and P_2O_5 vary over time, different analyses of fertilizer will produce given amounts of cotton for minimum cost at different prices.

The isoproduct contours increase by 300-pound intervals. The greater the distance between the contours, the greater the addition of the two inputs necessary to produce an additional 300 pounds of cotton. The distance between curves becomes greater as the amount of cotton represented by the contours increases. Thus, diminishing marginal returns to the two elements used together is also evident from these contours.

To demonstrate the selection of a least-cost combination for a specified amount of product, combinations of nitrogen and P_2O_5 which produce 1400 pounds of cotton are shown in Table 31. Notice how the

TABLE 31. Combinations of Nitrogen and Phosphoric Acid to Produce 1400 Pounds of Cotton and Corresponding Marginal Rates of Substitution

N (X_1), pounds	P_2O_5 (X_2), pounds	Marginal Rate of Substitution ($\Delta X_2/\Delta X_1$), pounds of P_2O_5 replaced by one pound of N
50	69.11	
60	43.66	2.545
70	27.59	1.607
80	16.77	1.082
90	9.70	0.707
100	5.62	0.408

rate of substitution changes as more N is added and P_2O_5 is replaced. With only 50 pounds of N, an additional 10 pounds of N replaces 25.4 pounds of P_2O_5; at 90 pounds of N, another 10 pounds replaces only 4.1 pounds of P_2O_5. This changing rate of substitution is characteristic of much agricultural production. In such cases, the proportion in which it pays to use inputs varies with changes in relative prices of the inputs.

Changes in the ratio of the price of N to the price of P_2O_5 alter the least-cost combination in the production of 1400 pounds of cotton. A change in the ratio of the price of nitrogen to the price of P_2O_5 from 2.0 to 1.0, for example, changes the minimum cost combination from 60 pounds of N and 44 pounds of P_2O_5 to 80 pounds of N and 17 pounds of P_2O_5.

11 | Choice of products affects net revenue

In previous chapters, we have discussed the choices associated with the amount of one input to use in the production of one product and with combinations of inputs to use in the production of one product. In addition to these problems, a producer must decide how to allocate the resources he owns, rents, or borrows to the alternative products which can be produced. This is a common problem. It involves choices, for example, between the number of hogs and sheep, the acres of tobacco and corn, or the acres of alfalfa and corn. Similarly, a grain merchant may be faced with choosing the amount of his facilities to use for storage and the amount to use for handling and processing of feed, and a poultry processor may be faced with decisions concerning the amount of broilers to market as dressed and drawn, cut up or frozen.

A producer may not wish to employ his resources in that combination of enterprises which yields maximum net revenue. As we have pointed out before, he wishes to obtain maximum satisfaction from the use of his resources. A farmer, for example, may not like hogs, chickens, or cows and may not want them regardless of net revenue. However, farmers usually wish to know how much revenue will have to be given up to have some combination of enterprises other than that which would give maximum net revenue. When a farmer states that he prefers chickens to cows, it is quite likely he means that, if chickens yield the same or greater net revenue from his resources

112

than cows, he will choose chickens. In most cases, there will be some difference in net revenue which will change his preferences. Therefore, we will follow previous procedure and assume that resources are allocated among uses on the basis of the net revenue that will be produced.

Factors to be considered in choosing a combination of products or enterprises to yield maximum net revenue are presented in this chapter. We still assume that the outcome of a production process is known with certainty. The effect that uncertain prices and yields have on production decisions will be discussed in Chapter 13.

Production Possibilities

A producer is interested in the effect that producing more of one product has on the production of alternative products. For example, he may be producing two products, Y_1 and Y_2, using the same resource X_1. The amount of X_1 that can be used to produce Y_1 depends upon the amount of X_1 used in producing Y_2. Since this is true, it follows that the amount of Y_1 that can be produced depends upon the amount of Y_2 that is produced, i.e., $Y_1 = f(Y_2)$.

The relationship existing between any two products can be shown graphically by considering the amount of resources or inputs used as constant. In this way, we can show what happens to the quantity of each product as resources are transferred from Y_1 to Y_2, or the reverse. We can describe the effect of producing more Y_1 on the production of Y_2 by a *production possibilities* or an isoresource relationship. It shows the maximum amounts of one product (Y_1) which can be produced for particular levels of another product (Y_2) from a given quantity of resources.

An example of a production possibilities function will now be developed. Two separate production functions in Table 32 show the

TABLE 32. Hypothetical Production Functions
for Two Products Using the Same Input

Input (X_1)	Product (Y_1)	Product (Y_2)
0	0	0
5	7	11
10	13	20
15	18	28
20	22	35
25	25	41
30	27	46

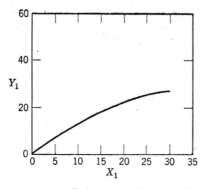

Figure 30. Relationship between X_1 and Y_1.

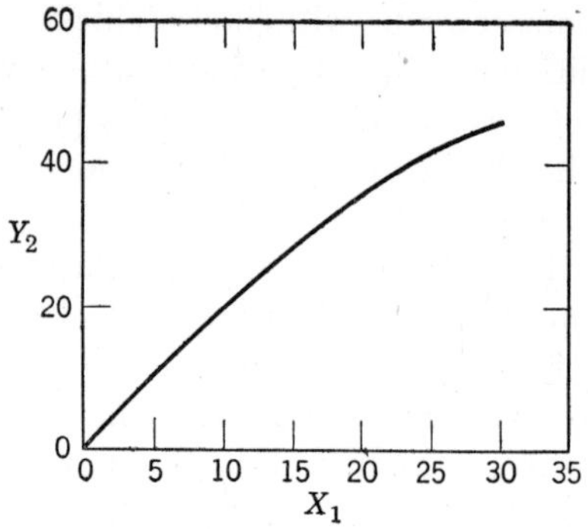

Figure 31. Relationship between X_1 and Y_2.

effect of adding the same input X_1 to either Y_1 or Y_2. A graphic presentation of these data is shown in Figures 30 and 31. The input X_1 can be used to produce either Y_1 or Y_2, or a combination of them.

If only 30 units of X_1 are available to the producer for production of Y_1 and Y_2, we can determine various combinations of the two products in such a manner that a maximum of one is obtained for any level of the other. Such combinations are shown in Table 33. If the producer

TABLE 33. Possible Product Combinations for 30 Units of Input

Units of X_1 Used in Producing		Output		Marginal Rate of Substitution
Y_1	Y_2	Y_1	Y_2	$(\Delta Y_2/\Delta Y_1)$
0	30	0	46	——
5	25	7	41	$-5/7$ or -0.71
10	20	13	35	$-6/6$ or -1.00
15	15	18	28	$-7/5$ or -1.40
20	10	22	20	$-8/4$ or -2.00
25	5	25	11	$-9/3$ or -3.00
30	0	27	0	$-11/2$ or -5.50

uses all 30 units of X_1 in the production of Y_2, he obtains 46 units of Y_2 but does not get any Y_1. He can shift five units of X_1 to the production of Y_1. In doing so, he receives seven units of Y_1, but only 25 units of X_1 are available to produce Y_2. He can produce only 41 units of Y_2 with these 25 units of X_1. In like manner, he can produce the other combinations shown in Table 33.

These data are shown as a production possibilities curve in Figure 32. That is, the columns Y_1 and Y_2 in Table 33 are plotted with Y_1

on the horizontal axis and Y_2 on the vertical axis. For example, when no Y_1 is produced, 46 units of Y_2 are produced, and, when 18 units of Y_1 are produced, 28 units of Y_2 are produced. The way in which two products compete or can be substituted for each other is important from an economic standpoint. The rate at which two products can be substituted in production shows how much one product must be reduced in order to produce one additional unit of the other product. That is, the marginal rate of substitution is $\Delta Y_2/\Delta Y_1$ or $\Delta Y_1/\Delta Y_2$, whichever is preferred.

There are as many production possibilities curves as there are input levels. The combination of products, as well as the amount of products to produce, depends upon the level of inputs used. Another point to notice is that the production possibilities curve of Figure 32 is of one particular type. Other types also exist, each of which has definite economic implications.

Joint products. This class of products includes such combinations as butter and buttermilk, lamb and wool, beef and hides, and cotton and cottonseed. In the short-run time period, at least, there is no substitution of one product for the other. That is, if a given quantity of one is produced, the amount of the other product is fixed by nature. The combinations of Y_1 and Y_2 obtainable are simply points,

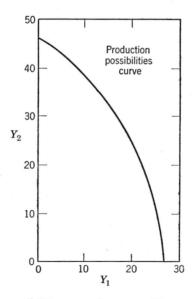

Figure 32. Production possibilities curve for competitive products substituting at an increasing rate.

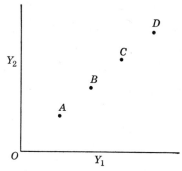

Figure 33. Production possibilities for joint products.

as shown in Figure 33, where points A, B, C, and D represent possible combinations of Y_1 and Y_2 at four different levels of resources.

In the case of joint products, there is no economic decision to make with respect to product combination, and the two products may be treated as one for purposes of economic analysis. However, decisions concerning how much of the joint output to produce are still important. For example, the cotton farmer does not have to determine the proportions of cotton and cottonseed to grow; he decides whether it will pay him to produce cotton, given the fact that a certain amount of lint and seed will be produced. Likewise, a broiler producer does not decide how many chicken legs and wings to produce; he decides whether it will pay him to produce chickens, given the fact that each chicken will have two legs and two wings.

In the long-run time period, however, changes in the relative prices of such joint products may bring about some shifts in product combination. For example, an increase in the price of wool as compared to lamb might cause a shift to breeds which produce a higher proportion of wool. Once this shift is made, however, the proportions of the two products are again fixed.

Competitive products. *Two products are competitive if an increase in production of one makes a reduction in the other necessary, given a particular level of resources.* The example in Figure 32 is of this type. When two products are competitive, some of one product must be given up to increase the quantity of the other product. Therefore, the marginal rate of substitution between the products is negative, as in Table 33. The two products, Y_1 and Y_2, in Table 33 substitute at a changing rate, and $\Delta Y_2/\Delta Y_1$ becomes larger as more Y_1 is produced from a given amount of resources. That is, the more Y_1 that is produced with 30 units of X_1, the greater the number of units of Y_2 which must be given up to produce an additional unit of Y_1. Most decisions of product choice involve competitive products.

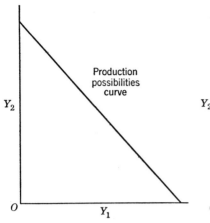

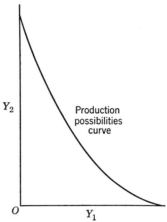

Figure 34. Production possibilities curve for competitive products substituting at a constant rate.

Figure 35. Production possibilities curve for competitive products at a decreasing rate.

There are two other general cases of competitive products which should be considered. The two products may substitute at a constant rate, as shown in Figure 34. Two varieties of the same grain belong in this category. That is, the marginal rate of substitution in production of two varieties is constant regardless of the proportion of land planted in one variety or the other. Where two products using the same resources can be substituted at a constant rate, only one of the products should be produced if maximum net revenue is to be obtained. For example, if one variety of oats yields 80 bushels on a particular soil and another variety yields 70 bushels, the first variety should be planted as long as production costs and price per bushel are equal for both varieties.

In any one year, with soils of equal productivity, and with land the input held constant, all crops belong in the category of products substituting at a constant rate. For example, if an acre of land produces 75 bushels of corn or 35 bushels of wheat, 10 acres produce 750 bushels of corn and no wheat, 350 bushels of wheat and no corn, 375 bushels of corn and 175 bushels of wheat, etc.[1] However, over a longer

---

[1] The case of competitive products substituting at a constant rate is common. In the use of budgeting to develop farm plans, which we discuss in Chapter 12, and in the more formal method of linear programming, the assumption of linearity between products is necessary. That is, we assume that products substitute at a constant rate. This linearity assumption merely means that, if one man produces 2 automobiles, 2 men produce 4 automobiles, and n men produce $2n$ automobiles.

period of time, a constant marginal rate of substitution between products may not hold. The effect of one crop on another in a rotation, for example, changes this rate of substitution. This is discussed in more detail below.

Where decreasing quantities of one product must be given up to obtain an additional unit of another product, as shown in Figure 35, only one of the products should be produced. A combination of two such products will never yield maximum net revenue, since successive increases of one unit in the production of one product require the sacrifice of smaller quantities of the other product.

One reason for a production possibilities curve as shown in Figure 35 is that the amount of resources used is so small that the production of both products is taking place in the region of increasing returns. It has been shown in Chapter 4 that a rational producer never operates in an area of increasing returns if he can avoid doing so. Another possible reason for a production relation as shown in Figure 35 is that two products may be detrimental to each other because of disease or similar factors. Where this is true, only one of the products should be produced.

Complementary products. *Two products are complementary when a transfer of resources to one product and an increase in the production of it are accompanied by increased production of the other.* Such a case is shown in Figure 36. The range of complementarity goes from point A to point B. In this range, the production of Y_1 can be increased and the production of Y_2 increased at the same time. The marginal rate of substitution between these two products is positive in the range of complementarity. At some point, this complementary relationship must end, as at point B, and the two products become competitive.[1]

Obviously, producers should transfer resources from the production of one product to another as long as doing so increases production of both. In Figure 36, for example, at least ON of Y_1 should be produced, even if Y_1 has no value. Beyond ON, any further increase in production of Y_1 must come at the expense of decreased production of Y_2. Hence, how much beyond ON it will pay to go in producing Y_1 will be determined by the relative prices of Y_1 and Y_2.

Rotations provide some examples of complementarity of products. The inclusion of legumes in rotations adds nitrogen and has a bene-

---

[1] This is to say that after some point, a transfer of resources from Y_2 to Y_1 must cause a reduction in Y_2. At least when all resources are employed in producing Y_1, there will be no Y_2 produced.

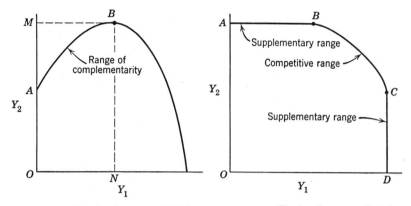

Figure 36. Production possibilities curve for two complementary products.

Figure 37. Production possibilities curve for two supplementary products.

ficial effect on soil condition in many areas. Where this is true, it is possible to increase total grain production over a period of years while increasing the production of hay. *In any one production period, however, hay and grain must be competitive.* Complementarity can only occur over a number of production periods, not within one production period.

An example of complementarity between clover and grain is shown in Table 34. A rotation with clover one year out of four increases the total production of grain from a given quantity of land. Note that complementarity is indicated by the positive marginal rate of

TABLE 34. Total Production per Acre of Grain and Hay under Different Rotations, Clarion-Webster Silt Loam, Ames, Iowa, 1915–48

	Per Acre Yields			Total Production*		Marginal Rate of
Rotation	Corn, bushels	Oats, bushels	Hay, tons	Grain (Y_1), pounds	Hay (Y_2), pounds	Substitution $(\Delta Y_1/\Delta Y_2)$, pounds
1. Corn	32.2	—	—	180,320	—	—
2. Corn, corn, oats, clover	60.6	59.6	1.70	217,360	85,000	+0.43
3. Corn, oats, clover	63.7	57.8	2.01	182,333	132,660	−0.74

Source: Earl O. Heady and Harold R. Jensen, "The Economics of Crop Rotations and Land Use," Iowa Agricultural Experiment Station, *Research Bulletin 383*, Ames, Iowa, Aug. 1951, p. 438.

* Based on 100 acres of land in the rotation.

substitution between the continuous corn rotation and the corn-corn-oats-clover rotation. This positive marginal rate of substitution occurs only in a limited range of production, however.

Increasing the proportion of land in clover to one-third increases hay production, but as this happens, total grain production is reduced. The marginal rate of substitution in this range is −0.74. That is, to produce an additional pound of hay, over this range, necessitates a reduction of 0.74 pound of grain. On soils such as this, farmers intending to farm for a period longer than one or two years will wish to include some clover in the rotation. Whether rotation 2 is superior to rotation 3 depends on the relative prices of hay and grain. Without knowing the prices, however, it can be seen that rotation 1 is inferior to rotations 2 and 3.

Another example of complementarity is found in the more arid portions of the Great Plains where summer fallow and wheat are complementary. Moisture is conserved by cultivating land for one summer and not planting a crop. Total wheat production is increased by fallowing land every third or fourth year. In this case, fallow itself has no value; it is practiced because of its effect on wheat yield.

Supplementary products. This fourth product relationship is a borderline case between products which are competitive and those which are complementary. *Two products are supplementary if the production of one can be increased without increasing or decreasing production of the other.* The two products in Figure 37 are supplementary in two places. Production of Y_1 can be increased without affecting production of Y_2 in the range AB. From D to C, production of Y_2 can be increased without any change in production of Y_1. The competitive range BC is the range within which the rational producer will operate. Any supplementary relationships should be taken advantage of by producing both products at least to the point where the products become competitive.

The utilization of labor and machinery on many farms provides examples of supplementarity. Using machinery on crop Y_1 for a certain amount of time may increase income from Y_1 but may not reduce income from an alternative crop Y_2. As more and more machinery time is spent on Y_1, however, a point will be reached where production of Y_2 is reduced because of lack of machinery services.

Farm labor requirements vary a great deal from one time of the year to another. One enterprise requires large labor inputs at one time; another requires little or no labor at this same time. A capable farm manager will study his labor situation carefully and combine enterprises which have different peak labor periods in order to increase farm income. Farm family labor is not completely utilized in many sectors of the United States, particularly in the Southeast. Small quantities of capital and land are combined with large amounts of labor on many farms. As a result, farm family members have, in many instances, taken jobs in industry in order to utilize their labor not used on the farm. The development of part-time farming has been rapid in the Southeast as well as in many other areas. It represents a good example of supplementarity. In this case, however, one of the enterprises is a nonfarm enterprise.

Supplementarity exists to some extent in many commercial enterprises. Grain storage and handling operations are good examples. Facilities and labor are available and not completely used during that part of the year when grain is not being brought in for sale. A common sideline operation for these businesses is the handling of mixed feed, concentrates, and seed. These products can be sold during the entire year and utilize resources which would otherwise be idle. If, however, a large portion of the resources are devoted to these enterprises, some reduction in storage and grain handling would be required. That is, the enterprises would become competitive.

Choosing the Optimum Product Combination

The rational producer operates in the range where products are competitive. The output at which he operates in the competitive range depends on the marginal rate of substitution and the price ratio. As we have seen, the marginal rate of substitution indicates the rate at which products can be substituted in production. The ratio of the prices of any two products shows how these two products can be exchanged in the market place.

The maximum net revenue obtainable with a given amount of inputs is where the physical rate of substitution between two products is equal to the rate at which the products exchange in the market, or where $\Delta Y_2/\Delta Y_1 = P_{Y1}/P_{Y2}$. If, as inputs are transferred from Y_2 to Y_1, $P_{Y1} \Delta Y_1 > P_{Y2} \Delta Y_2$, more inputs should be added to produce Y_1, and less Y_2 should be produced. On the other hand, if $P_{Y1} \Delta Y_1 < P_{Y2} \Delta Y_2$, adding inputs to the production of Y_2 will be profitable.

The condition necessary for maximizing net revenue from production of two products also can be shown graphically. In Figure 38, we have a production possibilities curve for two products, Y_1 and Y_2. Any combination of the two products represented by this curve can be produced with a given amount of inputs. Thus, any product combination on the curve can be produced for the same cost. For this

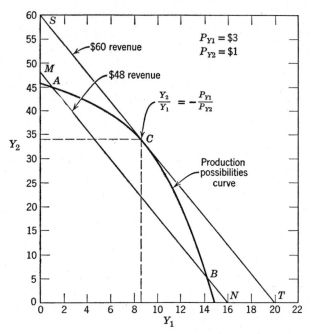

Figure 38. Net revenue maximization in production of two products.

reason, if we find that product combination which brings the greatest total revenue, that combination will also maximize net revenue.

In Figure 38, we assume the $P_{Y1} = \$3$ and $P_{Y2} = \$1$. With these prices, we can establish isorevenue lines representing all combinations of Y_1 and Y_2 which bring an equal total revenue. We can, for example, construct a line showing all combinations of Y_1 and Y_2 which can be sold for \$48.00. We find that 48 units of Y_1, 16 units of Y_2, or any combination of the two products on line MN will bring \$48.00. We can produce the combinations of Y_1 and Y_2 shown by points A and B and sell the quantities of the products for \$48.00. Any movement in the combination of the two products from A or B toward C on the production possibilities curve involves increasing the amount of one product and decreasing the amount of the other. These movements from A or B toward C also increase revenue.

The highest total revenue obtainable is found when the isorevenue line is tangent to the production possibilities curve. In this example, combination C yields the highest revenue. If 34 units of Y_2 and 9 units of Y_1 are produced, a total revenue of \$60.00 is received. At C, we notice that the slope of the production possibilities curve is equal to the price ratio, i.e., $\Delta Y_2/\Delta Y_1 = P_{Y1}/P_{Y2}$. Production of other combinations means that the loss in revenue from the reduction in the production of one product exceeds the gain in revenue from increasing the production of the other product.

As an example, the marginal rate of substitution of hay and grain between rotations 2 and 3 in Table 34 is −0.74. If the price of hay is more than 0.74 times the price of grain, the rotation producing the greatest amount of hay, the corn-oats-clover rotation, is most profitable. When the hay price is less than 0.74 times the price of grain, rotation 2 is more profitable than rotation 3.

In summary, it pays producers to take advantage of complementary and supplementary relations where possible by expanding production until the relation between the products becomes competitive. It will pay to produce competitive products in such proportions that the marginal rate of substitution is equal to the price ratio.

Optimum Combinations of Many Products

We have seen that $P_{Y1} \Delta Y_1 = P_{Y2} \Delta Y_2$ is a condition for the most profitable combination of products from a given quantity of inputs. This means that there are no benefits to be gained by transferring inputs from Y_1 to Y_2 or vice versa.

We saw in Chapter 5 that the optimum combination of products is achieved when the value of the marginal product of a unit of X_1 in the production of Y_1, that is, $P_{Y1}(\Delta Y_1/\Delta X_1) = P_{X1}$. It is also true that $P_{Y2}(\Delta Y_2/\Delta X_1) = P_{X1}$ for the most profitable use of X_1 in producing Y_2. We see that the value of the marginal product of X_1 in producing both Y_1 and Y_2 is equal to P_{X1}, when we maximize net revenue. It must be true then that the value of the marginal product of X_1 in producing Y_1 must equal the value of the marginal product of X_1 in producing Y_2 when we have the best use of X_1. Thus, when we are getting the maximum revenue from use of X_1, $P_{Y1}(\Delta Y_1/\Delta X_1) = P_{Y2}(\Delta Y_2/\Delta X_1)$.

Many inputs are used in the production of more than two products. When this is true, we obtain the most profitable combination of products when $P_{Y1}(\Delta Y_1/\Delta X_1) = P_{Y2}(\Delta Y_2/\Delta X_1) = \cdots = P_{Ym}(\Delta Y_m/\Delta X_1)$. That is, *the value productivity of the last unit of any one resource employed in producing any product must be equal for all products.* For example, if one hour of labor can be transferred from one use to another where the return is greater, revenue would be increased by transferring that one unit. Movement of the labor inputs should be continued until the return of the last unit of labor is equal in both uses. Then and only then is net revenue at a maximum.

A simple example can be used to tie together the concept of maximum net revenue developed in Chapter 5 with the concept developed in this chapter. Suppose that a farmer is faced with the production function of Table 35. Suppose also that the price of each unit of

TABLE 35.   Production Functions for Corn and Fertilizer on Two Different Tracts of Land

Fertilizer	Added Corn Due to Fertilizer		Value of the Marginal Product*	
	Tract 1, bushels	Tract 2, bushels	Tract 1, dollars	Tract 2, dollars
0	0	0	—	—
1	7	11	7	11
2	13	20	6	9
3	18	28	5	8
4	22	35	4	7
5	25	41	3	6
6	27	46	2	5
7	28	50	1	4
8	28	53	0	3

* Corn price is $1.

fertilizer is $3.50, and that the price of corn is $1.00. For simplicity, we assume that the farmer has 2 acres of land with different productivity, as shown in the table. He has enough money, $31.50, to buy nine units of fertilizer.

If this farmer had enough money, he would put four units of fertilizer on tract 1 and seven units on tract 2. Since he does not have sufficient money, however, he must decide how to divide the available fertilizer between the two tracts. There are numerous ways in which he can divide the nine units of fertilizer between the two tracts of land. For example, he could put seven units on tract 2 and two units on tract 1. This gives him a total of 63 bushels of corn. If he transfers one unit of fertilizer from tract 2 to tract 1, he reduces the yield on tract 2 by 4 bushels and increases the yield on tract 1 by 5 bushels. This gives him a total of 64 bushels from the use of his nine units of fertilizer. This is the greatest total production he can obtain. To transfer another unit involves reducing production by 5 bushels on tract 2 and increasing production by only 4 bushels on tract 1, a net decrease of 1 bushel.

Maximum net revenue is obtained when the value of the marginal product is equal to the price of the input. With a resource limitation, however, the input price which is relevant is not always the market price but is the opportunity return of using the resource elsewhere. In any event, maximum net revenue is obtained when the value of the marginal product of an input is equal in all uses. Both concepts are identical, of course, when we consider the price of the input to be the opportunity return.

Specialization and Diversification

We are now in a position to see why some farmers and some whole areas specialize or produce only one product and some farmers or areas diversify their production by having several major enterprises. Where complementarity or supplementarity among products exist, diversification tends to predominate. In other areas where most products are competitive and substitute at a changing rate, production is less diversified. If products are competitive and have a constant marginal rate of substitution, specialization is the general rule.

In much of the Great Plains, grain crops are competitive and can be substituted at a constant rate. Thus wheat, which yields the highest return per acre, tends to be the major and sometimes the only crop grown. However, there is supplementarity between wheat and other grains in some areas of the Great Plains because seeding and harvesting dates are not exactly the same. That is, although competitive with respect to the land input, wheat and other grains are supplementary with respect to labor and machinery services. To take advantage of this situation, grains other than wheat are grown in many portions of the Great Plains. Another reason that wheat is not the only crop produced in all of this area is that risk elements must be considered. In Chapter 13, we shall see that diversification is a means for reducing risk. As such, diversification may be practiced even though producing all of one product would produce the greatest net revenue over the long-run time period.

During the 1950's there has been a trend toward increased specialization of production. Farming is a very competitive business, and successful farmers must keep up to date on management practices. It is difficult to keep informed on new developments in numerous enterprises, and many farmers have found that they can do a better job of keeping up with new production and marketing information by concentrating on one or two main enterprises.

Also, the development of large-scale machinery and equipment has tended to promote increased size of farm enterprises. Producers who specialize in the production of a single commodity can take advantage of any economies of size which exist in producing that particular commodity. Recent technological advances have largely been in the form of new machinery and equipment, making it possible to reduce average costs at increased levels of output. For this reason, a firm which employs its inputs in the production of a single commodity, often greatly reduces the average cost of producing that commodity. If the same firm produces two commodities, the average cost of production for each commodity may be higher than for either commodity if it is produced alone and at a larger output.

An increase in capital investment often is required to purchase new equipment. Furthermore, as knowledge increases, and equipment becomes more specialized, the amount of capital needed for efficient production increases for each enterprise. Therefore, the increasing complexity of management, the increase in capital requirements, and economies to scale in production have created incentives for specialization in agricultural production.

Type-of-Farming Areas

If we look at the pattern of farming in the United States, we see that areas tend to specialize in the production of one or a few commodities. But we do not always find products being produced in areas where more of the product can be produced on a given unit of land than in another area. Illinois soil and climate, in general, produce more wheat per acre than can be grown in North Dakota. Yet, Illinois is primarily a corn state, and North Dakota's major crop is wheat. Corn is relatively more profitable than wheat in Illinois under present price and production conditions.

In general, we can say that a farmer does not grow corn or tobacco because his soil is "good corn land" or "good tobacco land." To say that soil is "good" for some product really has no meaning in terms of what should be produced. Net revenue is the important consideration in determining what will be produced. A farmer produces corn or tobacco because he thinks that it will yield the greatest net revenue for the inputs he controls.

Changes in prices and technology may occur over a period of years so that combinations of products which were at one time most profitable would be replaced by other products. Development of new technology may alter physical substitution rates among products. A new crop variety which is peculiarly adapted to one region, for example, may greatly increase production of this crop compared to other products in that region. This would tend to cause a larger pro-

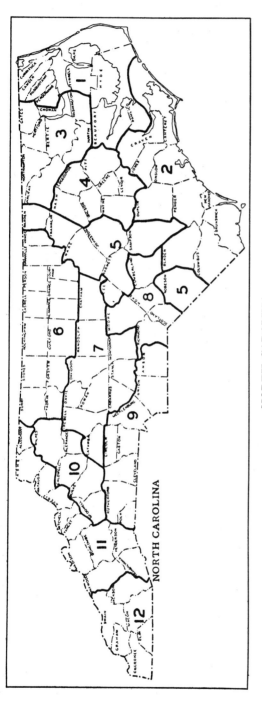

NORTH CAROLINA

1. Northern Tidewater—Corn, *soybeans, Irish potatoes,* hay, *vegetables, hogs.*
2. Southern Tidewater—Corn, *tobacco,* hay, cotton, vegetables, peanuts, soybeans, hogs.
3. North-Central Coastal Plain—Corn, *peanuts,* hay, cotton, tobacco, soybeans, hogs.
4. Central Coastal Plain—*Corn, tobacco,* cotton, hay, soybeans, small grains, *peanuts.*
5. Upper Coastal Plain and Eastern Piedmont—Corn, *cotton, tobacco,* hay, small grains.
6. Northern Piedmont—Corn, hay, *tobacco,* small grains, home gardens, lespedeza seed, *dairying,* beef cattle.
7. Central Piedmont—*Small grains,* hay, corn, *lespedeza seed,* cotton, tobacco, *dairying, poultry, beef cattle.*
8. Sandhills—Corn, *cotton,* hay, small grains, tobacco, *peaches,* soybeans.
9. Southern Piedmont—*Cotton,* corn, small grains, hay, *lespedeza seed, poultry,* dairying.
10. Foothills—Corn, hay, small grains, cotton, tobacco, home gardens, *vegetables, apples, dairying, poultry.*
11. Northern Mountain—Hay, corn, *vegetables,* small grains, home gardens, *tobacco, Irish potatoes, apples, dairying, beef cattle.*
12. Southern Mountain—Corn, hay, home gardens, small grains, *vegetables, poultry, dairying,* beef cattle.

Figure 39. Type-of-farming areas, North Carolina. Italics indicate important cash crops or livestock.

portion of resources to go into production of the more profitable crop.

A change in relative prices tends to bring about shifts in production to increase production of those products whose prices are relatively highest. No one area has a permanent advantage over another area in the production of any commodity. The combination of products which will be produced depends on the physical substitution rates and relative prices.

We know that changes in substitution rates and relative prices do occur. These changes are generally not rapid, however, and areas do tend to specialize in a certain product or in a combination of products. This fact has led to the establishment of type-of-farming areas. Type-of-farming area designations have been set up to distinguish areas where the major products produced are similar. These areas for North Carolina are shown in Figure 39. In each area, relative prices and physical rates of substitution have tended to bring about a similar pattern of production.

12 | Farm organization affects farm income

Net revenues vary widely from farm to farm. Differences in net revenues of farm families result from differences in kinds and quantities of resources which they own or control and differences in the use which they make of these resources. Farmers can often improve their incomes by using the types of analyses which we have discussed earlier. They can compare the costs of different methods of performing operations, or they can compare net revenues from producing different kinds of products. In order to make these comparisons, farmers must have information in regard to the consequences of alternative choices. Construction of enterprise budgets is one method by which producers can compare directly the revenues and cost of alternative enterprises.

Enterprise Budgets

A budget is a plan or a record of what one might expect to obtain from particular production practices. An *enterprise budget* consists of a statement of expected revenues and expenses from the production of a particular product. Development of a budget requires information pertaining to the amount of product which should be expected from particular quantities of inputs and information in regard to the expected prices of the product and of the inputs.[1]

One of the major problems involved in enterprise budgeting is the lack of information concerning the amount of products which will result from particular combinations of inputs. In other words, it is seldom that the producer has complete information pertaining to the production function for a particular commodity. Also, producers do not have complete information in regard to conditions in product and input markets. Typically, the producer has more information regarding prices of inputs than he has in regard to prices of products. This is due to the fact that inputs are purchased during one time period, and products are sold at a later period. Therefore, there is more uncertainty as to prices of products than prices of inputs.

Although they lack information needed to make perfect decisions, producers are forced to make decisions on the basis of the information they possess. An enterprise budget is shown in Table 36 for cotton

TABLE 36. Cotton: Estimated Variable Expenses and Net Revenue Above Variable Expenses per Acre with Specified Inputs and Outputs, Southern Piedmont Area, North Carolina

Item	Description	Price, dollars	Unit	Quantity	Amount, dollars
Income					
Yield: Lint		0.315	pounds	625	196.88
Seed		0.031	pounds	1060	32.86
Total					229.74
Expenses					
Seed	Coker 100 wilt	2.75	bushel	1	2.75
Fertilizer					
Nitrogen		0.15	pounds	50	7.50
Phosphate		0.07	pounds	70	4.90
Potash		0.055	pounds	70	3.85
Poison	3 per cent Gamma BHC–5 per cent DDT	0.26	pounds	60	15.60
Ginning					9.75
Workstock		0.05	hours	45.5	2.28
Direct cash expenses					46.63
Net revenue to operator's labor and capital					183.11
Family labor used			hours	138.4	

[1] We can express an enterprise budget in equation form. If $Y_1 = f(X_1, X_2 \cdots, X_n)$, then $Y_1 P_{Y1} - [X_1 P_{X1} + X_2 P_{X2} + \cdots + X_n P X_n]$ equals the net revenue from resources used in the production of Y_1.

produced with production practices recommended by the North Carolina Agricultural Experiment Station for use in the Southern Piedmont
Area of that state. This budget shows the amount of cotton which
might be expected, over the long run, from particular levels of application of nitrogen, phosphorus, potash, and other inputs. The budget
specifies the kind and amount of seed used, the kind and amount of
poison used, and makes an allowance for ginning expenses and for
the use of the tractor in production. It is assumed that enough culti-
vations are made to be consistent with the specified yield.

The items which should be included in an enterprise budget are those
variable inputs which are used in the production of the particular
commodity under consideration. For example, if a farmer were going
to buy a combine to harvest several grain crops on his farm, he would
not charge all of the combine expenses to wheat. Combines and many
other items of machinery and equipment, as well as buildings, are
typically used by more than one enterprise. When an investment in
these items has been incurred, it is in the category of fixed cost and is
not relevant in influencing the farmer's production decisions as to
choice of enterprises. For example, in Table 36 only the variable
expenses were charged to the cotton enterprise. No charge was made
for the fixed expenses of land, equipment, and family labor. On the
other hand, if a farmer is giving consideration to the question of
whether it would pay him to farm or to go out of farming, the costs
of land and equipment are pertinent in making this decision.

A farmer can construct budgets for each enterprise he wishes to
consider on his farm. He needs to obtain information as to the amount
of product to be expected from particular amounts of inputs and information as to input and output prices. He can tell from the construction of a budget whether he could obtain a positive net revenue from
the production of a commodity. This does not tell him, however,
whether it would be more profitable to produce other commodities.
If a farmer wishes to know which commodities will be most profitable
for him to produce, he had to compare one enterprise with another
and determine what the effects would be on the net farm revenue from
changing the production of one enterprise relative to another.

Table 37 shows summary budgets for seven commodities for a typical farm in the Southern Piedmont Area of North Carolina. The
columns in the table indicate inputs and outputs for particular enterprises and the net revenue for each enterprise. For example, one acre
of cotton is expected to yield 625 pounds of lint cotton and 1060 pounds
of cottonseed. In order to obtain this yield, it is necessary to use
inputs consisting of 50 pounds of nitrogen, 70 pounds of phosphoric

acid, and 70 pounds of potash fertilizers, and to spend $30.28 for insecticides, ginning, and other cash expenses. In the table, negative numbers denote inputs, and positive numbers denote outputs.

TABLE 37. Basic Input-Output Data Summarizing Enterprise Budgets*

						Enterprises				
Item	Price, dollars	Unit	Cotton, 1 acre	Corn, 1 acre	Oats and Lespe- deza, 1 acre	Alfalfa, 1 acre	Layers, 1000 hens	Hogs, 5 sows	Dairy, 8 cows
Cotton	0.315	pound	625						
Cottonseed	0.031	pound	1,060						
Corn	1.50	bushel		75			−652	−885	−217.5
Oats	0.86	bushel			65		−578		−149.5
Alfalfa	30.88	ton				3			−13.2
Lespedeza	27.80	ton			1.25				−2.9
Eggs	0.43	dozen					15,000		
Hens	0.25	pound					4,920		
Hogs	16.80	cwt						146.25	
Sows	11.75	cwt						22.50	
Milk	5.64	cwt							720
Cows	150.00	number							1
Veal calves	25.00	number							3
Other calves	50.00	number							2
Baby chicks	0.28	number					−1,125		
Chick mash	4.69	cwt					−160		
Laying mash	4.64	cwt					−550		
Protein supplement	4.50	cwt						−94	
Cottonseed meal	3.49	cwt							−76
Minerals	2.45	cwt					−7		
Pasture	19.04	acre						−2.5	−16
Corn silage	31.00	acre							−2.5
Marketing	1.00	dollar						−141.00	−324.00
Fixed capital†	0.05	dollar					−2,068.25	−1,440.00	−4,200.00
Depreciation	1.00	dollar					−206.83	−122.30	−296.00
Maintenance	1.00	dollar					−75.00	−21.21	−185.00
Nitrogen	0.15	pound	−50	−100	−70	−3	0	‡	‡
Phosphate	0.07	pound	−70	−50	−68	−74	0	‡	‡
Potash	0.055	pound	−70	−50	−60	−170	0	‡	‡
Other expenses	1.00	dollar	−30.28	−3.27	−22.56	−25.87	−39.39	−52.65	−313.80
Net revenue	xx	dollar	183.11	87.98	49.51	51.79	2,162.89	496.97	1,466.48

* Negative (−) values are enterprise inputs; positive values are outputs.
† Exclusive of fixed costs of land, workstock, and horse-drawn equipment; five per cent of the average investment.
‡ Included in cost of pasture, winter grazing, and corn silage where applicable.

Enterprise budgets, as shown in Table 37, present a summary to the farmer of the results from choices of particular enterprises. This information alone does not tell him which combination of enterprises is most profitable. Different enterprises give different returns for particular inputs. In order to determine his most profitable enterprise

combination, a farmer must give consideration to the quantities of the
various inputs which he has on his farm and try to find that combination of enterprises which makes best use of his resources as a whole.

Enterprise Combination

The available inputs on a particular farm are shown in column 3 of
Table 38. The data in columns 4 through 8 indicate the quantities of

TABLE 38.   Input Requirements and Expected Net Revenues
from Alternative Enterprises

Item (1)	Unit (2)	Quan- tity (3)	Cotton, 1 acre (4)	Corn, 1 acre (5)	Oats and Lespe- deza, 1 acre (6)	Layers, 1000 hens (7)	Hogs, 5 sows (8)
Cash expenses*	dollar	3000	−47	−25	−41	−5132	−2020
Labor							
Dec.–Jan.	hour	580	−1.1	0.0	0.0	−184.0	−58.0
Feb.–Mar.	hour	580	−4.8	−9.0	−1.2	−256.0	−71.5
Apr.–May	hour	650	−8.1	−10.8	0.0	−244.0	−74.0
June–July	hour	910	−29.6	−6.9	−4.6	−184.0	−69.5
Aug.–Sept.	hour	850	−19.3	0.0	−9.9	−184.0	−77.5
Oct.–Nov.	hour	800	−75.5	−12.0	−6.0	−172.0	−72.6
Land							
Cropland	acre	50	−1.0	−1.0	−1.0	0.0	−2.5
Cotton allotment	acre	15	−1.0	0.0	0.0	0.0	0.0
Net revenue†	—	0	183	88	50	2163	497

* Costs associated with fixed investment have been omitted.
† These estimates of net revenue have been rounded to the nearest dollar.

inputs required to produce the amounts of commodities shown in Table
37. The figures in the bottom row indicate the approximate net
revenue expected from production of one unit of the particular enterprise. The farmer must choose a combination of these enterprises
that will maximize the net revenue, using the inputs which he has on
the farm.

The possibilities available to a farmer are determined by the inputs
he has for use in farm production. Suppose, for example, that we
consider the case of the production of corn or oats with lespedeza.
Each of these alternatives requires land, expenditures of capital, and
labor. The farmer must decide whether he thinks it will be more
profitable to grow corn or oats and lespedeza with his inputs. Suppose
the farmer has the quantities of inputs shown in Table 39. We can
now determine the maximum quantities of oats with lespedeza and
of corn which can be produced from the inputs on this farm. The
maximum quantity of oats with lespedeza which can be produced from

100 acres of cropland is determined by multiplying the yield per acre times the number of acres of land. The maximum acreage of oats with lespedeza which can be produced with the available capital is determined by dividing the cash expenditures per acre into the total amount of working capital available to the farmer. Since $41 of direct cash expenses are required per acre of oats with lespedeza, the maximum acreage which can be produced from $4000 of working capital is 97.6. Since the yield per acre of oats is 65 bushels, 6344 bushels can be produced on 97.6 acres. Oats and lespedeza are grown together, i.e., they are joint products. We assume that 1.25 tons of lespedeza and 65 bushels of oats are obtained from each acre. Therefore, 97.6 acres planted in oats also produces 115.4 tons of lespedeza.

TABLE 39.   Maximum Quantities of Corn and Oats with Lespedeza Which Can Be Produced from a Farm with Specified Inputs

Input		Input Used per Acre		Maximum Quantity Which Can Be Produced		
Item	Quantity Available	Corn	Oats with Lespedeza	Corn, bushels	Oats, bushels	Lespedeza, tons
Cash expenses	$4,000	$25.00	$41.00	12,000	6,344	115.4
Land	100 acres	1.0	1.0	7,500	6,500	125.0
Labor, hours						
Dec.–Jan.	579	0.0	0.0	*	*	*
Feb.–Mar.	576	9.0	1.2	4,800	31,200	592.8
Apr.–May	650	10.8	0.0	4,515	*	*
June–July	913	6.9	4.6	9,924	12,900	245.1
Aug.–Sept.	850	0.0	9.9	*	5,584	107.4
Oct.–Nov.	800	12.0	6.0	5,003	8,665	166.6

* Input is not limiting.

Table 39 shows the maximum quantities of oats with lespedeza and of corn which can be produced with each of the inputs listed in the table. By connecting the points of maximum yield from specified inputs, the limits to production of oats and corn on the farm from all inputs can be obtained, as shown in Figure 40. These lines indicate production possibilities for the two products for each of the limiting inputs. Lines are not drawn for Dec.–Jan. labor or June–July labor since other inputs are more limiting for both corn and oats with lespedeza.

For example, the labor requirements for the Oct.–Nov. period are higher for both enterprises than the labor requirements for June–July. Thus, we know that June–July labor will not be a limiting factor for either corn or oats with lespedeza. We also see that cash expenses do not limit either corn or oats with lespedeza. Other inputs are more limiting than cash expenses at all other points. The curve for Feb.–Mar. labor has also been omitted since production of the two products is limited by other inputs before Feb.–Mar. labor is used up.

Since the production of oats and lespedeza does not require labor in April and May, the relationship between corn and oats is supplementary for this input. The amount of corn which can be produced with Apr.–May labor does not depend on the amount of oats which is produced. On the other hand, during August and September, corn requires no labor, and the relationship between oats and corn is supplementary; the amount of oats and lespedeza which can be produced is independent of the amount of corn produced. We have learned earlier that in such a range of supplementarity it pays a producer to expand the supplementary product.

Production of oats on this farm is limited at 5584 bushels by the amount of August and September labor available. Corn production

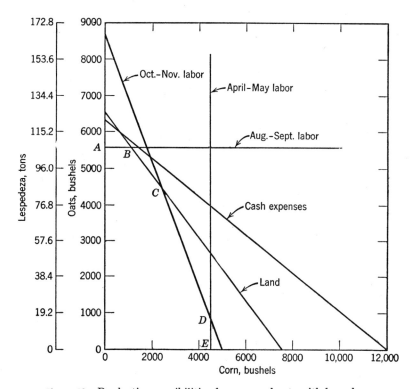

Figure 40. Production possibilities for corn and oats with lespedeza.

can be expanded up to 1057 bushels or from A to B without decreasing the amount of oats produced. After corn production is expanded beyond 1057 bushels, production of corn and oats becomes competitive for the use of land. That is, if corn production is to be expanded in the segment BC, production of oats must be decreased. If corn production is expanded beyond 2503 bushels or from C to D, corn and oats with lespedeza compete for Oct.–Nov. labor. The maximum amount of corn which can be produced on the farm is limited by the supply of Apr.–May labor to 4500 bushels.

The $ABCDE$ curve is the production possibilities curve when all limiting inputs are considered. Combinations of corn and oats with lespedeza beyond this curve cannot be obtained because one or more of the inputs is limiting. The rates of substitution of corn and oats with lespedeza on this production possibilities curve are presented in Table 40.

TABLE 40.   Rates of Substitution of Corn for Oats
on a Farm with Specified Inputs

Combination	Corn	Oats*	ΔOats/ΔCorn
A	0	5584	—
B	1057	5584	$\dfrac{0}{1057} = 0$
C	2503	4330	$\dfrac{-1254}{1446} = -0.87$
D	4515	845	$\dfrac{-3485}{2012} = -1.73$
E	4515	0	$\dfrac{-845}{0} = -\infty$

* Lespedeza and oats are produced in fixed proportions at a rate of 19.2 tons of lespedeza with 1000 bushels of oats.

Now that we have the production possibilities curve, we can use the procedure developed in Chapter 11 to determine the combination of products which will maximize net revenue. We simply find the combination where the marginal rate of substitution is equal to the ratio of the prices. This combination will maximize net revenue.

Suppose that we want to determine the most profitable combination of corn and oats with lespedeza from the data in Table 40. Information on the product prices is needed in addition to the data shown. Since oats and lespedeza are jointly produced, we need a single price for the two products together in order to compare the profitability with corn. For each bushel of oats produced, 38 pounds of lespedeza are produced. If the price of lespedeza hay is 1.5 cents per pound, the value of hay for each bushel of oats produced is $0.57. If oats is $0.85 per bushel, we get $1.42 for each bushel of oats produced when we include the value of hay.

Suppose the price of corn is $1.50 per bushel. For each bushel increase of corn, we gain $1.50; for each bushel decrease in oats, we lose $1.42. That is, the ratio of the price of corn to the price of oats is 1.06. Going from *B* to *C*, we give up 0.87 bushel of oats for each additional bushel of corn we produce. This will obviously increase net revenue since a bushel of corn is worth 1.06 times a bushel of oats. Going from *C* to *D* is not profitable, however, since we must give up 1.73 bushels of oats for each extra bushel of corn. We conclude from this that, with these prices, the combination of products at *C* maximizes net revenue.

Farmers usually have more than two alternative enterprises, however. Where this is true, the budgeting technique is useful in the process of farm planning. Several methods of going about budgeting a farm might be used. One procedure is to determine the maximum quantity of each enterprise which can be produced with the available inputs and then to determine which enterprise will give the maximum net revenue when limited by the available inputs. Choose this enterprise first; then see if there are other enterprises which are complementary or supplementary to this enterprise with respect to the input which limits the production of the most profitable commodity. If there are other enterprises complementary or supplementary for the limiting resource, add such enterprises to the farming system. Thereafter, the process of determining which products to produce involves comparing the effects of changes in the number and size of enterprises on the net revenue to the farm family. From here on the selection of enterprises becomes a method of trial and error.[1]

To see how budgeting might be used in a simple case, we can refer to our example in Table 38. First, we look for the one enterprise which gives greatest net revenue if used alone. We find that at least one input will restrict the number of units of each enterprise which can be produced. Cash expenses will limit the layer enterprise, for example. We find that 3000/5132 or 0.585 units of layers is the maximum which can be produced because of the capital limitation. Labor requirements would not limit layers below about 3000 hens. As a next step, we find that the most net revenue we can get from layers alone

[1] A more exact procedure called "linear programming" provides a method of systematically choosing enterprises to maximize net revenue. This procedure, however, should be left to more advanced courses.

TABLE 41. A Budgeting Example

Enterprise	Amount	Inputs	Cash, dollars			Labor, hours				Land, acres	Cotton Allotment, acres	Net Revenue, dollars
				Dec.–Jan.	Feb.–Mar.	Apr.–May	June–July	Aug.–Sept.	Oct.–Nov.			
		unused	3000	580	580	650	910	850	800	50	15	—
					Trial 1							
Corn	50 acres	used	1250	0	450	540	345	0	600	50	0	4400
		unused	1750	580	130	110	565	850	200	0*	15	—
					Trial 2							
Corn	50 acres	used	1250	0	450	540	345	0	600	50	0	4400
Layers	340 hens	used	1745	63	87	83	63	63	58	0	0	735
		total used	2995	63	537	623	408	63	658	50	0	5135
		unused	5*	517	43	27	502	787	142	0*	15	—
					Trial 3							
Corn	48 acres	used	1200	0	432	518	331	0	576	48	0	4224
Layers	330 hens	used	1694	61	84	81	61	61	57	0	0	714
Cotton	2 acres	used	94	2	10	16	59	39	151	2	2	366
		total used	2988	63	526	615	451	100	784	50	2	5304
		unused	12*	517	54	35	459	750	6*	0*	2	—

* This input is limiting.

138

is 0.585 × $2163 or $1265.36. Checking all five enterprises in a similar way, we find that land is the limiting input for corn and for oats with lespedeza; Oct.–Nov. labor limits cotton; and capital limits hogs.

If we check the maximum net revenue obtainable from all enterprises, we find that corn would yield more net revenue than any other single enterprise. We use 50 acres of corn as our first trial budget. Inputs used, inputs unused, and net revenue from 50 acres of corn are given in Table 41. The production of all the corn that can be produced from the available inputs will yield $4400 net revenue. We see that there are many unused inputs, however. If we can find an enterprise that is supplementary with corn for labor, adding this enterprise will increase our net revenue. Looking again at Table 38, we see that the layer enterprise does not require land. We add the layer enterprise to the corn enterprise in our second trial. Again, we need to know which input will limit the size of our layer flock. Now, we look at the inputs unused by corn in trial 1. We divide the unused inputs by the requirements for layers to find the limiting input. We find that capital is that limiting input. With the $1750 unused in trial 1, we can have 0.34 of a unit of layers or 340 hens, without reducing the amount of corn.

In trial 2, or our second budget, we now have 50 acres of corn and 340 layers. We total the inputs used by the two enterprises and subtract from the total inputs available to find the amount of unused inputs. Both capital and land are now found to be limiting. Further examination shows us that no enterprise is supplementary to both corn and layers with respect to the two limiting inputs, land and capital. If we add another enterprise now, we will have to decrease the amount of corn, layers, or both.

As a next step, we examine the unused inputs from trial 2. Notice that there is a large amount of surplus labor. Cotton gives a larger net revenue than corn on a per-acre basis and requires a large amount of labor. We can add cotton and reduce corn until labor in some two-month period becomes limiting. The amount of unused Oct.–Nov. labor limits cotton production at about 2 acres. To produce 2 acres of cotton, it is necesssary to reduce corn by 2 acres in order to make land available. The reduction in corn also frees 24 hours of Oct.–Nov. labor and $50 of capital. However, cotton requires more capital than corn, and capital is also limiting. If we are to add 2 acres of cotton, we need to reduce corn by more than 2 acres, or we can reduce the size of the laying flock so that enough capital is available to add the 2 acres of cotton. An additional $50 becomes available if we reduce layers by 10 hens or if we reduce corn by 2 more acres. We need to compare the loss in net revenue from reducing the laying flock by 10 hens with the loss from reducing corn by 2 acres. Each hen yields a net revenue of $2.16; each acre of corn brings $88.00. Therefore, the loss due to reducing the laying flock is much less than the loss we would have if we reduced corn by 2 more acres in order to free needed capital. For this reason, we reduce corn by 2 acres to free land for cotton. We obtain the additional needed capital for the cotton by reducing the laying flock by 10 hens. The $50 freed by reducing the laying flock plus the $50 available by reducing corn by 2 acres is a large enough amount so that the 2 acres of cotton can be included in our trial 3. This plan calls for 48 acres of corn, 2 acres of cotton, and 330 laying hens. Capital, land, and Oct.–Nov. labor restrict further increases.

If any more combinations are tried, we find that it is impossible to increase the farm's net revenue. If more inputs were available, we could change the size or combination of enterprises, but the combination of enterprises in trial 3 gives us as much net revenue as can be obtained with the given inputs.

As more alternative enterprises are considered, we encounter much more difficulty in choosing combinations. However, a procedure such as that used in our example is helpful in finding the direction of changes in enterprise combinations which will increase net revenue. We must remember that budgeting involves trial and error. In most cases, we will not be sure that we have the best combination. On the other hand, a person skilled in the use of budgeting can find this technique to be very satisfactory in working out product combinations which tend to maximize net revenue.

We have assumed that we know with certainty the outcome of production practices in this and preceding chapters. However, some types of productive operations may be more risky than others. Uncertainty is a very important aspect in agricultural production. For this reason, we will examine in Chapter 13 some of the reasons for, effects of, and alternative remedies for uncertainty or risk in agriculture.

13 | Time and uncertainty are important in production decisions

Production decisions are influenced by time in that transformation of inputs into outputs requires time. After producers receive information from the market indicating that production of particular commodities is profitable, time is required to organize the factors of production to produce the commodities. The amount of time involved in production is different for different commodities. Hence, funds are tied up for varying time periods in the production of different commodities.

The longer the time period of production, the more uncertain producers are of the prices which may be received for their products. Often there is little relation between prices at the time production is planned and prices at the time of sale of the product. Also, in farming, there is a great deal of uncertainty as to the amount of product which will result from a given amount of inputs. In the production of most nonfarm products, the output can be predicted with certainty once the kinds and quantities of inputs to be used are known. A shirtmaker, for example, knows how many shirts he will receive from a given quantity of cloth, thread, buttons, and labor. In the production of farm commodities, however, the exact output which will result from particular combinations of inputs is seldom known. Rather, the most that a farmer can hope for is that over the long pull some average production can be predicted. Usually, a farmer has some idea of the range of results to be expected from combining particular quantities of inputs in the production of a commodity. That is, he has an idea of the highest and lowest yields that he might receive, but he must estimate what yield may be expected during each production period.

Present Value of Future Income

Even when the returns from alternative uses of inputs are known with certainty, they must be converted to a comparable time period before decisions can be made concerning the most profitable uses. In the production of many farm commodities the period of production is more than one year. In comparing the returns from investments which require different amounts of time, it is necessary to convert future incomes to present values. Since money obtained at some future date has less current value than money owned at present, some method must be available for *discounting* future incomes to obtain present values. Discounting is a process by which incomes received at some future time are converted to present values. For example, the present value of $100 ten years from now, in the form of a United States Government bond, is $75. This is obtained by discounting the $100 future return by a 3 per cent rate of interest. The present value of $100 ten years later at a 3 per cent rate of interest is obtained as follows: $75 = 100/[(1 + 0.03)^{10}]$. The present value of a future return is obtained by the use of the formula $V = R/[(1 + i)^n]$, where V is the present value of the future return R, and i is the rate of interest received over a period of n years.

If we invest $75 currently, it is obvious that $100 received five years from now represents a larger rate of earnings than does $100 received ten years from now. But it is not so obvious whether $100 received ten years from now is worth more than $85 five years from now. The answer can be determined by discounting the future returns over the specified time period, using the appropriate rate of interest.[1]

One example of the effects of time on the present value of earnings from farm commodities is the case of production of forest products. The data in Table 42 present the quantity and estimated value of forest products harvested from an acre of short-leaf pines in North Carolina.[2]

---

[1] In the event that the income is received in each of several years over a period of time, the present value of the income is obtained by use of the formula $V = R/[(1 + i)] + R_2/[(1 + i)^2] + \cdots + R_n/[(1 + i)^n]$.

[2] W. H. Pierce, M. S. Williams, and John E. Ford, "Forest Farming Can Pay," *Tarheel Farm Economist*, Oct. 1954.

TABLE 42.   Earnings from Short-Leaf Pine, North Carolina

Thinning	Years	Quantity	Esti-mated Price, dollars	Actual Returns per Acre, dollars	Discounted Return, dollars*
1	15	Mostly pulp and fuel wood		10	6.41
2	25	Mostly pulp and fuel wood		24	11.46
3	35	3,600 board feet	20	72	25.58
4	45	7,000 board feet	20	140	37.02
Harvest	55	24,000 board feet	25	600	118.02
Total return per acre				846	198.49

* Present value of return discounted at 3 per cent rate of interest.

The value per acre from forest products is comparatively high when not discounted. In this case, the average return per acre over the 55-year period is $15.39. However, if a farmer had the alternative of investing his funds in some other use which would yield a rate of return of 3 per cent per year, the total discounted return from forest products would be only $198.49. The present value of $198.49 is equivalent to the present value of $7.43 received each year for a period of 55 years.[1] If a farmer could expect more than $7.43 each year from another use of his land, he would make more net revenue from this alternative than from production of forest products.

In summary, the information needed to convert future incomes to present values includes the amount of the future income, the time at which the income is expected, and the rate of interest which the producer is willing to accept. The appropriate rate of interest depends upon the earning power of investments in alternative uses. With high rates of interest, short-term investments are relatively more profitable than long-term investments. On the other hand, a decrease in the rate of interest will tend to cause people to invest in enterprises with longer production periods.

Future Value of Current Investment

An alternative means of comparing net revenues received over different periods of time is to compare the future value of present costs with future incomes. Converting present expenditures to future values

[1] That is, using the formula for present value, $198.49 = 7.43/1.03 + 7.43/[(1.03)^2] + \cdots + 7.43/[(1.03)^{55}]$.

is called *compounding of costs*. As an example of the costs involved in the production of a commodity which will be sold several years later, consider the case of production of apples. In the production of apples, it is necessary to incur considerable expense in the preparation of land, purchasing and planting of young trees, and culture of trees prior to bearing age. Apples are planted with the expectation of receiving profits from the sale of fruit. Since several years elapse between planting of trees and harvesting of the fruit, a producer needs information concerning future value of present investments in order to make rational decisions regarding these investments. That is, he needs to know how much he will have invested at the time of harvest of the crop.

Suppose that a farmer must choose between investing in the production of apples and in another alternative which yields 3 per cent return per year. In terms of the income sacrificed, the farmer must give up the amount expended in cash for the planting and culture of apple trees during the first year plus an interest charge of 3 per cent for each year until harvest. That is, if the farmer invests $100 in the alternative use, he will have $103 from the investment at the end of the first year. Therefore, the value of $100 present investment, one year later, is $103.

In the event that an investment of funds is made in the production of a commodity which has a production period of several years, costs are *compounded* from the initial investment, using the rate of interest and the time period under consideration. For example, at the end of the first year, $100 invested currently at 3 per cent would be worth $103. At the end of the second year, the original investment is worth $103 plus 3 per cent interest, or $106.09. Using the principle of opportunity return, we see that by the end of the second year, the farmer has given up $6.09, the return which he would have received in the alternative use for his $100. We see, therefore, that the value one year hence, C, of some cost currently incurred, E, is obtained as follows: $C = E + Ei = E(1 + i)$, where i is the appropriate annual rate of interest. The compounded value two years hence is $C = E(1 + i)^2$.[1] The value n years hence is $C = E(1 + i)^n$.

Most investments in agricultural production are not made all at one time. Typically, investments are made over a period of years. In the event that production involves expenditure of funds at several

---

[1] $C = E(1 + i) + E(1 + i)i$. If we factor out $E(1 + i)$ from the right side of the equation, we obtain $C = E(1 + i)(1 + i)$.

different times prior to the sale of the commodity, the compounded total cost can be obtained as follows: $C = E_1(1 + i)^n + E_2(1 + i)^{n-1} + \cdots + E_n(1 + i)$, where C is compounded cost at the time of sale, E_1, E_2, and E_n are actual expenditures in the various years, n is the number of years, and i is the rate of interest. Using this procedure, the cost to any date in the future for an investment incurred at any point prior to that date can be computed.

Valuation of an Input

In the estimation of the value of an input, producers make use of the *discounting* principle. A producer is concerned with the amount which he expects the input to add to his income and the time period during which this income is expected to be received. In the event that an input is expected to yield a perpetual annual income, the value of the input may be estimated by dividing the annual net income by the rate of interest the producer is willing to take for his investment. That is, the value of an input is $V = R/i$, where V is the present value of the input, R is the net income expected each year, and i is the annual rate of interest. For example, a farm from which a farmer could expect a net revenue of $20 per acre per year would be worth $400 per acre to one who was willing to accept a 5 per cent return on an investment of his funds. If the farmer were willing to accept a 4 per cent return on his investment, the farm would be worth $500 per acre. If he were not willing to take less than a 10 per cent return on his investment, he could not afford to pay more than $200 per acre for the farm. We can see from these examples that the rate of interest an individual is willing to accept for use of his funds has a great effect on the value he places on an input.

The value of an input to a producer is also related to the value of the marginal product of that input. In estimating whether the purchase of an additional unit of an input would be to his advantage, a producer estimates the amount he expects the additional unit of the input to add to his revenue. This additional revenue must be estimated not only for a one year period but for the expected life of the input. Valuation, therefore, involves discounting expected net revenue to a present value. By comparing the discounted value of the additional income he expects, as a result of using the inputs, with the price, the producer can determine whether the purchase of an input is profitable.

Depreciation

Depreciation refers to the loss in value of an input due to age and use of the input. Depreciation has two components—time and use. That part of depreciation which is related to use is a variable expense and is a cost item which should be considered in making production decisions. Use depreciation is dependent on the amount of time that the resource is used. Time depreciation, on the other hand, occurs as a result of obsolescence and occurs regardless of the amount of use of the input. Time depreciation results largely from changes in techniques of production and is a fixed cost. It will be recalled from Chapter 7 that fixed costs do not influence production decisions. Therefore, time depreciation has no bearing on production decisions if the input is already owned.

It may be asked whether time depreciation will not influence production decisions in that there are alternative uses for the input. For example, the owners may give consideration to the question of whether to use an input on their farm or to sell it to other producers. When making decisions in regard to selling inputs, farmers compare the discounted returns which could be expected from the use of the inputs and the sale price. If the sale price is greater than the discounted return, it pays the farmer to sell the input.

From the standpoint of the buyer, the problem is comparable. The relevant question to him is whether the discounted value of the return from the input will be greater than the price of the input and greater than the return from alternative uses of his funds. If the answer to both of these questions is positive, it pays the buyer to purchase the item. Note, however, that this is a problem of input valuation rather than a problem of depreciation. The decisions are based on the amount by which revenues are expected to be increased as a result of purchasing the input in comparison with the price of the input. The amount of time the input has been used in the past enters into consideration only indirectly insofar as it affects expected future productivity.

Depreciation does have one significant effect on income. It is very important in determining the amount of property and income taxes paid by individuals and firms. Depreciation allowances are made in computations for both property and income taxes. Although depreciation is a fixed cost and as such does not affect decision-making, we see that it does affect annual net incomes as a result of the taxing procedures.

Conservation of Resources

Conservation of resources is another problem involving time. Conservation refers to the maintenance of the real-value productivity of a resource.[1] When the value productivity of a resource is increased through capital investment, the resource is said to have appreciated in value. When the value productivity decreases as a result of use, the resource is said to have depreciated in value.

Soil conservation is one case of resource conservation. The value productivity of soils depends on how the soils are used. Continuous row cropping of some soils will result in decreased physical productivity over time. If productivity falls, the value of the land will fall. In this case, part of the income of the producer is received by depreciating the value of his assets.

We must remember, however, that the capitalized value of a resource depends upon the rate of interest which the individual is willing to take for his investment. People on small farms often encounter difficulty in earning a subsistence from the land resources that they control. They frequently exploit the land or depreciate it by employing production methods which result in decreased productivity over time. Furthermore, from the standpoint of the individual, it may not be profitable to conserve his resources.

But, conservation of land resources is a problem of significance not only to the individual but to the nation at large. Future generations must have assurance of an adequate supply of food and fiber if the nation is to survive. The Government has seen fit to grant subsidies to farmers for employing their land in particular uses in order to insure future productivity. These subsidies are called conservation payments. They are made with the idea that they provide an incentive for farmers to use production practices which will maintain the physical productivity of soils at some specified level.

Major Types of Imperfect Knowledge

The valuation of farm inputs often is more difficult than the valuation of inputs used in nonfarm production. When the future is not known with certainty, the producer is faced with the problem of determining the most probable value of future returns from alternative uses of his inputs. The distribution of income over time is also important to the producer. If he should incur large losses during the

[1] Real value refers to value in terms of a constant price level.

early years of his business, it might be impossible for him to continue to produce. Thus, in considering the available alternatives, producers are sometimes inclined to choose enterprises which are expected to have small year-to-year variation in the returns. They choose these enterprises even though the average returns over a period of years may be lower than the average returns from other enterprises which have relatively large year-to-year variation in net returns.

Farmers face two major types of imperfect knowledge. These are yield uncertainty and uncertainty with regard to price conditions in product and input markets.

Yield uncertainty. Yield uncertainty refers to the fact that the farmer cannot accurately predict the yields he will receive from combining particular quantities of inputs in the production of a farm commodity. Yield uncertainty stems from variation in conditions beyond the control of the farmer. For example, even though the farmer uses the same inputs in one time period as in another, the yields of crops may be quite different because of differences in weather conditions. Likewise, yield uncertainty may result from disease or infestation of insects in the production of farm commodities. Farm commodities are different from the products of most other industries in that they are living products, that is, plants and animals. As such, they are subject to damage by disease and by insects to a greater extent than are the products of most other industries.

Imperfect knowledge regarding conditions in product and input markets. Prices of individual farm commodities are highly variable. Production tends to fluctuate more than would be the case if producers had complete control over the quantity of product produced. When the quantity of product varies, price of the product also changes. With large crops, prices fall; with small crops, prices rise.

Farmers are faced with additional uncertainty because many products which they produce become inputs in the production of other farm commodities. Uncertainty as to the quantity of these inputs available for use in farm production affects production decisions. For example, livestock producers frequently limit their livestock numbers to the minimum expected feed production. In so doing, they sacrifice the possibility of obtaining a greater income.

Changes in demand and supply conditions for inputs and products and changes in technology alter the most profitable combination of enterprises to producers. In making production plans and committing inputs to the production of particular commodities during future time periods, the producer must take into consideration changes expected in technology and prices. Once inputs are committed to the production of particular commodities, and specified techniques are used, it may not be possible to reorganize inputs in such a way as to produce efficiently other products with different techniques of production. For this reason, some producers are hesitant to go into enterprises requiring a large investment in specialized inputs.

Producers tend to discount returns to adjust for uncertainty of production and prices. Since the production period for some commodities is longer than that for other commodities, producers discount returns from products with longer production periods at a higher rate than products produced in short periods. Producers may have less knowledge and less confidence in predictions in regard to prices and production conditions over a 5-year period, for example, than for a 1-year period.

Farmers Can Reduce Risk by Altering Production Plans

Farmers can reduce the variability of income through insurance, diversification, production on a contract basis, and through maintaining flexibility and liquidity.

Insurance. Insurance involves the substitution of a small known cost for the possibility of a larger but uncertain loss. In the production of some products, farmers may insure against loss due to weather hazards and destruction from insects and diseases. In purchasing insurance, the farmer incurs a cost. In effect, the farmer pays someone else to assume the risk of loss from the production of particular commodities on his farm.

Other persons or insurers are able to accept the risk of loss from weather hazards, insects, and other uncontrollable conditions on individual farms because they are able to spread their risk over a large number of farms. Although the probability is quite high that some farms will have yields damaged by unpredictable weather conditions in a given year, the probability is low that any particular farm will have yields damaged by unfavorable weather conditions. Insurance companies are able to predict what percentage of farms, in the aggregate, will suffer damages as a result of weather and other conditions beyond the farmers' control. As a result of spreading their risk over a large number of producers, insurance companies are able to absorb the risk of loss on individual farms.

Diversification. Farmers may also carry a form of insurance of their own by diversifying the production of farm commodities. Diversification is the production of several products at the same time or the production and sale of the same product at different times during the year. Through diversification, farmers spread the risk of loss over several commodities and may reduce the risk of loss from the farm as a whole. Farm products respond differently to the same weather conditions. Weather conditions which greatly reduce the production of some farm commodities will actually increase the production of others. For example, cool weather is beneficial in the production of some vegetables, but it reduces cotton yields. Also, prices of some farm commodities increase when the prices of other farm commodities decrease, and vice versa. Because of these conditions, farmers are often able to reduce the variability in their incomes by producing several commodities. Variation in the aggregate value of several products will usually be less than the variation of each product taken separately. This is due to the fact that yields and prices of all commodities do not vary in the same direction at the same time.

Diversification with respect to time evens out the seasonal distribution of income. It also reduces the possible effects of changes in prices during the year.

We must recognize that diversification may involve cost and reduce average income. We know that in the production of some commodities there are advantages to specialization because of economies of size. Also, we saw in Chapter 11 that net revenue is maximized by specializing in one product if the alternative products are competitive and can be substituted for each other at constant rates. We see that, like insurance, diversification reduces the variability of income. But it may do this at a cost of reducing average income over time.

Contract. By including in the production program some commodities which have a high degree of price stability, farmers also may reduce income variability. An obvious example is the production of a commodity grown on a contract basis. This type of arrangement is particularly common in the production of broilers and in the production of some vegetables for canneries. Many processors prefer to know in advance about how much of a commodity they will have for processing. In order to assure themselves of the volume of product they desire, they often contract for the production of a specified amount to be purchased at a guaranteed price. The processors often specify the characteristics of the product which will be accepted in order that they may standardize the quality of their product. Production on a contract basis removes uncertainty as to price of the product at the time of sale.

Contract farming has expanded rapidly since World War II. The development of modern supermarkets as the major retail outlets for food products has altered market conditions for farm products. These stores handle large volumes of standardized food products. Their sales are fairly uniform over time. Hence, supermarkets must obtain a large volume of products of standardized quality in a fairly uniform flow for profitable operation. To assure the needs of modern market outlets, the production of more farm products is being done on a contract basis. In many instances, production and marketing have been *vertically integrated*. That is, production and marketing decisions have been coordinated by some firm or firms in the industry. These firms are able to specify the kind of product that will be produced, the production practices that will be employed, when the product will be sold, and the terms of the sale. This type of arrangement results in a more uniform product and provides a high degree of control over the flow of the product through the marketing system.

When products are grown under contract, the producer shifts the risk associated with changes in the price level to the buyer. The buyer, however, is not likely to absorb all the risk of price changes. Rather, he is likely to offer somewhat lower prices on the average than he expects at the time of harvest. In effect, the producer pays the buyer to accept part of his risk.

Flexibility. Flexibility refers to the ease with which the organization of production can be changed. A flexible organization is one where changes in production can be readily made so as to take advantage of improved knowledge in regard to economic and technological conditions.

If a farmer knew with certainty that one product would be the most profitable in the future, a specialized production organization would be more efficient than an organization with considerable flexibility. If conditions in input and product markets are expected to change over time, or if the farmer is uncertain as to what conditions will be in these markets, a flexible production organization may be more profitable.

The market reflects supply and demand conditions at a particular time. The market does not transmit information to producers regarding the production intentions of other producers. Hence, there may be little correlation between prices existing in the market at one point in time and prices existing at another time. To make good decisions, a producer needs information concerning the production plans of other producers. Government agencies publish information in regard to production plans for some commodities. For example, government agencies periodically publish information with respect to the breeding intentions of hog producers. Some farmers organize their farms on a flexible basis and postpone decisions in regard to the marketing of their gilts until they obtain information concerning the breeding intentions of other producers.

As another example of flexibility, some farmers have found it wise to construct buildings that have more than one use. Poultry houses have been built which can be used for broilers or layers. In this way, farmers can produce either layers or broilers depending on which enterprise appears to be relatively most profitable at a given time.

Liquidity. To take advantage of changes in market information, it is necessary that producers have access to sufficient liquid funds to make effective use of the knowledge which they receive. Liquidity refers to the maintenance of balances of money or assets that can be readily converted into money.

Liquidity is a form of flexibility. The assets of farm firms are of such form that they cannot be readily converted to cash. Thus, farmers find it necessary to hold some of their assets in cash in order to take advantage of changes in economic conditions. Liquidity would not be necessary if the individual farm firm could obtain from existing capital markets the capital needed to take advantage of improvements in information. Because uncertainty does exist, and because credit cannot always be readily obtained, it is often desirable for a farmer to hold some liquid assets. We should note that costs also may be involved in maintaining liquid assets. To maintain these funds, a farmer must give up the revenue he would receive by investing the funds in other uses.

In summary, insurance, diversification, contract farming, and the maintenance of flexibility and liquidity may all involve costs and influence a farmer's return. Whether a farmer will want to adopt any of these measures will depend on his estimate of the relation between cost and returns from doing so.

14 | Land tenure arrangements affect use of inputs

Land tenure refers to the possession of rights to the use of land. People hold varying kinds of rights in the use of land and are said to belong in different tenure classes. Although it is difficult to rank tenure classes according to the degree of rights which are held, we generally recognize that the owner-operator without debt has the most freedom of action with respect to the use of his inputs. At the other end of this scale of rights in land are found the hired farm laborers and sharecroppers. Between these two extremes are share tenants, cash tenants, mortgaged owners, part-owners, and numerous combinations of these groupings.

Many farmers have climbed the "agricultural ladder" from the unpaid family worker to a hired laborer status, through tenancy, and finally to owner-operatorship. In earlier stages of United States history, this was considered to be an ideal way to get started in farming. It is still possible to move from a hired laborer status to a full owner situation. However, the larger farms and greater use of machinery needed for efficient farming today make it more difficult to climb the "ladder" than was true some years back.

There are many different types of tenure arrangements in our agricultural economy today. These arrangements influence the efficiency with which inputs are used. They also affect the degree of uncertainty encountered in the operation of a farm. In this chapter we will examine the most common tenure arrangements with respect to their effects on the use of resources.

Tenure Classes

Although innumerable breakdowns are possible, most tenure arrangements can be placed in one of three main classes: owners, part-owners, and tenants.

Owners. This group includes those who have title to all of the land they operate. This is known as ownership in fee simple. It entitles the owner to sell or use his land as he sees fit within the limits of the law. In 1954, over one-half of all farms were owner-operated, and 34.2 per cent of all farm land in the United States was farmed by owners.[1] Owners as a group generally have more freedom in their production plans than any other tenure class. However, in order to obtain ownership, many owners have had to be satisfied with relatively small farms because of the small amount of capital available to them. Many farmers are capable of managing larger farms than they are able to buy. Also, where these owners have a large debt, they may have to adjust their production so that their short-term income will be sufficient to meet living expenses plus payments on their debt obligations. This may mean that a farming pattern will be necessary which will not yield the greatest long-term income for the family. For this reason, we may find that ownership does not always guarantee the most efficient organization of resources.

Part-owners. This group includes those farmers who own some land and rent additional land in order to enlarge their farming units. In 1954, 40.7 per cent of all farm land in the United States was operated by part-owners.[2] Part-owners have, on the average, larger farms in terms of acres and in value of land and buildings than do owner-operators or tenants. Renting additional land is a way of gaining control of larger quantities of resources without increasing risk by going further into debt. With the relatively high capital requirements needed for efficient farming, many farmers have found this form of tenure to be very satisfactory. The problems of part-owners in terms of allocation of resources are largely the same as those of tenants. These problems are discussed below.

[1] U. S. Bureau of the Census, 1954 Census of Agriculture.
[2] *Ibid.*

Tenants. Tenants are those farmers who rent all of the land they operate. In this group are slightly less than one-fourth of all farmers operating 16.4 per cent of all farm land.[1] Several different tenant categories exist. Sharecroppers, for example, are tenants who pay a particular type of rent, a share of the crop. They do not own much, if any, of the farming equipment. In this chapter, we will see how the kind of rent paid by tenants affects the use of inputs on tenant-operated farms.

Some people in our society believe that tenancy, in itself, is evil and that farmers should be owner-operators if the best interests of farmers and society are to be served. This idea is based on a belief that, by owning property and making their own decisions, farmers make better use of their property and take a more active part in community affairs and democratic government. For people holding these views, the solution of all problems of tenancy is simple; tenancy should be abolished. Whether this view is sound must be judged from viewpoints other than those of economics. From an economic standpoint, we can examine tenure arrangements as to their effects on resource use and income distribution. People can then decide whether they regard the effects as desirable or undesirable.

Effects of Specified Leasing Practices

The basic function of tenancy is to allow two or more people to combine their inputs into a single producing unit. Unfortunately, conflicts between landlord and tenant can arise within leasing arrangements. We have learned that an owner-operator who is attempting to maximize net revenue will carry production to the point where the value of the marginal product is equal to the price of the input. In landlord-tenant arrangements, both landlord and tenant are utilizing inputs belonging to the other party. Each party may consider the inputs contributed by the other party to have a zero price. In this case, there will be a tendency to use the other person's inputs up to the point where the value of the marginal product is zero. For example, the tenant's labor has no price to the landlord. The landlord tends to push the use of the tenant's labor, insofar as he is able, to the point where additional labor brings no return. That is, the landlord would like to see enough labor used so that the value of the marginal product would be zero. The tenant, on the other hand,

---

[1] U. S. Bureau of the Census, 1954 Census of Agriculture.

considers the price of the land to be zero. He has an incentive to use additional land as long as the value of the marginal product of the land is greater than zero. But the land has a cost to the landlord. For this reason, a conflict of interest may develop.

In the development of rental arrangements, much discussion takes place concerning a "fair" rent. Unfortunately, "fair" implies some judgment involving considerations of income distribution. The word has different meanings to different individuals. From an economic standpoint, rent would be equal to the value of the marginal productivity of land if the forces of competition operated effectively. If rent were too high, no tenants would be available; if rent were too low, the abundance of tenants would bring about an increased rent. Where competition does not operate effectively and either tenants or landlords are able to obtain monopoly power, the question of "fairness" almost certainly is relevant.

However, our major concern here is to investigate leasing practices and see how they might be improved in terms of the effect on resource use. As a goal, we can say that we wish to improve leasing arrangements so that rented farms can be operated at least as efficiently as owner-operated farms. In saying this, we recognize that it is possible that leasing may even provide a means of farming in a more efficient manner than would owner-operatorship. If there are any economies of size, a farmer may receive more net returns from renting than from ownership of a farm which is too small to utilize efficiently his labor and capital.

Another way in which renting may be beneficial to resource owners is that it provides a means of attaining flexibility. Where land is rented, it is relatively easy to reduce the amount of land if opportunity returns to some other input should change. For example, a couple can rent out their land and live from the rent when they become too old to farm it themselves. Other farmers who find oportunities for off-farm work more profitable than farming can rent out their land. Later, if farming appears more profitable than off-farm work, they can return to farming.

In the establishment of leasing arrangements, some sort of bargaining between tenant and landlord takes place. The give and take of the bargaining process results in some variations in leasing terms in a given area. Generally, however, leasing provisions are quite similar, regardless of land productivity, within any one area. The bargaining which takes place seems to occur on the basis of trying to get better tenants for better land and buildings, or conversely, the better tenants will likely get the better farms. Also, some side concessions are often made in terms of who pays for fertilizer, seed, or repairs.

Rents are of two general types, fixed rent and rent which is a function of output, a share rent. Both of these types of renting may bring about certain problems in terms of resource use. Yet, neither lease type is necessarily bad or good. The specific provisions are important. These are the items which we examine below.

Fixed rent. Farming under a cash rental system is not nearly as widespread as it was in the period before the depression years of the 1930's. In 1954, however, nearly 14 per cent of all tenant farms were operated under cash rental contracts. That is, these farmers paid a fixed amount each year as rent, paid for all inputs, and received all of the proceeds from their production. Another 14 per cent of all tenants paid part of their rent as a share of production and also paid some cash rent. These share-cash renters are faced with some of the problems of both cash and share renters.

Cash renting has one big advantage over share renting. Once the cash payment is decided upon, the tenant can farm according to his plans.[1] The tenant pays all expenses and receives all returns. In many respects, his incentives to produce are the same as those of the owner-operator.

Having a fixed amount of money which must be paid each year has a risk-increasing effect, however. The rent must be paid even if yields and prices are low. Knowing this, the cash tenant is inclined to choose enterprises which yield a relatively stable return year after year. This may mean that he must accept a smaller average income over a long term in order to be sure of meeting his rental payment each year. In this respect, a fixed cash rental has the same effect on resource use as does the fixed payment obligation of an owner-operator with a mortgage. Both increase risk and tend to force inclusion of less uncertain enterprises in the farming system.

Most farmers will only rent for cash if they can do so for a lower price than they would expect to pay if they rented on a share basis. That is, they discount the rent to be paid because of the additional risk involved with cash rents. The risk-increasing effect of a fixed cash payment can be reduced, if not altogether eliminated, by providing for a flexible cash rent. The first step would be for tenant and landlord to agree upon a base rent. This base rental rate could be raised or lowered each year depending on weather conditions and yields

[1] Of course, some restrictions may be placed on the tenant by the landlord, such as prohibiting more than a given amount of land from going into soil-depleting crops. However, the tenant is aware of these restrictions when he rents, and, as a result, resource use should not be adversely affected.

in the local community and on prices of inputs used and prices of products produced. This can be stated as:

$$R_1 = R_0 \left(\frac{Y_1 \, P_{Y1} \, P_{X0}}{Y_0 \, P_{Y0} \, P_{X1}} \right)$$

where R_1 is the rent to be paid in the present year, R_0 is the base rent agreed upon, Y_1 is the average crop yield in the local area in the present year, Y_0 is the average yield for the base year, P_{Y1} and P_{Y0} are prices of some main product or indexes of prices received for the present year and the base year respectively, and P_{X0} and P_{X1} are indexes of prices paid for farm inputs in the base year and the present year respectively. If yields or prices received rise, the rent to be paid goes up. On the other hand, if the index of prices paid for inputs rises, the cash rent is reduced.

We can use an example of a western Kansas wheat farm to show how a flexible cash rent might work. Suppose that a tenant and landlord have agreed on a base rent (R_0) of \$7 per acre if the average wheat yield (Y_0) in the township is 15 bushels per acre, the price of Kansas wheat (P_{Y0}) is \$2 per bushel, and the government index of prices farmers pay (P_{X0}) is 300. Now suppose that, in the year for which the rent is being determined, the township wheat yield (Y_1) is only 12 bushels per acre, the price of wheat (P_{Y1}) is \$2.20 per bushel, and the index of prices that farmers pay (P_{X1}) is 305. The cash rent paid in this case would be

$$R_1 = 7(12 \times 2.20 \times 300/15 \times 2.00 \times 305) = \$6.06 \text{ per acre}$$

The advantage of a flexible cash rent is that initiative is not hampered, since the farmer receives all of the return. Risk is reduced, enabling the tenant to proceed with production plans involving risky products where such products will yield the greatest long-term income.

Rent as a function of output. Crop-share, livestock-share, crop-share-cash, and cropper arrangements belong in this class. For each of these types of lease, rent is paid as some portion or share, such as one-half or one-third of the production of the farm. Since rent is a share of production, risk of poor crops or prices is shared by tenant and landlord.

As share contracts are commonly set up, there is a tendency for the profitability of the use of some inputs to be reduced. Since the tenant and landlord receive only a given percentage of the production, the marginal revenue curve of each is lowered as compared to that of an owner. In Figure 41, MC_1 and MR_1 refer to the cost and revenue curves for a farm operated by an owner or by a cash tenant. The marginal revenue for each output is the price of the product. An output of OB, determined by the interesection of MC_1 and MR_1, is the most profitable under this condition.

Suppose, on the other hand, that the tenant pays one-half of the crop as rent. His revenue per unit of output is reduced to MR_2. If the tenant pays all of the variable costs, his costs are as shown by MC_1. The optimum input would be that amount to produce an output of OA, determined by the intersection of MC_1 and MR_2. Thus, it is seen that share contracts can lead to a reduction in output and a decreased income for the farm.

The remedy is quite simple. If landlord and tenant share variable costs in the same proportion as they share the returns from the farm, optimum use of the inputs is the same as for an owner-operated farm. If the tenant and landlord share variable costs equally, the tenant's marginal cost curve for Figure 41 is MC_2. The two curves MC_2 and MR_2 intersect at a point where OB is the most profitable output, the same output as if the farm were owner-operated. In many respects, this amounts to nearly the same thing as a partnership arrangement.

The effects of not sharing variable costs are shown in Table 43. If corn were \$1.50 per bushel, 160 pounds of nitrogen is the most profit-

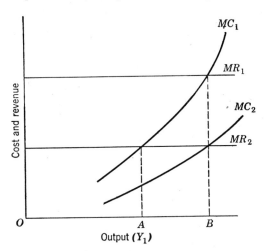

Figure 41. Marginal revenue and marginal cost curves for a common one-half share rental arrangement.

able application. If, however, the landlord pays for all of the fertilizer and receives one-half of the corn, he receives only $0.75 for each bushel of corn produced. He prefers to use only 120 pounds of nitrogen; the tenant wants to add nitrogen until the marginal productivity of nitrogen is zero. If they share nitrogen costs equally, the marginal cost to both landlord and tenant is one-half of the firm's marginal cost. The added cost per bushel is only $0.61 at 160 pounds of nitrogen, and an application of this amount is profitable to both tenant and landlord.

TABLE 43.   Cost and Production Data for Nitrogen and Corn

Nitrogen	Corn, bushels	Marginal Cost, dollars	One-half of the Marginal Cost, dollars
0	26	—	—
40	54	0.34	0.17
80	74	0.44	0.22
120	85	0.70	0.35
160	91	1.22	0.61

One study shows that conflicts of this nature do arise. In a sample of Iowa farms, 60 per cent of the rented farms, where the landlord shared fertilizer costs, employed fertilizer on corn compared to only 6.9 per cent of the farms fertilizing corn where the tenant paid all fertilizer costs.[1] Furthermore, the average amount of fertilizer used per farm was more than six times as great on the farms where the landlord paid part of the costs of fertilization.

Leasing conflicts arise because one of the parties of the lease does not receive the marginal productivity of the inputs he contributes. Landlord and tenant should realize this and avoid provisions within leases which have bad effects on use of inputs. Share-renting can be an efficient means of farm production. To avoid almost inevitable conflicts between landlords and tenants, variable costs, such as seed and fertilizer, should be shared in the same proportion as returns. For example, if the tenant gets two-thirds of the crop, he should pay two-thirds of the variable costs. Although a tenant and landlord do not share the labor and land costs, sharing of as many costs as is feasible, and sharing costs in the same proportion as they share the return will tend to bring about greater profit for the farm and for each individual.

[1] Earl O. Heady and Earl W. Kehrberg, "Relationship of Crop-Share and Cash Leasing Systems to Farming Efficiency," Iowa State College Agricultural Experiment Station, *Research Bulletin 386*, Ames, Iowa, May 1952, p. 662.

Length of Tenure and Capital Improvements

Problems common to all types of rental arrangements include the improvement of land and buildings and the insecurity and shortness of tenure on rented farms. Both problems are interrelated. Most leases in the United States are not written. If written, most are for a period of only one year. Tenants have little assurance, under such conditions, that they will be on a farm for more than the one year.

The insecurity and shortness of leases may have beneficial as well as harmful effects upon the efficiency with which a firm's inputs are used. Short-term leases may bring about increased effort on the tenant's part in order to increase his chances of staying on the farm. This may be advantageous to both the landlord and the tenant. It is expensive for both tenant and landlord when a tenant moves and a new tenant takes over. The tenant incurs the actual cost of moving and the cost of learning about the new farm. The landlord loses, since he must find a new tenant. Also, the new tenant will need some time to become acquainted with the farm so that he can do a good job of farming.

Tenants do not stay on one farm for as long a period as owners. In 1954, in the United States, full owners had been on their farms for an average of 17 years. All tenants had only been on their farms for 7 years, and croppers had an average tenure of only 6 years.

Besides moving costs and the effect on tenant incentive, short tenure has another effect on input use. Where tenants have no security of being on a farm for many years, they tend to produce commodities requiring short periods of production. They have no incentive to invest in buildings or conservation practices which yield income over a number of years. Landlords also have little incentive to make improvements for which they receive no direct return. For example, landlords receive no direct return from dwellings or barns on crop-share farms. For this reason, dwellings are usually in a poor state of repair on rental farms.

On rented farms, a useful method for obtaining input use similar to that of owner-operated farms is to provide for compensation for unexhausted improvements. A tenant can make the building or land improvements, and the landlord can promise to pay the tenant varying amounts, depending on the time period involved, if the tenant should leave. For example, a tenant might want a poultry house costing $10,000. The landlord and tenant could agree on some depreciation schedule based on the expected life of the building. If the building were expected to last 10 years, the landlord would pay the tenant $9,000 if the tenant should move after one year, $8,000 after two years, and so on up to a time when the house would have no residual value.

As another alternative, landlords can pay for improvements wanted by tenants. If an improvement increases the productivity of the tenant's inputs or improves his living conditions, the tenant should be willing to pay an additional annual cash rent for it. This alternative is generally preferable to compensation for unused value in those cases where the tenant does not have sufficient funds to make the improvement himself.

We found in this chapter that some provisions of leases can be changed so that both landlords and tenants can have increased incomes from their farming operations. Other adjustments in leasing arrangements may result in the lowering of one party's income and the raising of income to the other party. Since one party gains and one party loses, we cannot determine through economic analysis whether such an adjustment is beneficial. Income distribution adjustments must be judged by people in general as to the benefits obtained by changing the distribution.

15

Supply of individual farm products varies

We have placed a great deal of emphasis on the behavior of individual producing units in order to obtain an understanding of how changes in economic conditions affect the actions of producers. We are also interested in the firm from the standpoint of obtaining knowledge as to the effects in the aggregate of changes in production of individual firms. Most consumers, for example, have very little interest in whether farmer Brown produces milk. These same consumers, however, become greatly concerned if enough farmers alter their production to cause the prices of milk to rise. In this chapter, we will look at total supply of products in an effort to explain changes in aggregate production and prices.

Changes in Supply from Firms

The total supply of a commodity is the sum of the quantities produced by individual units during any production period plus carry-overs from preceding production periods. If producers are motivated by net revenue, changes in the quantity of farm products will be brought about by changes in relative prices of these products. The supply curve for a firm represents the maximum quantities of product which the firm is willing to produce for sale per unit of time at various product prices. Costs of production affect the quantity supplied by a firm.

In Chapter 7, we learned that, when a firm is unable to influence the price of its product, the most profitable level of output is that output at which the price of the product is equal to the marginal cost. We also saw that firms cease production when the price of the product is less than the average variable cost. Thus, when price is greater than average variable cost, the marginal cost curve is the supply curve for the firm.

Changes in Total Supply

There are two factors which cause the aggregate supply of a product to increase when its price increases. First, when price increases, it usually pays the firms in the industry to increase output. Second, when price increases, there is a tendency for new firms to enter the industry. That is, when the price of commodity Y_1 increases relative to the price of commodity Y_2, some firms cease production of Y_2 and begin production of Y_1. The supply curve, from the standpoint of the industry, represents the maximum quantities that firms in the aggregate are willing to supply at alternative prices under given cost conditions. It represents both the changes in output of firms in the industry and changes in output due to changes in number of firms.

The extent to which output changes in response to a change in price varies among commodities. The concept of *elasticity* is used to provide us with information about the responsiveness of changes in quantity produced to changes in price. *Elasticity of supply* is the percentage change in quantity in response to a given percentage change in price.

Elasticity may be computed from two observations of prices and quantities. On any supply curve, the formula for *arc* or *average*[1] elasticity is

$$\frac{(Q_2 - Q_1)/(Q_2 + Q_1)}{(P_2 - P_1)/(P_2 + P_1)}$$

or inverting, $$\left(\frac{Q_2 - Q_1}{Q_2 + Q_1}\right)\left(\frac{P_2 + P_1}{P_2 - P_1}\right)$$

In this formula, P_1 represents the price in one time period, and Q_1 represents the quantity supplied at that price. P_2 is the price in another time period, and Q_2 is the quantity supplied at that price.

We normally expect that, as price increases, the quantity of farm commodities produced will increase; that is, under normal conditions

---

[1] Arc elasticity is only an average. The elasticity at any point on a supply curve is equal to $(dQ/dP)P/Q$.

the elasticity of supply of farm products will be positive. In the period when the quantity of farm products available is fixed, there is no additional product forthcoming as a result of an increase in price, and the elasticity of supply is zero. That is, there is no change in quantity in response to a change in price. Over a period of time, when farmers have an opportunity to adjust their production to changes in relative prices, the elasticity of supply is expected to be greater than zero.

If elasticity is greater than one, supply is said to be *elastic*. If, on the other hand, quantity supplied responds relatively little to price changes, elasticity is less than one and is said to be *inelastic*. That is, if the percentage change in quantity is greater than the percentage change in price, supply is elastic; if the percentage change in quantity is less than the percentage change in price, supply is inelastic.

Elasticity of supply from the standpoint of an industry is affected by the shape and position of the marginal cost function of firms in the industry and by the position of the average cost of other firms which might potentially produce the product. If the marginal cost function for firms producing a product is relatively flat, the elasticity of supply for this product will be rather large. On the other hand, if the marginal cost of producing an additional unit of output increases sharply as output increases, the elasticity of supply will be rather small.

The elasticity of supply for many farm commodities is undoubtedly very high since the number of potential producers for these commodities is great. A small rise in price leads to a large expansion in the number of producers, even though relatively small increases may be made in the production of each firm formerly producing the product. This results in a highly elastic supply from the standpoint of the industry as a whole.

Elasticity of supply may be different when price rises and when price falls. This difference is caused primarily by differences in the length of planning period. For example, when the price of a commodity increases relative to the prices of other commodities, it may be necessary for firms to purchase specialized inputs in order to expand production. This expansion of production may involve long-run decisions and will not be undertaken unless the firm expects to gain from the expansion. After having made the change, however, those costs which were for specialized inputs become a part of fixed costs and are no longer relevant in production decisions. Hence, prices may fall considerably without altering production of commodities, although these same commodities are rather sensitive to price increases. We find, partly for this reason, that the supply elasticity of many farm commodities is extremely low over short periods of time. Over the long pull, however, when firms have depreciated out their investments in specialized inputs, production of commodities will decline in response to continuation of relatively low prices.

Optimum Output from the Standpoint of the Industry

A firm is producing an optimum output and is said to be in equilibrium when there is no incentive to change its output. Likewise, an industry, the aggregate of firms, is said to be in equilibrium when there is no tendency for the output of the industry to change. Thus, an industry is in equilibrium when there is no incentive for firms in the industry to change their production and there is no incentive for the number of firms in the industry to change.

Individual firms in an industry producing Y_1 are operating at an optimum level of output when marginal cost is equal to marginal revenue, or when value of the marginal product is equal to the price of the inputs. This condition of optimum production may occur when individual firms in the industry are making large profits. These profits provide an incentive for additional firms to enter the production of Y_1. If we consider a period of time long enough for other firms to purchase specialized inputs, expansion will occur as long as the returns to firms producing Y_1 are greater than the returns which firms can get from the production of other commodities. The industry is in equilibrium, therefore, when the least profitable firm producing Y_1 is receiving a return just high enough to keep it in the industry. If this firm is receiving less than can be received from producing other commodities, the firm will have an incentive to change to the production of other commodities. On the other hand, if firms not producing Y_1 can receive a greater net revenue from entering the industry than from the production of other commodities, there is an incentive for these firms to change to the production of Y_1.

Cost structures for three hypothetical firms are shown in Figure 42. When P_{Y1} is $1, firm 1 is making a profit from the production of Y_1. Since firm 1 is making profits from the production of Y_1, it has no incentive to change production unless it can make a greater profit from the production of other commodities. Firm 3, on the other hand, is not able to cover its costs of producing Y_1 when P_{Y1} is $1. Thus, this firm will not produce Y_1 and will engage in the production of other commodities. Firm 2 is receiving a *normal* return, a return which is just large enough to keep it in the industry. This firm is producing

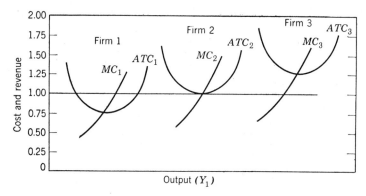

Figure 42. Cost curves for three firms in an industry.

where price equals average cost. Firms with costs greater than those of firm 2 will not enter the production of Y_1. Although firm 2 is producing Y_1 under conditions where P_{Y1} is equal to the ATC, it would prefer that the price be higher. That is, the firm does not seek to produce at an output where price equals average cost but is forced to by virtue of the fact that, when price is higher, other firms enter the industry causing the price to fall. All firms which are motivated by net revenue seek to equate marginal cost and marginal revenue, but some firms are forced to equate marginal revenue and marginal cost at an output where these are equal to average cost.

If we know the marginal and average cost relations for individual producers in an industry, we can estimate the change in production which will occur in response to a change in price for the commodity. The total supply of a commodity is the sum of the quantities produced by all firms in the industry. The aggregate change in output brought about by a change in price is the sum of the changes made by the individual firms. We see then that, other things being equal, the aggregate supply curve of a commodity is equal to the sum of the supply curves of the individual firms.

Input Prices May Increase When Production Increases

The conditions facing a producer in input markets may be quite different from those which he thinks exist. In the evaluation of returns from an increase in the production of a product, a producer must give consideration to the expected price of the product and the expected price of the inputs needed. As pointed out above, if the price of the product rises, there is an incentive to expand production. An expansion in production by one firm will have little bearing upon the prices firms have to pay for inputs. On the other hand, an expansion in production by firms in the aggregate probably will lead to an increase in the price of inputs. This means that the marginal cost to firms will be greater than expected and also that average cost will rise as a result of the increase in input prices. Thus, an individual firm in deciding to expand its output in an effort to increase its net revenue may find its cost increasing and the price of the product decreasing to such an extent that the actual changes in net revenue are disappointing.

Changes in the Supply of Particular Farm Commodities Over Time

Production of agricultural products varies substantially over time. Some of the changes in quantities of commodities produced likely result from changes in uncontrollable conditions such as weather. On the other hand, many changes in production result from changes in relative prices and costs. Changes in production of major classes of livestock from 1925 to 1955 are shown in Figure 43. In general, there are fairly definite cycles of production of livestock. During the 30-year period under consideration, there was a peak in numbers of all cattle and calves about every 10 to 11 years and a trough about every 10 to 11 years. The number of cows and heifers kept for milk followed a pattern quite similar to that of beef cattle. Numbers of sheep

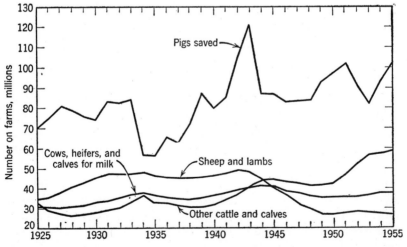

Figure 43. Production of major classes of livestock in the United States, 1925–1955.

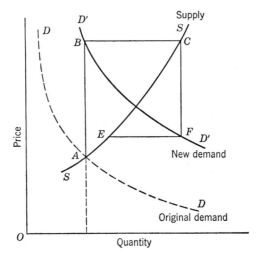

Figure 44. Cobweb behavior in production.

and lambs have decreased greatly during the last decade, but, in general, a cyclical pattern similar to that for beef and dairy cattle is apparent. The variation in hog numbers is greater than that of other classes of livestock. There seems to be a 2- to 4-year increase in number of hogs followed by a 2- to 4-year decrease.

The cyclical variation in livestock numbers results in large part from mistaken expectations regarding the relative profitability of livestock. A possible explanation of the cyclical behavior is demonstrated by what is called the "cobweb" theorem of production. There are several conditions necessary for a cobweb type of behavior to result. According to the cobweb theorem, producers of a commodity expect the price in the next period of production to be the same as the current price and make production plans accordingly. The cobweb theorem is most appropriate in the case of nonstorable goods. Also, a cobweb type of behavior is influenced by the length of the production period. A commodity which has a short production period so that producers can get into and out of production quickly is usually subject to more violent fluctuations in production and prices than a commodity which has a long period of production.

An example of the cobweb type of behavior is shown in Figure 44. The industry is in equilibrium at *A*, i.e., the consumers are willing to purchase the same quantity that the producers are willing to supply. The original demand curve *DD* shows the maximum quantities of the good that consumers are willing to purchase at alternative prices. Suppose that the demand shifts to *D′D′* because people's preferences change so that they are willing to buy more of the good at all prices. Now the consumers are willing to pay the price at B for the same output for which they originally were willing to pay the price at A. In planning their production, producers consider the current price at B as the future price and make plans to increase their production to C accordingly. When production has been increased, however, it is necessary to take a lower price for the product than was anticipated. Consumers are willing to pay a price equal to that at F for the new output. In view of this, producers plan to decrease their production in the next time period to the amount at E. In some cases, this process continues until an equilibrium level of output at the intersection of the supply curve and the new demand curve is reached. In other cases, an equilibrium is never reached, and we have a continuous fluctuation in prices and production.

An equilibrium condition for the major livestock classes does not continue for long even if it is reached. There may be two reasons for this. It is possible that the supply and demand relationships may be such that a continuous fluctuation in prices and quantities takes place. Even if there is a tendency toward equilibrium, as in Figure 44, shifts in demand or supply may cause a new cobweb to be set in motion.

Estimates of Supply of Farm Commodities

Several attempts have been made to estimate the extent to which farmers respond to changes in the prices of particular farm commodities. Since production of many commodities is highly variable as a result of changes in weather and other factors beyond the control of farmers, most of the estimates of elasticity of supply of crops have been estimates of the responsiveness of acreage to price rather than quantity to price.

In one recent study, elasticities of supply were derived for wheat, cotton, and corn.[1] The following estimates of the elasticities of acreage with respect to price were obtained: wheat 0.93; cotton 0.67; and corn 0.18. We see from these data that the elasticity of supply may vary greatly among commodities. This should not be surprising, however, since the difficulty of changing the level of production varies among commodities. Some commodities use essentially the same inputs as are used in the production of other commodities, and a large proportion of their production costs are variable. Where this is true, we expect to find rather high supply elasticities. Examples of agricul-

---

[1] Marc Nerlove, "Estimates of the Elasticities of Supply of Selected Agricultural Commodities," *Journal of Farm Economics*, Vol. 38, May 1956, pp. 496–509.

tural products expected to have relatively large changes in production in response to changes in price are eggs and some vegetables.

Other products use a high proportion of inputs which are specialized, and a high proportion of the costs are fixed. In these cases, such as corn, purebred cattle, and fluid milk, the short-run response of production to price changes is relatively low.

16 | Aggregate supply of farm products also varies

Year-to-year changes in production of individual farm commodities are much greater than changes in production of farm commodities in the aggregate. This difference is principally due to the fact that expansion in production of some commodities is partially offset by contraction of production of others. A farmer may reduce his corn acreage in one year, but he will probably produce soybeans or some other product on the land which he withdraws from corn. Also, unplanned changes exert more influence on the production of individual farm commodities than on total agricultural output. For example, good weather conditions in one area may increase production of commodities in that area enough to offset the effects of adverse weather conditions in other areas and leave total agricultural production unchanged.

We expect that short-term changes in production of agricultural commodities will be quite different from long-term changes. It takes time for information concerning changes in consumption patterns and prices to reach farmers in order that they can plan changes in production of individual commodities. Additional time is required to implement their plans to bring about these changes. When the demand falls for some agricultural products, farmers tend to shift from production of one product to another without decreasing aggregate production. In the short run, an expansion of total farm output requires an increase in total inputs. For this reason, if demand rises for some agricultural products, inputs will not be added if they are inputs which yield income over a period of years, and if the farmer does not expect a price rise to be permanent.

Aggregate Agricultural Production Is Highly Stable

In the aggregate, agriculture supplies a stable, dependable source of food and fiber. We see in Table 44 that year-to-year variations in

TABLE 44. Year-to-Year Variability in Aggregate Production

Change in Production from Preceding Year, per cent	Price Received for All Farm Products* 1910– 1954, years	Farm Output 1910– 1954, years	Livestock and Livestock Products 1910– 1954, years	All Crops 1910– 1954, years	Total Industrial Production 1919– 1954, years	Durable Manufac- turing 1919– 1954, years	Non- durable Manufac- turing 1919– 1954, years
+31 and over	1	0	0	2	0	4	0
+21 to +30	5	1	0	0	3	8	1
+16 to +20	3	1	0	0	6	1	1
+11 to +15	2	2	1	3	5	4	4
+6 to +10	4	5	5	5	4	5	6
+1 to +5	12	15	23	11	5	1	10
0	1	2	2	4	1	0	1
−1 to −5	7	12	12	12	1	2	9
−6 to −10	3	4	1	2	3	3	2
−11 to −15	2	2	0	4	2	0	1
−16 to −20	1	0	0	1	2	0	0
−20 to −30	2	0	0	0	3	3	0
−31 and less	1	0	0	0	0	4	0
Average vari- ation, per cent	12.07	5.36	3.40	7.31	13.35	21.89	7.27

Source: Agricultural Statistics, 1954, pp. 456, 457, and 473. 1947–1949 = 100.
* 1910–1914 = 100.

aggregate production of farm products are small in comparison with year-to-year variations in production of industrial products. During the period 1910 to 1954, year-to-year changes in output of agricultural products were less than 5 per cent in 29 years. In contrast, between 1919 and 1954, year-to-year changes in output of industrial products were less than 5 per cent in only 7 years. In only 2 years, 1921 and 1934, did farm output decrease more than 10 per cent, and the decrease in 1934 resulted largely from a severe drought. It did not occur primarily in response to a change in prices for agricultural products. The largest increases in farm output followed the droughts of 1934 and 1936. The next largest increases occurred in 1912 and 1942.

The average annual variation in industrial output is about 2.5 times as large as the average annual variation in farm output. In 1921, 1932, and 1938 industrial production decreased more than 20 per cent from the preceding year. In 5 years between 1919 and 1954, industrial production increased more than 20 per cent.

We note also that year-to-year variation in production of crops is greater than year-to-year variation in production of livestock products. This is due to the fact that smaller investment in specialized inputs is necessary in crop production than in production of livestock and livestock products. Furthermore, weather has a greater influence on crop production than on production of livestock. Also, the production period for most livestock products is longer than one year. The production of most crops, on the other hand, can be changed within a year.

Year-to-year changes in production are influenced to a large extent by factors beyond the control of individual producers. Perhaps a better indicator of production intentions is furnished by the stability of inputs used in agricultural production. There have been only two periods in the history of United States agriculture in which there were substantial decreases in inputs in agricultural production. Professor Schultz has pointed out that, during the period 1920 to 1924, there was a decrease of approximately 5 per cent in the inputs used in agriculture. In the period from 1931 to 1934, there was a decline of approximately 11 per cent in inputs.[1] Major periods of expansion in the use of agricultural inputs were 1917 to 1920 and 1942 to 1949. In the first of these periods, agricultural inputs increased 8 per cent; in the second, 9 per cent. Both of these periods, however, were wartime periods, and the expansion in agricultural production was brought about in part by patriotic motives in connection with war efforts. Thus, the large changes occurring in agricultural production during these periods should not be attributed entirely to changes in prices of farm commodities. On the other hand, it should be noted that the prices of farm products increased rapidly during the period of 1917 to 1919 and again in the period of 1942 to 1948. Also, during the two periods in which inputs declined, prices for agricultural products decreased substantially.

Although agricultural output has been relatively stable during the twentieth century, prices of farm products have been very unstable. Between 1910 and 1955, farm product prices increased more than 20 per cent in 7 years and decreased more than 20 per cent in 4 years. The largest price increases occurred during World Wars I and II and

[1] T. W. Schultz, *The Economic Organization of Agriculture*, McGraw-Hill Book Company, New York 1953, pp. 210–212.

following the drought of 1934. The largest decreases in prices were in 1921 and in 1931 and 1932.

The stable production of feed and fiber is undoubtedly an asset to the nation. The high stability, however, raises questions as to why farmers do not respond to a greater extent to the large changes in prices of farm commodities.

Reasons for Low Elasticity of Supply of Agricultural Products in the Short Run

The low elasticity of supply of agricultural products in the short run has long been a puzzle to students of economics. The forces which contribute to the stability of agricultural output when prices rise are somewhat different from those which contribute to the stability of agricultural output when prices fall. Prices of agricultural commodities have in the past generally risen when production and prices of nonfarm commodities rose. Hence, prices of agricultural commodities were rising when opportunities for additional employment in nonfarm sectors were expanding. The response of farmers to increases in prices of farm commodities was tempered by the transfer of labor from farm to nonfarm sectors of the economy.

Uncertainty as to the duration of high prices when prices of farm products rise also restricts expansion in the production of agricultural commodities. A farmer would not be expected to invest in a layer house, for example, if he did not expect egg prices to remain at a relatively high level for some time. The longer the period of rising prices, therefore, the greater is the production response to the increase in prices.

Another factor which restricts expansion of agricultural production during periods of rising prices is the limitation placed on agricultural production by the investment capital available to farmers. As a result of experiences encountered in granting loans to farmers, lending agencies are reluctant to make loans for investment in agriculture when price increases are expected to be temporary. Also, farmers may be reluctant to borrow capital to invest in agriculture if they expect high prices to be temporary. A shortage of capital, whether brought about by a refusal of lending agencies to lend or by a refusal by the farmer to borrow, contributes to the low short-run elasticity of supply during periods of increasing price.

Many reasons are offered to explain the stability of aggregate agricultural production during periods of falling prices of farm products. Some people contend that farmers try to offset the effects of falling prices by increasing the production of farm products. This explanation does not appear completely satisfactory. In order for it to be plausible, it is necessary to assume that farmers are willing to work more for a lower wage than for a higher wage. That is, it must be necessary that a supply curve for farm labor is "backward-sloping" so that when prices of farm labor increase, farmers work less and take more leisure. This means that when the returns for farm labor decrease, farmers work more in an effort to maintain their income at something approximating a constant level. This assumption is probably correct for some people and for certain ranges of income. However, there is too much evidence to the contrary to consider this to be a complete explanation of stable production of farm products during a period of falling prices. For example, during World War II, when prices were relatively high and the nation needed more agricultural products, an incentive for additional production was provided by guaranteeing higher prices to farmers than had existed in preceding years. These high prices provided an incentive to expand production. If the hypothesis that farmers would work more with lower prices were correct, then one approach which the government might have taken in obtaining an increased production of agricultural products would have been to decrease the prices of farm products.

Another reason which is often advanced in an explanation of the low elasticity of supply of agricultural products is that fixed costs are relatively important in agriculture. Persons using this argument emphasize the close association of the household and the firm in agriculture. They point out that household expenditures for subsistence purposes constitute a high proportion of expenditures and must be incurred irrespective of the level of farm production. They also argue that investments in land and buildings and in machinery and equipment are fixed. As a result, the same inputs are used regardless of the price paid.

Perhaps a more realistic appraisal is to consider the supplies of the inputs to agriculture as a function of the opportunity return for these inputs in other uses.[1] During periods when prices of farm products are declining, the level of employment and wages in nonagricultural sectors of the economy may also be falling. Hence, when prices of farm products are falling, there are few opportunities for labor to transfer from agriculture to industry. The use of inputs, as we have learned earlier, is determined primarily by the opportunity return which can be obtained for inputs in alternative uses. When there are

[1] D. Gale Johnson, "The Nature of the Supply Function for Agricultural Products," *American Economic Review,* Vol. XL, No. 4, 1950, pp. 539–564.

no jobs in the nonfarm sector of the economy, the opportunity return for labor used in farming may be zero. In view of this, labor stays in agriculture and continues to produce even though the returns for labor are low. Likewise, the opportunity return for land in the aggregate is very low. There is no alternative to farming or forestry for most land. Therefore, the stable production of agricultural commodities during periods of falling prices is explained in large part by the inelasticity of supply of the inputs used in agricultural production.

Where conditions are favorable, that is, where opportunity returns for agricultural inputs are high, we expect that supply elasticity of inputs would be somewhat greater. We do note that, as a result of relatively more profitable jobs in industry, agricultural employment has dropped from 9.3 million in 1950 to 7.9 million in 1956.[1] Agricultural incomes were relatively unfavorable during this same period. Had it not been for the job opportunities in industry, the movement of people from rural to urban employment would likely have been much slower if not actually reversed.

The explanation which has been advanced for the stability of agricultural production also applies to those industries processing agricultural products. For example, the stability of production in canned milk, meat packing, beet sugar, and other industries which process agricultural products is about the same as in agricultural production. This is due, in large part, to the fact that agricultural commodities are inputs used in the production of the processed products. During periods in which prices of processed, agricultural commodities fall, farm prices of these commodities are also low. Therefore, the input costs to the processing firms are decreased, and they continue to produce at about the same level as was true before prices fell. In other words, prices of the inputs fall in about the same proportion as prices of the product, leaving the optimum level of production, from the standpoint of the firm, unchanged.

[1] U.S.D.A., "Farm Labor," Jan. 1957 and Jan. 1954.

Part **III**

CONSUMPTION AND DEMAND

17 | Consumer demand is important to farmers

Farmer's income possibilities are affected by wants of consumers. All producers expect their products to be consumed. Through their purchases in the market place, consumers transmit knowledge to farmers relative to the kinds and amounts of farm products they want. Changes in consumer desires are reflected to farmers through changes in prices and quantities of goods purchased by consumers. Our principal concern in this chapter is to determine why consumers vary their purchases. This information will help us to understand the reasons for changes in the demand for farm products.

Consumers Have Preferences Among Goods

Consumers gain utility or satisfaction from consumption of goods. In purchasing goods, they attempt to buy those goods from which they get the greatest satisfaction in relation to the prices of the goods. All consumers are limited in the amount of goods which they can purchase and, as a result, must make choices among various goods. These choices are influenced by preferences, income, and by the prices of the goods available. The problem of choice in consumption is similar to the problem of choice in production. In production, the producer bases his choice of production alternatives on physical production relationships and on relative prices. In making consumption decisions the consumer is also concerned with relative prices; in addition, she is concerned with her preferences for various goods.

In purchasing goods, consumers buy some combinations of goods instead of others which they also could purchase. No housewife spends all of her budget on one commodity. Rather she purchases combinations of goods. Furthermore, she chooses some combinations of goods in preference to others. If a consumer can substitute one commodity for another, she can usually find many combinations of the two commodities which are equally satisfactory to her. The consumer is said to be indifferent to those combinations which are equally satisfactory.

We can illustrate the idea of consumer preferences graphically. We can construct a boundary line, like the two lines in Figure 45, which separate those combinations of goods and services considered preferable from those considered inferior. We call this line an *indifference curve*. It represents those combinations of goods and services to which the consumer is indifferent. That is, it represents those combinations which are equally satisfactory to the consumer.

We now see that indifference curves are comparable to isoproduct contours which we studied in Chapter 9. Just as there are different ways in which inputs can be substituted in the production of a commodity, there are also different ways in which commodities substitute for each other in consumption.

Some commodities may be substituted at a constant rate in consumption. If commodities substitute at a constant rate, a consumer

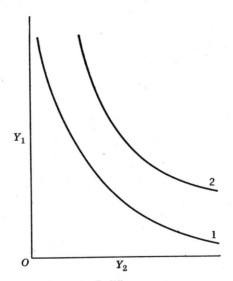

Figure 45. Indifference curves.

is willing to trade a given number of units of one good for a given amount of another. Under such conditions, we would expect to find consumers using only one of these goods. However, most commodities which consumers purchase are not substituted at a constant rate. A consumer with ten apples and ten oranges may be willing to give up one orange for one additional apple. But, the same consumer with 16 oranges and one apple would hardly be expected to give up one apple for one more orange. The rate at which the consumer is willing to trade apples for oranges depends upon the number of oranges and apples which she possesses.

As a general rule, when a consumer is trading commodity Y_1 for commodity Y_2, she asks increasingly larger quantities of Y_2 for a unit of Y_1 as the amount of Y_2 which she has increases relative to the amount of Y_1. This means that we expect indifference curves to be convex to the origin, as shown in Figure 45.

We normally regard consumers as preferring more goods and services to less. In other words, we say that consumers seek to attain the highest indifference curve possible, given the amount of money available for the purchase of consumer goods. Because of this fact that more of one good is preferred to less, indifference curves must have a negative slope. An upward-sloping indifference curve would indicate that a consumer was indifferent to consuming more goods. This seems to be in conflict with reality.

An indifference curve which lies above another represents a greater amount of satisfaction. For example, the combinations of goods along indifference curve 2 in Figure 45 give the consumer greater satisfaction than the combinations on curve 1. Just as we do not expect product contours on production functions to cross, we do not expect indifference curves to cross. Since combinations above an indifference curve are, by definition, preferred to combinations below the curve, these curves cannot intersect.

The indifference curve tells us the rate at which consumers are willing to trade one good for another according to their individual preferences. Yet, we do not know which combination will be purchased unless we know something about prices of the two goods. The combinations of goods which consumers can purchase depend upon their incomes and the prices of the goods. Suppose that commodity Y_1 costs $1 and Y_2 costs $2. If a consumer has $100 to spend, the maximum amount of Y_1 she can purchase is 100 units, and the maximum amount of Y_2 is 50 units. The price of Y_2 is twice as much as the price of Y_1. Thus, she can substitute the commodities in the market in the ratio of two of Y_1 to one of Y_2, as shown by MN in Figure 46. This line, which

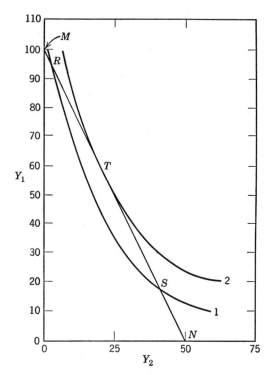

Figure 46. Optimum combination of consumer goods.

shows the combinations of goods that can be purchased is called the *price line*. The slope of the price line, as we have learned in preceding chapters, is equal to the ratio of prices of the two goods, or P_{Y2}/P_{Y1}. There is a price line for every amount of money available to spend, but all price lines are parallel.

Two of many possible indifference curves of an individual are shown in Figure 46. The price line MN represents the quantities of Y_1 and Y_2 which can be purchased for $100. We want to know which combination of Y_1 and Y_2 which can be purchased with $100 will bring the most satisfaction. The points R, S, and T represent combinations of goods which can be purchased for $100. But T lies on a higher indifference curve and will be preferred to R and S. The consumer maximizes satisfaction by choosing a combination of two goods such that the rate at which she is willing to substitute two goods in consumption is just equal to the rate at which she can substitute the goods in the market. That is, satisfaction is maximized when $\Delta Y_1/\Delta Y_2 =$

P_{Y2}/P_{Y1}. Unless this condition is fulfilled, it is possible for the consumer to receive the same amount of satisfaction for less cost or to receive more satisfaction for the same total expenditure.

For example, at point R, the consumer is willing to give more units of Y_1 for Y_2 than she has to give in the market place. She is willing to trade three units of Y_1 for one unit of Y_2. But Y_2 costs only twice as much as Y_1. By giving up two units of Y_1, she will have enough funds to buy a unit of Y_2. Since she is willing to trade on a three for one basis, this is a good trade. She will continue to trade Y_1 for Y_2 until she reaches the point where she no longer is willing to give up two or more units of Y_1 for an additional unit of Y_2. There is no combination of Y_1 and Y_2, other than that at point T, which gives her as much satisfaction for $100.

Income and Price Changes Affect Consumption

Changes in price and in income affect the quantities of goods which consumers buy. An increase in income, for example, makes it possible to purchase additional quantities of goods and services. We normally expect consumers to increase purchases when their incomes increase. If purchases of a particular good do increase with increased income, the good is said to be a *normal good*. On the other hand, if the quantity of a good purchased decreases when income rises, that good is said to be an *inferior good*.

The effects of a change in the price of a good upon its consumption are somewhat more complex than the effects of a change in income. A change in the price of a commodity has two distinct effects upon an individual's behavior—an income effect and a substitution effect. A change in price of a commodity affects the value of an individual's income, since the purchasing power of his income is changed. Likewise, a change in the price of a commodity relative to other commodities makes it desirable for an individual to change his consumption pattern. For example, if the price of Y_1 rises relative to the price of other goods, we expect less of Y_1 to be purchased, ignoring the income effects. On the other hand, a decrease in the price of Y_1 makes this good more favorable relative to other goods, and more will be purchased.

To illustrate the income effect of a change in price, suppose that an individual has an income of $2000, and that she has been purchasing 400 quarts of milk per year at a price of 24 cents per quart. Assume now that the price of milk drops to 20 cents per quart, but the prices of all related commodities remain unchanged. Previously, the individual had been spending $96 per year on milk. Now she can purchase the same quantity of milk for $16 less. Clearly, there has been an apparent increase in her income of $16 as a result of the decline in the price of milk. This extra $16 will be treated like any other increase in income. It will lead the consumer to change her expenditures on the various goods and services, including milk, that she purchases.

With a normal good, the income and substitution effects operate in the same direction. If the price decreases, consumers will substitute this good for other goods. The decrease in price, as we saw above, also has the effect of increasing consumers' incomes. Consumption of normal goods is increased when income rises. Thus, both the income and substitution effects cause an increase in consumption of a normal good when its price decreases. On the other hand, both the income and substitution effects of a price increase for a normal good cause a decrease in consumption of that good.

A price decrease for an inferior good, however, brings about two opposing influences. The substitution effect causes an increase in

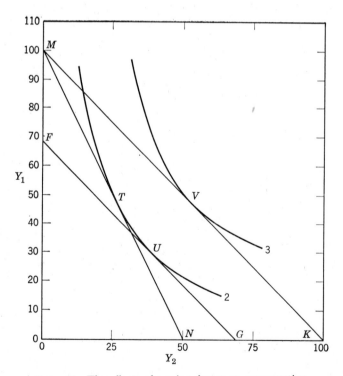

Figure 47. The effects of a price change on consumption.

purchases of the good, as with normal goods. The price decrease, in effect, results in an increased income. Since the good is inferior, purchases of the good are expected to decrease. Thus, whether a price decrease for an inferior good results in an increase or a decrease in purchases depends upon the relative strength of the income and substitution effects. If the substitution effect is stronger, as is nearly always the case, more of the good will be purchased. If the income effect predominates, purchases will decrease.

An example of a price change and its effect on quantities purchased is shown in Figure 47. We start with the same price line and indifference curve of Figure 46, and the satisfaction-maximizing combination at T. Suppose that the price of Y_2 now falls from \$2 to \$1. More of Y_2 can now be purchased for the same income, and the slope of the price line decreases from 2/1 to 1/1. The new price line is MK. As a result of the new price ratio, the satisfaction-maximizing combination will be at V. The price decrease brings about a substitution of Y_2 for Y_1. The substitution effect alone can be shown by finding the combination of Y_1 and Y_2 which would give the same satisfaction at the new prices as combination T gave at the old prices. The substitution effect of the price decrease for Y_2 is shown by the change from T to U. There is an increased consumption of Y_2 and a decreased consumption of Y_1. The income has been increased as a result of the price decrease. Both Y_1 and Y_2 are normal goods, and the consumption of both is increased as a result of the income effect. The income effect is the change from U to V.

From information similar to that obtained in Figure 47 we can estimate the effects of changes in the price of a product upon consumption. In Chapter 18, we will be concerned with demand elasticity with respect to price and income. What we have learned in this chapter is essential to a thorough understanding of what will be discussed in the next chapter.

18 | Market demand for farm products affects farm incomes

Indifference curve analysis has shown how an individual's preferences affect demand for goods. Farmers are interested not so much in how one individual behaves but rather in the *market demand* for the products which they produce and the inputs which they use. Market demand is the sum of all individual's demands and shows the aggregate relationship between quantities offered for sale and the price paid for the various quantities. Specifically, *a demand curve shows the maximum quantities which will be purchased at alternative prices of a good for a given period of time.* When we speak of the demand for a given product, we refer to the relationship between quantities and prices of that product and assume that prices of other products do not change.

Price Elasticity Defined

Demand curves are generally considered to slope downward to the right as *DD* in Figure 48. Logic and experience tell us that lower prices are necessary to bring about consumption of larger quantities of a good or service. The extent to which consumption responds to changes in price varies among commodities. We use the concept of *price elasticity of demand* to measure the extent of this responsiveness. We define price elasticity of demand as the percentage change in

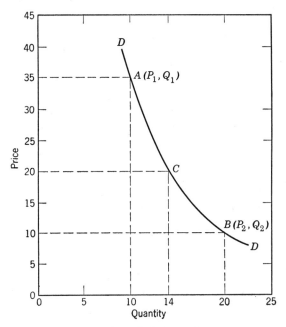

Figure 48. A typical demand curve.

quantity taken as a result of a 1 per cent change in price. The formula for computing this elasticity is the same as that for elasticity of supply. For example, to determine the *arc* or *average*[1] price elasticity between any two points such as *A* and *B* in Figure 48, the formula is

$$\frac{(Q_2 - Q_1)/(Q_2 + Q_1)}{(P_2 - P_1)/(P_2 + P_1)} \quad \text{or} \quad \left(\frac{Q_2 - Q_1}{Q_2 + Q_1}\right)\left(\frac{P_2 + P_1}{P_2 - P_1}\right)$$

The arc elasticity between *A* and *B*, for example, is $[(20 - 10)/(20 + 10)][(10 + 35)/(10 - 35)]$. This is $(10/30)(45/-25)$, which is equal to $-9/15$ or -0.6. In this case, a decrease in price of 1 per cent brings about an increase in quantity taken of only 0.6 per cent. We say that the demand curve is inelastic between these two points. Demand is said to be inelastic if elasticity is less than one; if greater than one, it is elastic. If a 1 per cent decrease in price causes a 1 per cent increase in quantity taken, demand is said to be of unit elasticity. Price elasticity of demand is usually negative since demand curves generally slope downward. Because demand elasticity is nearly always negative, the negative sign is often omitted in common usage.

---

[1] Arc elasticity is only an average. The elasticity at any point on a demand curve is equal to $(dQ/dP)\ P/Q$.

We need to recognize that the arc elasticity of any given segment of a demand curve may be different from that of some other segment. For example, the price elasticity of demand between C and B in Figure 48 is $(-6/34)(30/10) = -0.53$. The elasticity of the shorter arc is smaller than that of the whole arc AB. This indicates that the elasticity varies at different points on the curve. We may need to consider the elasticities for short segments of the curve in order to obtain the most useful information.

Price Elasticity and Total Revenue

Price elasticity of demand is important to producers because of the interrelationship between elasticity and total revenue for alternative quantities of goods. Much of the present argument about agricultural policy involves the effect on farmers' revenue of reducing agricultural output. Historically, attempts have been made to decrease the production of agricultural commodities in an effort to bring about an increase in the total revenue which farmers receive. Whether total revenue will be increased when production is decreased depends upon the price elasticity of demand.

To illustrate this point, consider a straight-line demand curve such as FH in Figure 49. The elasticity of demand for any straight-line demand curve depends upon the segment of the curve under consideration. This is because elasticity is a relative concept. In the segment of the demand curve FG, the percentage change in price is less than the percentage change in quantity. For example, from point F to point G the change in price is 50 cents. This is a percentage change of 67 per cent relative to the average price of 75 cents. The change in quantity is 40 units or 200 per cent of the average of 20 units. Thus, the elasticity of demand is greater than unity. In this case, it is 200/67 or 3.0, and this segment of the demand curve is elastic.

In the lower portion of the demand curve, from G to H, demand is inelastic. The change in price is 50 cents, as it was from F to G. However, on a percentage basis, the change in price is 200 per cent of the average price of 25 cents. The percentage change in quantity is only 67 per cent. Thus, the percentage change in quantity is less than the percentage change in price, and the demand curve is inelastic. Since this demand curve is elastic in the upper portion and inelastic in the lower portion, there is a point between these two segments at which the elasticity of demand is unity. In the case of a straight-line demand curve, this point is the mid-point of the demand curve. In Figure 49, the elasticity of demand at point G is unity.

The important relationship for the farmer to know is how these elasticities are related to total revenue. In Figure 49, the total revenues for various quantities of a commodity are shown as they correspond to the demand curve. Total revenue increases as quantity increases from 0 to 40, is at a maximum when the quantity is 40, and decreases to 0 at a quantity of 80. Maximum total revenue from production of this commodity would be received if production were controlled at the output where elasticity of demand is unity. Where demand is inelastic, as in the segment of the demand curve GH, total revenue is increased by reducing production. This is due to the fact that in an area where demand elasticity is less than unity, a given percentage decrease in quantity is accompanied by a greater percentage increase in price. This, of course, increases total revenue.

If a farm product has an elasticity of demand less than unity, farmers producing this commodity receive greater total revenue if output is restricted. It costs less to produce less. Therefore, farmers in

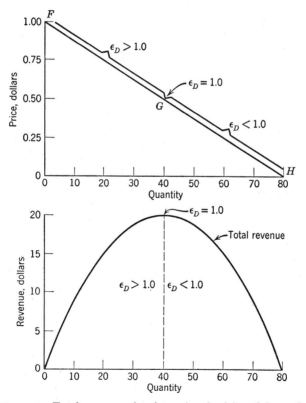

Figure 49. Total revenue related to price elasticity of demand.

the aggregate also would receive greater net revenue by restricting production.

In Table 45 the three general cases of price elasticities of demand

TABLE 45. Effect on Total Revenue of Restricting Production for Alternative Price Elasticities of Demand

Elasticity	Total Revenue	Net Revenue
<1.0	increases	increases
1.0	stays the same	increases
>1.0	decreases	uncertain

are considered. We see that total revenue is increased by reducing production if elasticity is less than unity. Net revenue also is increased because costs are decreased when production is decreased. If the demand curve is of unit elasticity, total revenue is the same regardless of the quantity produced. However, the decrease in production is accompanied by a decrease in cost, and net revenue to farmers is increased. On the other hand, if a commodity has a price elasticity of demand greater than unity, total revenue is decreased by restricting production. Whether net revenue is increased or decreased depends upon whether the decrease in total revenue is greater or less than the decrease in cost which accompanies decreased production.

Examples of Price Elasticity of Demand

When commodity prices change, people change their consumption of some commodities by a larger amount than they do for others. In general, we can say that if a good has no close substitutes, consumption of this good changes very little when price changes. Salt, for example, is essential to diet and has no other close substitute. Thus, the demand for salt is highly inelastic.

In a recent study, elasticities of demand were calculated for various livestock products from observations of price and quantity for the period 1922–1941. The price elasticity shown in Table 46 for all meats is −0.62. If prices of meat rise, other foods can be substituted for meat. However, it is easier to find a substitute for pork, for example, than for meats as a whole. This is borne out by the fact that the price elasticities of demand for pork, beef, and lamb are all greater than the elasticity for all meats taken together. Also, the price elasticity for food as a whole should be less than for individual commodities within the aggregate. This is because there are no substitutes for food as a whole, but one food product may substitute readily for another.

TABLE 46.   Estimated Price Elasticities of Demand for Various Food Products, United States, 1922–1941

Commodity	Price Elasticity
All meat	−0.62
Pork	−0.81
Beef	−0.79
Lamb	−0.91
Eggs	−0.26
Milk for fluid use (farm price)	−0.30
Evaporated milk	−0.84

Source: Karl A. Fox, "Factors Affecting Farm Income, Farm Prices, and Food Consumption," *Agricultural Economics Research*, Vol. III, No. 3, July 1951, p. 76.

The elasticity of demand for milk is less than the elasticity of demand for meat. Since milk is regarded as an essential item in our diets, particularly for families with children, we expect the elasticity to be small. A price increase of 10 per cent for milk results in a decrease of only about 3 per cent in consumption, according to these estimates. Evaporated milk, on the other hand, responds more to price changes. An increase in the price of evaporated milk of 10 per cent brings about a decrease in consumption of slightly more than 8 per cent.

In summary, we expect those commodities to have a rather low elasticity of demand for which there are no close substitutes and which are generally regarded as necessary to our way of life. The grains, for example, belong in this category. On the other hand, the consumption of meats and vegetables is affected more by price changes.

Changes in Demand

In our discussion of price elasticity of demand, we have been considering relationships between prices and quantities on a particular demand curve, such as *DD* in Figure 50. Demand curves shift over time. When a demand curve shifts, the quantity taken at any particular price is changed. For example, if demand increases from *DD* to *D'D'*, greater quantities will be taken at each price than was the case on *DD*. We also note that a greater price will be paid on *D'D'* for each quantity.

Shifts in demand are brought about by changes in the basic conditions underlying consumer purchases. The factors which exert the greatest influence on demand changes are: changes in taste and preferences, changes in population, changes in income, and changes in prices of other products. We will examine in more detail the effects of changes in tastes, income, and population on changes in demand in later sections.

Income Elasticity of Demand

Farmers are concerned not only with the effect of price changes on the quantity consumed but also with the effects of income changes on the consumption of their products. To determine these effects on the most profitable pattern of production, farmers need to know how much consumption of particular commodities will change as the income of the consuming population changes over time.

We measure the responsiveness of consumption relative to income changes by *income elasticity* of demand, which is the percentage change in quantity for a 1 per cent change in income. This can be written as $[(Q_2 - Q_1)/(Q_2 + Q_1)][(I_2 + I_1)/(I_2 - I_1)]$.

Ordinarily, we expect that, as incomes increase, consumption of goods also increases. As we learned in Chapter 17, this is not always the case. If a good is a normal good, income elasticity of demand is positive. That is, an increase in income brings about an increase in consumption. On the other hand, if a good is inferior, an increase

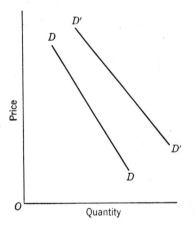

Figure 50. A change in demand.

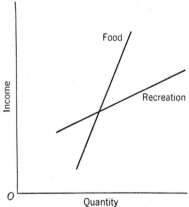

Figure 51. Relationships between income and the consumption of food and recreation services.

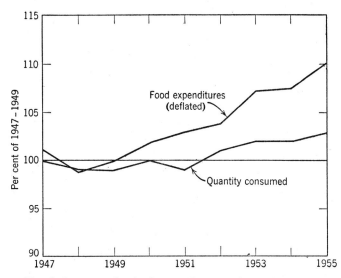

Figure 52. Trends in per capita food expenditures and quantity consumed, 1947–1955.

in income brings about a decrease in consumption, and income elasticity is negative.

Some years ago, Engel put forth the idea that, as incomes increase, the percentage of incomes spent on food decreases. This idea is known as Engel's law. He also suggested that, as incomes increase, a larger percentage of income would be spent on "luxuries," such as amusements and recreation of all types. This concept can be seen graphically in Figure 51. The curve for food shows that, as income rises, quantity consumed increases but by a small amount. That is, the income elasticity of demand is low. Expenditures for recreation increase more in response to increases in income than do expenditures for food, and the income elasticity is greater.

Income elasticity of demand can be used to refer to a *change in expenditure* or to a *change in quantity consumed* as related to changes in income. These two elasticities are not necessarily the same. In Figure 52, the difference between changes in food expenditures and quantity consumed in response to income changes is quite evident. Expenditures have risen since 1947 by a great amount, while the quantity consumed per capita has remained almost constant.[1] Much of this increase in food expenditures comes about as a result of the

[1] *Agriculture Outlook Charts, 1956*, U.S.D.A., Washington, D. C. November 1955, p. 84; *Employment and Earnings*, U. S. Department of Labor, Bureau of Labor Statistics, Jan. 1957, p. IX.

purchase of more services with the food items. For example, more brown-and-serve rolls, frozen, concentrated orange juice, and frozen chicken pot pies are now being purchased. Consumers are buying more services along with the food. This results in an increased expenditure for food items but does not mean that more pounds or calories of food are being consumed.

Fox, in a study of the effect of price and income changes on consumption, determined income elasticity of demand on the basis of both expenditures and quantity purchased. He found the income elasticity of demand for all food expenditures to be about 0.4, as shown in Table 47. That is, as incomes increase by 10 per cent, expenditures

TABLE 47. Effect of Income Change on per Capita Expenditures for Food and Quantities of Food Purchased, Household Budget Survey, United States, 1948*

Commodity	Effect of a 1 Per Cent Change in Income on	
	Expenditure	Quantity Purchased
All food expenditures	0.42	—
At home	0.29	—
Away from home	1.14	—
All livestock products	0.33	0.23
Meat	0.36	0.23
Dairy products	0.32	0.23
Eggs	0.22	0.20
Fruits and vegetables	0.42	0.33
Grain products	0.02	−0.21
Fats and oils	0.13	−0.04
Dry beans, peas, and nuts	−0.07	−0.33
Potatoes and sweet potatoes	0.05	−0.05

Source: Karl A. Fox, "Factors Affecting Farm Income, Farm Prices, and Food Consumption," *Agricultural Economics Research,* Vol. III, No. 3, July 1951, p. 81.

* All elasticities with the exception of the ones for "All food expenditures" are based on 21 meals at home.

on food increase by only about 4 per cent. Separating this expenditure for food into expenditure at home and expenditure in restaurants, the income elasticity at home was about 0.3, while the income elasticity for expenditures away from home was greater than 1.0. Apparently, people eat a larger percentage of their meals in restaurants as their incomes increase.

Income elasticities are greater for livestock products and for fruits and vegetables than for grain products and fats and oils. The income elasticity for livestock products is slightly over 0.3 when elasticity is calculated on the basis of expenditure. When quantity purchased is considered, elasticity of demand is only a little over 0.2. We see that, as incomes rise, more meat and livestock products are consumed, but the increase in expenditure is greater than the increase in quantity purchased.

The income elasticity for fruits and vegetables is higher than for any of the other individual products shown in Table 47. An increase of 10 per cent in income brings about an increase of 4 per cent in expenditures for fruits and vegetables. On the other hand, the income elasticities for grain products, fats and oils, dry beans, and potatoes are all low. In fact, on the basis of quantity purchased, income elasticities for this group of products are less than zero. On the basis of quantity purchased, we would say that grain products, fats and oils, beans, and potatoes are inferior goods. As incomes rise, per capita quantities consumed of these products decrease.

Long-Term Changes in per Capita Consumption

Over a period of years, changes have occurred in consumption patterns of the population in the United States. Primarily, these changes in consumption have resulted from changes in peoples' preferences and from changes in income. Peoples' preferences have been changed

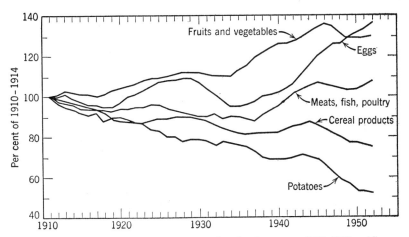

Figure 53. Per capita consumption of major food groups, 1910–1955. (*Source:* U.S.D.A., *Agricultural Outlook Charts, 1955*, Washington, D. C., Oct. 1954, p. 39.)

by education as to the importance of different products in the diet. Also, in the period since 1900, incomes in the United States have risen substantially. In Figure 53, it is evident that per capita consumption has been increasing for fruits and vegetables and eggs relative to the per capita consumption of cereal products and potatoes. Also, the per capita consumption of meat has increased greatly in the last 10 years. This bears out our previous observations that there is a higher elasticity of demand for meat and vegetables than for cereals and potatoes. In fact, per capita consumption of the two latter foods has fallen since 1910.

The differences in income elasticities of demand have implications as to the direction to be followed by agricultural production in the future. We all believe that incomes in the United States will continue to increase. The shift to meat and vegetables and away from cereals, potatoes, and fats indicates that, in the long run, it will pay farmers to increase their production of meats and vegetables relative to the products containing more calories.

We also know that an increase in income for the United States would tend to increase the consumption of nonfarm commodities relative to the consumption of farm products. As was pointed out above, people tend to buy more services and to spend a greater proportion of their income on recreation and entertainment as their incomes increase. This indicates that the industrial sector of our economy is faced with a more rapidly expanding demand than agriculture. Productive inputs will likely continue to be shifted to nonagricultural industries as national income rises.

19 | International trade increases the demand for U. S. farm products

The Nature of Trade

Trade consists of the exchange of goods and services by two or more parties. Trade may be conducted on two bases. One of these methods is to trade on a barter basis. In this case, no money is exchanged, but goods and services owned by one party are exchanged for goods and services owned by another party. A more common means of trading is to exchange goods and services for money. Actually, money is a commodity which is accepted universally within a country in exchange for goods and services. Nations have different currencies, however, and the money of one nation is not normally accepted by another nation in exchange for goods and services.

We learned in Chapter 11 that it usually pays each geographical area to concentrate on the production of certain commodities and to exchange them for commodities produced in other areas. We learned that concentration of production of certain commodities in agricultural areas has resulted in what is known as type-of-farming areas. Areas tend to specialize in the production of particular commodities and to trade with other areas.

Nations may also gain from specialization of production and trade. International trade is concerned with transactions among nations. Although governments may trade commodities on a barter basis, trade among individuals within a nation is not usually conducted in this manner. Rather, individuals sell goods and services to some people and purchase goods and services from others. The amount of goods and services an individual can purchase over time, therefore, depends upon the amount of goods and services he sells. The basic nature of trade among nations is the same as trade between two individuals or two geographic areas within a country. The amount of goods a nation is able to purchase from other nations depends upon the amount of goods it can sell to other nations. The major difference is that two countries do not use the same money. The United States needs pounds, for example, to purchase commodities produced in England. England, on the other hand, needs dollars to purchase commodities produced in the United States.

Trade Balance

Goods sold from one country to other countries are called *exports*. Goods purchased from other countries are called *imports*. When the amount purchased by a nation from other nations equals the amount sold to those nations, the trade between nations is said to be in balance. Therefore, when exports equal imports, we say that there is a *trade balance* between the nations.

Basically, trade between nations consists of the transfer of goods and services produced, the granting of capital loans, the payment of interest on loans and dividends on investments in foreign countries, and expenditures by tourists in foreign countries. Gold is internationally accepted as money. It also is sometimes exchanged directly for goods and services traded among nations. Where the monetary standard of a nation is based on the amount of gold it has, however, it is reluctant to purchase commodities involving the transfer of gold to other nations.

It is not necessary that the exports from any one country exactly balance the imports from another country for trade to continue to take place between the two countries. What is important is that the total amount of exports and imports of a particular country over time must tend to balance. It is the total exports that constitute receipts to a nation and determine its purchasing power. Imports constitute expenditures. Although the exports and imports between two countries need not balance for trade between these countries to continue at a high level, it is necessary for the trade of a group of nations to balance. Suppose, for example, that a country wishes to purchase goods produced in the United States and does not have the dollars to purchase those commodities. It may be able to obtain dollars by selling goods to another country which has sold goods to the United States for dollars. For example, suppose that England wanted to purchase commodities produced in the United States, but that England was short of dollars. She might obtain these dollars by selling British goods and services to African countries which have sold more commodities to the United States than they have imported from the United States, thereby enabling them to have a surplus of dollars.

Since World War II, the quantities of products the United States has exported to foreign countries have greatly exceeded the imports of the United States. This has meant that foreign countries have had difficulty in obtaining the dollars needed to buy United States products. Countries desiring to purchase goods from another country but lacking a balance of currency for that country may be able to obtain credit for additional purchases. Various credit arrangements have been worked out which enable other countries to obtain imports from the United States. The continuation of trade, however, must ultimately involve the creation of the ability of other countries to obtain dollars with which to purchase United States goods. If we desire that other countries consume large quantities of United States products, there are only two ways of obtaining this objective: (1) We must permit these countries to pay for United States products; or (2) we must give these products to them. There are no other ways of trading goods and services. The continuation of a large volume of international trade for United States products, therefore, ultimately must depend upon the level of imports of the United States. If other countries cannot earn dollar credits to enable them to purchase United States goods, trade cannot be maintained at a high level without outright grants of money or goods to foreign nations.

The Gains from Trade

It is necessary that we understand the basic reasons for trade in order to appreciate the gains that may be derived from international trade. Trade does not take place unless it is expected that all parties will gain from the trade. Although it is theoretically possible that trade can occur and leave each party only as well off as before the trade, there is little incentive for trade under such conditions. The incentive for trade lies in the fact that the parties engaged in the trading expect to gain from the transactions.

Gains from trade arise out of the fact that the relationship between the cost of producing products differs among countries. This statement will bear some reflection. It does not imply that one country is able to produce goods and services for a lower absolute cost than another country. In order for two countries to gain from trade, the basis of trade rests on the fact that one country can produce commodities for relatively different costs than they can be produced in the other country.

Let us consider the production of two commodities in two countries and inquire into the conditions under which these countries can profitably engage in trade. Let the two commodities be Y_1 and Y_2. The cost of producing these commodities is shown in Table 48. The

TABLE 48.   Costs of Producing Two Products in Two Nations

Cost of Production

Unit of Product	United States	Other Country
Y_1	C	C
Y_2	C	$2C$

production of a unit of Y_1 in the United States requires C resources. Production of a unit of Y_2 also requires C resources. Now, looking at the quantities of resources required to produce Y_1 and Y_2 in the other country, we find that it takes C resources to produce a unit of Y_1, but that it requires $2C$ resources to produce a unit of Y_2. We see that a unit of Y_1 and Y_2 can be produced with the same amount of resources in the United States. Note, however, that it costs twice as much to produce a unit of Y_2 in the other country as it does to produce a unit of Y_1. There would be a gain in the amount of products that could be produced by these two countries in the aggregate if the United States would concentrate on the production of Y_2 and exchange it for Y_1 produced in the other country. By transferring resources from Y_2 to Y_1, the other country is able to increase the production of Y_1 by two units for each unit decrease in the production of Y_2. The United States, on the other hand, is able to transfer resources from Y_1 to Y_2 on a one-for-one basis. We must conclude that the United States and the other country will gain by trade unless the cost of sending a unit of Y_2 from the United States to the other country, plus the cost of sending a unit of Y_1 from the other country to the United States, is greater than C.

The extent to which countries can gain from trade depends on the relative cost of production of commodities in those countries and on the cost of transporting and selling goods. A change in the cost of production in one country relative to the cost of production in another

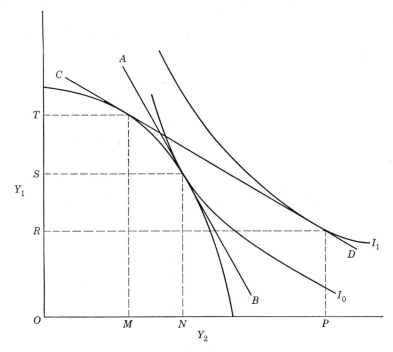

Figure 54. Gains from trade.

country changes the gains from trade. Likewise, alteration of the transportation cost and selling cost among countries changes the gains from trade.

The graphic analysis we have used earlier in this book can be employed to demonstrate the gains from trade. Suppose that the quantities of products Y_1 and Y_2 that can be produced by the United States are as shown by the production possibilities function in Figure 54. The highest level of utility, or national satisfaction, that can be achieved from the production of Y_1 and Y_2 is indicated by the indifference curve I_0, where the production possibilities function is tangent to the highest possible indifference curve. We are considering here a case where we consume what we produce. If there is no trade allowed between countries for these two products, the domestic price ratio would be as shown by the line AB. If the United States produced all the Y_1 and Y_2 that it consumed, the maximum level of utility available to the public would be achieved when OS of Y_1 and ON of Y_2 have been produced.

This, however, may not be the combination of Y_1 and Y_2 that would maximize national welfare if trade is allowed. Ordinarily we expect trade to alter the price ratios among products. In fact, there is no justification for international trade unless prices of some goods are reduced. Suppose trade causes the price of Y_2 to be reduced relative to the price of Y_1. The new price line is represented by CD. The level of utility or satisfaction in the United States can now be increased by expanding the production of Y_1 from OS to OT and reducing the production of Y_2 from ON to OM. The United States could then exchange TR of Y_1 for MP of Y_2. This would enable a higher level of satisfaction to be reached through trade than would be true if the nation relied entirely on its own productive capacities to produce the products it consumed.

The subject of trade is often discussed, but the basis of discussion differs greatly among people. Some people take an isolationist viewpoint and argue that a particular country or geographic region should strive to produce all of the goods and services it consumes. In other words, it is argued that the particular geographic region should strive to be self-sufficient. Others argue that all barriers to trade among regions and countries should be removed, and that we should have free trade.

Historically, we find that very few countries have followed the principles of free trade to the extent of removing all governmentally constructed barriers to trade. This has been especially true of countries having relatively high levels of living. It is argued in these countries that removal of trade barriers will reduce the returns for inputs, especially labor, and, consequently, will reduce the level of living. These countries sometimes control trade by imposing a form of taxes, called tariffs, on goods imported from other countries. Also, countries often place quotas on the amount of goods that may be imported. Both tariffs and quotas tend to increase domestic prices for imported goods and, therefore, encourage domestic production.

As an aftermath of World War II, many countries placed a great deal of emphasis on self-sufficiency in the production of agricultural commodities. During and shortly after World War II, critical shortages of food products developed in some countries because of the breaking down of international markets. In an effort to become more nearly self-sufficient with respect to the production of food, many of these countries restricted the imports of agricultural commodities and subsidized domestic production. The United States government, for example, has taken steps in this direction in the case of wool and sugar. Also, synthetic production of rubber has been subsidized in the United States as a precautionary measure against a reduction in imports in time of national crisis. Another striking example is drawn from the experiences of Great Britain. During World War II, Britain found herself faced with critical food shortages. As a result, Britain has subsidized the production of agricultural products since the war to avoid a recurrence of possible food shortages in times of emergency.

Another argument often used in justification of trade restrictions, particularly in underdeveloped nations, concerns the establishment of a new industry in a nation. As we learned in Chapter 7, the average cost of production of a commodity tends to decline over some range of output. Therefore, firms in a young industry may have higher costs than would be true after the industry is well developed. It is often argued that these "infant" industries must be protected from foreign competition until they have developed to a point which would permit them to realize their natural competitive advantage in world markets. One of the obvious major weaknesses of this argument is the fact that, once protection for an industry becomes established, it is seldom taken away.

In studying the effects of trade restrictions, we must recognize that, when a nation restricts the imports of goods it receives from other countries, it reduces the ability of other countries to purchase its goods. Hence, it must expect other countries to reduce their imports. When the United States increases its tariffs on goods which it imports, it reduces the dollar earnings of the exporting countries and reduces their ability to purchase United States goods. When this happens, countries are forced to trade with nations other than the United States.

United States Exports and Imports of Major Commodities

Farmers in the United States have always taken a keen interest in international trade and in trade barriers. Many of the first settlers of the United States were engaged primarily in the production of agricultural commodities for shipment back to the countries from which they came. Exports of cotton and tobacco grew rapidly in the early history of the country. For a long period of time, the United States was primarily a producer of raw materials to be used for manufacturing in the more highly developed countries of western Europe. Under these conditions, farmers were keenly aware of the importance of international trade as a market for their products.

The position of regions of the United States with respect to the advocation of trade restrictions varied with the importance of the export of agricultural commodities as a source of income. The South, for example, was primarily a producer of agricultural commodities and exported these commodities to western European countries. This

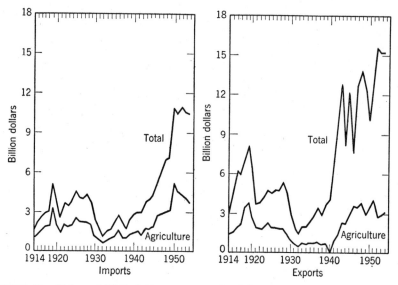

FIGURE 55. Value of United States exports and imports, 1914–1954. (*Source:* U.S.D.A., "Foreign Agricultural Trade Statistical Handbook," *Statistical Bulletin No. 179,* Aug. 1956, pp. 1, 20.)

fact was responsible for the advocacy of free trade which existed in the South through much of the 19th and early 20th centuries.

Exports of agricultural commodities became relatively less important as the manufacturing industries in the United States developed. We see in Figure 55 that the relative decline in agricultural exports was steady from World War I to World War II, but that exports increased greatly during World War II. The big increase during the war was primarily due to foreign aid programs. Since this time, agricultural exports as a percentage of total exports have fallen to about 20 per cent.

Total and agricultural imports have increased greatly since the turn of the century. In contrast with the behavior of exports, the relative importance of agricultural imports compared to nonagricultural imports has remained nearly constant during this time.

During the 1950's, United States exports have generally amounted to about $15 billion annually, and imports have amounted to slightly more than $10 billion. Food exports, including crude foodstuffs and manufactured foodstuffs, amounted to approximately $1.5 billion. Almost half of the value of total exports of United States commodities is to other American countries, especially Canada and the American republics. Most of the exports of agricultural commodities, however, go to western Europe and the Far East.

The major agricultural commodities exported by the United States consist of wheat, cotton, and tobacco. The percentage of total production of some of these commodities which are exported has changed considerably over time. For example, flue-cured tobacco exports have fallen from 60 per cent of production in the 1920's to 35 per cent in the 1950's. Cotton exports also were about 60 per cent of total production in the 1920's. This percentage had fallen to about 25 per cent in the 1950's. Wheat and rice exports as a per cent of total production, on the other hand, dropped until World War II. After this, the percentage of the crop exported rose again to levels equal to or higher than those of the 1920's.

Imports of foodstuffs amounted to approximately $3.3 billion in 1954. The major imports of agricultural commodities consist of cocoa, coffee, and tea. Sugar and wool are also imported in large quantities, along with selected meat products and fish. Most of the imports of agricultural commodities come from the American republics and from the Far East.

Outlook for Exports and Imports

The outlook for exports of agricultural commodities from the United States is not clear. Currently, exports of several agricultural commodities are subsidized by one or more types of government programs. Since World War II, many countries have had difficulty obtaining sufficient dollars to buy agricultural commodities in large volume from the United States. The position of the United States in the international market has been altered rather drastically by our rapid rate of development in industrial production. We now occupy a major role as a producer of machinery and equipment. Agricultural products, on the other hand, often can be obtained at less cost from countries other than the United States. Many countries, therefore, have restricted use of dollars to the purchase of nonagricultural commodities from the United States and have increased their purchases of agricultural products from other countries. To offset this difficulty, the United States has taken steps to subsidize the exports of agricultural products and, in some instances, has accepted payment for agricultural products in the currency of the importing country.

In the future, the level of exports of agricultural commodities from the United States will be determined by the progress made in the efficiency of producing agricultural commodities in other countries relative to the United States. The level of exports will also depend on the ability of other countries to obtain dollars with which to purchase United States commodities. This means that the amount of products we can expect to export in the future will depend on the amount of products we are willing to import.

20 | Our economy is subject to large price movements

In this chapter some of the reasons for price changes are examined. We also look at what has happened to prices of some commodities in the past. We begin by examining price movements over a period of years and move from this to an examination of seasonal price movements and price differentials which exist at any point in time.

Long-Term Price Movements

One thing which we note by looking at Figure 56 is that rather pronounced price cycles are in evidence, and both farm and nonfarm prices go up and down together. We do note, however, that agricultural prices have fluctuated to a greater degree than have nonagricultural prices. We also noted this relatively greater price variability for agricultural products in Chapter 16. It was pointed out that production of agricultural products tends to be relatively stable, whereas the industrial sector of our economy reduces its production more readily in periods of falling demand. As a result, farm prices tend to rise and fall faster than nonfarm prices.

Since the Korean War, agricultural prices have fallen relative to prices of nonagricultural commodities. Whether or not the recent relative price decline of agricultural commodities will continue is not

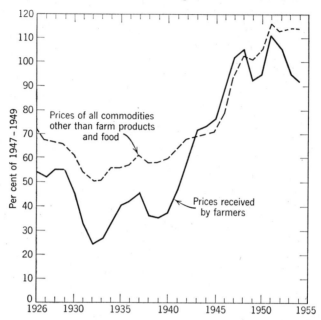

Figure 56. Wholesale prices for farm and nonfarm commodities, 1926–1954 (1947–1949 = 100). (*Source:* U.S.D.A., *Agricultural Outlook Charts, 1955*, Washington, D. C., Oct. 1954, p. 11.)

certain. This depends upon the shifts in supply and demand for agricultural and nonagricultural commodities. Technological change is now taking place at a rapid rate in agriculture, shifting the supply curve to the right. On the other hand, the income elasticity of demand for agricultural products is generally lower than for industrial products. With incomes of American consumers increasing at a rapid rate, shifts in demand brought about by rising incomes are greater for industrial products than for food and other agricultural commodities. Whether prices of agricultural products will rise or fall relative to nonagricultural prices depends upon the relative movements of supply and demand for both types of goods. If the rate of movement of supply relative to demand in agriculture is greater than the rate of movement of supply relative to demand in industry, agricultural prices will continue to fall in relation to nonagricultural prices.

Cycles

In Chapter 15 we investigated some of the causes of cycles in production and in prices. The cobweb theorem was used to demonstrate how these cycles come about. Cyclical behavior is largely a result of incorrect expectations by consumers and producers. A producer may expect a high price for his product and will plan to increase his production. Other producers may have similar expectations and plan accordingly. For this reason, production may be larger than anticipated when the time arrives to sell the product, and, as a result, the actual price may be much lower than expected. The lower price, in turn, causes a reduction in future production. As a consequence, the price of this product rises.

Cyclical price patterns are fairly well established for some commodities. The fact that somewhat definite price cycles exist provides an opportunity for some producers to take advantage of the cycles and increase the net revenue they receive. That is, they can attempt to plan so that their production is high when aggregate production is low and prices are high, and vice versa.

As more producers become acquainted with the cyclical nature of some agricultural production and learn how to take advantage of such cycles, we can expect that cycles in production and prices will become less distinct. The fact that producers do learn how to profit from cyclical behavior tends to reduce the variability of agricultural prices and production over time.

Seasonal Price Variation

Prices of many agricultural commodities follow a definite pattern within a one-year period. Commodities which exhibit this seasonal price pattern are those for which the production varies substantially over the year. Prices of corn, for example, are lowest in the period just following the harvest. Immediately after harvest, a large amount of corn comes to market, and the markets are often temporarily glutted. Farmers who store their corn until later in the year or until the following summer can ordinarily obtain a higher price for the corn at that time. Of course, there are costs associated with storing grain after the harvest period. This was pointed out in one of the examples in Chapter 8. If the person storing the grain is to increase his net revenue, these costs of storage per bushel must be smaller than the rise in price expected between harvest and the time at which the grain is sold.

Another factor in storing grain is that the producer assumes a certain amount of risk in that price could go lower rather than rise, as would normally be expected. If the price does not increase as much as the storage costs, the producer will lose money by storing. Therefore, a producer may not store grain in any one year because of the added risk, even if he anticipates an increase in his net revenue if he stores grain each year for several years.

As another example, the number of hogs marketed is greater in some months than in others. We know that prices tend to vary inversely with marketings. Hogs provide an example of a commodity which exhibits a moderately predictable seasonal pattern. In Figure 57, we notice that the number of hogs going to market increases very rapidly from September through January. As a result of this large supply of pork coming to the market, prices usually fall off to their lowest point in December. Farmers getting their hogs to market before the rapid decline in prices stand to get a higher revenue than if they put their hogs on the market at the time when marketings are greatest. However, we should recognize that there is a reason for this seasonal pattern of production. Weather conditions are such that more shelter is required to farrow pigs in early spring or in the winter. Furthermore, corn prices are generally lower in the fall than at any other time. We expect, therefore, that it costs more to raise pigs farrowed at this early date. If it costs more to raise early pigs, farmers who do this must receive a higher price for their product in order to make a profit. Some farmers have been able to produce early hogs and increase net revenue by so doing. The added cost of producing early hogs has been less for these farmers than the additional revenue they obtained by selling early and receiving a relatively more favorable price.

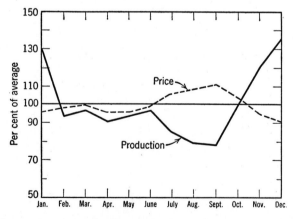

Figure 57. Seasonal variation in hog production and prices, percentage of or 12-month moving average. (*Source:* Fred V. Waugh, "Graphic Analysis in Economic Research," U.S.D.A., *Agricultural Handbook No. 84,* Washington, D. C., June 1955, p. 23.)

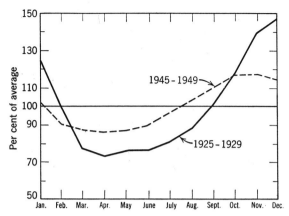

Figure 58. Seasonal variation in egg prices. (*Source:* Fred V. Waugh, "Graphic Analysis in Economic Research," U.S.D.A., *Agricultural Handbook No. 84,* Washington, D. C., June 1955, p. 23.)

As farmers become aware of seasonal price patterns, and as new techniques are introduced which allow farmers to produce commodities at a time when they can take advantage of higher prices, seasonal variations in production and price will be reduced. The magnitude of the seasonal variation will be reduced until price differences reflect only differences in cost of production at the various time periods. We can see from Figure 58 that much progress has been made in reducing seasonal variation in production and prices of eggs. The solid line shows the seasonal price pattern for eggs for the period 1925–1929. The broken line, on the other hand, shows the seasonal price pattern for eggs for the later period 1945–1949. We notice that the variation in the later period is considerably less than the price variation of the 1925–1929 period. Egg producers apparently have seen and taken advantage of the additional income to be gained by getting their pullets in the brooder house earlier, getting them in production faster, and receiving the benefit from the higher price for eggs to be obtained in the fall and early winter.

Other Factors Affecting Price Variation

There are several other reasons why prices for various commodities vary, even at one point in time. Factors which appear to be of major importance are differences in grade, location, and services associated with the products.

Grades. There are quality differences in nearly all agricultural commodities. Usually, these differences can be identified, and they provide a basis for separating the commodity into grades. We are all familiar with the fact that cattle are sold as prime, choice, good, standard, commercial, utility, canner, or cutter. In the same way, wheat may sell as no. 1, no. 2, or no. 3 dark Northern Spring. Each of these grades ordinarily brings a different price and may require different production costs. The fact that prices and production costs differ for different grades means that additional decisions are required. Producers are faced with the decision of which grade to produce, and consumers must decide which grade to buy. For example, a cattle feeder must decide whether the additional feed necessary to change the grade of his cattle from good to choice will bring back a return greater than the additional feeding cost.

We should point out that, if grades are justified in an economic sense, they should represent differences apparent to the consumer and for which she is willing to pay different prices. In some cases, grading of commodities is extremely complex. An outstanding example of grade complexity is found in flue-cured tobacco, where there are approximately 150 different grades, each carrying a separate Government support price. If the Government support prices for a grade at any point in time do not represent accurately consumers' or manufacturers' relative preferences for these grades; whether it is tobacco, wheat, or cotton, certain grades tend to pile up as surpluses.

Location. The distance separating a commodity from its final point of consumption affects the price received by the producer for that commodity. Costs of transporting and selling goods are incurred between the processes of production and consumption. The nearer a good is to its point of ultimate consumption, the greater will be its price. As an example, cattle fattened on farms near Chicago bring a somewhat higher price than cattle of the same quality produced in western Iowa. This price differential due to location approximates the differences in cost of transporting the good to the consuming points.

A striking example of price differentials due to location is shown in Figure 59. New York City is the major milk-consuming center in the north-eastern section of the United States. The lines in Figure 59 represent locations at which the farm prices for milk are equal. The numbers associated with each line represent the amount by which the farm price is less than the New York City price. As the distance from the city increases, the price paid for milk decreases because of additional transportation costs. The farm price does not always decrease in proportion to the distance from New York City. Other relatively large consuming centers exist in the Northeast. In order to obtain milk, these smaller consuming centers will bid the price up above the New York City price, less transportation costs. We see that, as we move westward from New York City toward Pittsburgh, the price of milk decreases steadily, except for the areas surrounding the smaller cities. As we near Pittsburgh, the price differential decreases from 90 cents to only 36 cents at Pittsburgh.

We recall from Chapter 11 that production possibilities relationships and relative prices determine what products will be produced in given areas. The milk price example should help us further in understanding why certain type-of-farming areas tend to exist. Certainly, it is evident that, other things being equal, milk production becomes relatively less profitable as distance from the major points of consumption

Figure 59. Theoretical equal milk price lines, farm price differentials from New York City. (*Source:* William Bredo and Anthony S. Rojko, "Prices and Milk-sheds of Northeastern Markets," *Northeast Regional Publication No. 9;* University of Massachusetts Agricultural Experiment Station, *Bulletin No. 470,* Aug. 1952, p. 53.)

increases. Therefore, we find that milk for fluid consumption is generally produced near cities. On the other hand, production of less perishable products, for which the price differential due to transportation is not as great, tends to take place in areas farther from population centers.

Services. The trend in recent years has been for consumers to buy more and more services along with the commodities they purchase. Obviously, production of these additional services costs money. Grocery stores are full of such items as cake mixes, TV dinners, and brown-and-serve rolls. With more and more services being sold with farm commodities, the percentage of the money spent by consumers going to the farmer decreases. That is, the "farmer's share of the consumer's dollar" decreases as consumer incomes rise and more services are purchased with agricultural commodities. That the "farmer's share of the consumer's dollar" has been decreasing is shown in Figure 60.

Not all additional services purchased with food need to increase costs. For example, one study has shown that the cost of prepackaged or self-service meat is, for certain volumes, no more than the cost associated with the former method of cutting meat at the request of

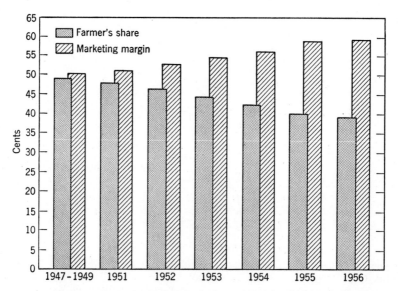

Figure 60. Farm and marketing shares of consumer's food dollar. (*Source:* U.S.D.A., *Agricultural Outlook Charts, 1957,* Washington, D. C., Nov. 1956. p. 5.)

the consumer.[1] The case in which additional services associated with agricultural commodities do not increase cost is not the normal case, however. The housewife obtains more leisure time by purchasing foods which have more of the preparation done, but she must also expect to pay for the added services.

We saw in Chapter 18 that the income elasticity of demand for food services is substantially greater than that for food itself. As incomes will rise in the future, the farmer will get smaller and smaller proportions of the amount of money spent by consumers for the products he grows. This, of course, does not indicate that the farmer is in any way being deprived of income he should receive. It merely suggests that looking only at the farmer's share of the consumer's dollar as a criterion of fairness is insufficient. From an economic standpoint, we can say that the farmer is not getting a fair share of the consumer's dollar only where certain of the services which are being provided are not really desired by the consumer. That is, with the food she buys, the consumer may be forced to purchase additional services which she does not feel are worth the additional cost. This, of course, can happen only if a company or companies control most of the supply of some commodity, and the goods are difficult to obtain without the additional services. Under such conditions, extraordinarily high markups may be found, and both the consumer and the farmer may be taken advantage of.

Parity Prices

The concept of parity prices was developed in order to compare the purchasing power of farm and nonfarm goods. The Agricultural Adjustment Act of 1933 states that parity prices were set up to "reestablish prices to farmers at a level that will give agricultural commodities a purchasing power, with respect to articles that farmers buy, equivalent to the purchasing power of agricultural commodities in the base period." The period of 1910–1914 was chosen as the base period because of the stability of prices during this period and because of the relatively favorable relationship of agricultural to nonagricultural prices. The basic idea behind parity prices is that a farmer with a bushel of corn in 1958 should be able to purchase the same

[1] Fred H. Wiegmann, "Comparison of Costs of Service and Self-Service Methods of Selling Meat in Retail Food Stores," Unpublished Ph.D. thesis, Iowa State College Library, Ames, Iowa, June 1953.

amount of commodities with the proceeds from the sale of this corn as would have been possible in the 1910–1914 base period.

It is essential that we know something about the construction of index numbers if we are to understand how parity prices are derived. An *index of prices received* tells us how much prices have changed relative to prices in some base period. Suppose that we wish to compute an index number of prices received by farmers in an area where the four commodities produced are corn, wheat, hogs, and cotton. An example of the construction of one type of prices received index is given in Table 49. A simple (unweighted) index is obtained by adding

TABLE 49.   Example of Index Number Computation

Commodity	Weighting Factors (W_0)	Base Period Price (P_0), dollars	P_0W_0, dollars	Present Price (P_1), dollars	P_1W_0, dollars
Corn	40	1.00	40.00	1.60	64.00
Wheat	20	2.00	40.00	2.30	46.00
Hogs	10	14.00	140.00	18.00	180.00
Cotton	8	30.00	240.00	34.00	272.00
Total	—	47.00	460.00	55.90	562.00

Unweighted Index = 55.90/47.00   Weighted Index = 562.00/460.00
                 = 118.9   = 122.2

the prices received for the four products in the base period and in the period for which we wish the index number. If we divide the sum of the prices in the period for which we are computing the index by the sum of prices in the base period, we have an index of 55.90/47.00 = 118.9. This tells us that prices are 118.9 per cent of prices in the base period.

In the above index all commodities have equal weights. However, all commodities are not of equal importance in determining costs and incomes. For example, a producer who annually sells about 100 bushels of wheat and 5000 bushels of corn is certainly more affected by a given price change for corn than for the same price change for wheat. For this reason, we often wish to *weight* the various commodities making up our index according to their relative importance. Choice of the weights to be used is a difficult problem, however. The relative importance of commodities changes over time, and the choice of using base period weights or other weights affects the index number. In our example in Table 49, base period weights are used in calculating the weighted index. These weights represent the relative quantities of the four commodities sold in the base period. For example, half as much wheat as corn was sold in the base period since the weight for wheat is 20, and the weight for corn is 40. If we multiply these base period weights times the prices in the two periods, we obtain weighted price figures for the two periods. If we divide the sum of the weighted prices in the one period by the sum of the weighted prices in the base period, we obtain a weighted price index. In our example, this is $562.00/460.00 = 122.2$, a slightly higher index than we obtained by using the unweighted prices. It is higher because the price of the relatively important item, corn, increased more than the prices of the other commodities.

The United States Department of Agriculture calculates up-to-date price and cost series from which parity prices are computed. To calculate parity prices, an index of prices paid is first computed. This index includes items in farmers' cost of living as well as items used in producing farm products, including wages, interest, and taxes. If costs, after being weighted according to their relative importance, are twice as much as they were in the base period, for example, the index of prices paid would be 200. In the same manner, *the index of prices received* by farmers is a composite of all agricultural prices in a given time period relative to their price in the base period. The *parity ratio*, which we hear so much about, is the index of prices received divided by the index of prices paid. For example, on January 15, 1957, the index of prices received by farmers was 238, and the index of prices paid by farmers was 292. The parity ratio at this time

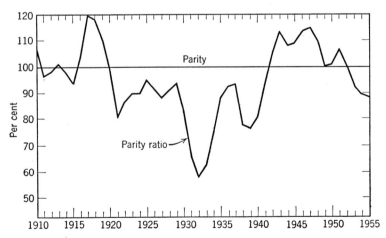

Figure 61. Parity ratio, 1910–1955. (*Source:* U.S.D.A., *Agricultural Outlook Charts, 1957,* Washington, D. C., Nov. 1956.)

was 238/292 or 82. Farmers in general were receiving 82 per cent of parity for the composite of all products which they sold.

In Figure 61, we see that the parity ratio has changed considerably over time. The period after World War II and to the end of the Korean War found the prices of agricultural products relatively high compared to nonfarm prices. Since the Korean War, however, agricultural prices have fallen, and the parity ratio has fallen to the low 80's.

It should be emphasized that the parity price concept is not equivalent to the idea of parity incomes. Parity prices refer to the ability of a given unit of some product to purchase equivalent quantities of goods at different times. Income, however, depends on quantity produced as well as on price. Where farmers have been able to increase farm production at the same or lower cost per unit than was true in the base period, their incomes may have improved even though the price per unit is less than parity.

Many of our agricultural commodities are supported at some percentage of the parity price. For example, the average price of American upland cotton in the base period was $12.52 per cwt, as shown in Table 50. The index of prices paid by farmers was 292 on January 15,

TABLE 50. Base Period and January 15, 1957, Parity Prices
for Certain Agricultural Commodities

Commodity (and Unit)	Base Period Prices*	Effective Parity Price, January 15, 1957
Wheat, bushel	0.884	2.49†
Cotton, American upland, cwt	12.52	36.56
Rice, cwt	1.95	5.69
Corn, bushel	0.642	1.80†
Peanuts, cwt	4.80	13.50†
Tobacco, types 11–14, cwt	19.10	55.80
Beef Cattle, cwt	7.58	22.10
Hogs, cwt	7.40	21.60

Source: U.S.D.A., *Agricultural Prices*, Jan. 30, 1957, p. 5.

* Adjusted for a 10-year moving average of prices received from Jan. 1947–Dec. 1956.

† Transitional parity, 95 per cent of parity calculated prior to Jan. 1, 1950.

1957. Therefore, the parity price for cotton was 12.52 × 292 or $36.56 per cwt. Since cotton was supported at 77 per cent of parity, the actual price at which cotton was supported was $28.15 per cwt.

The effective parity prices for some commodities such as corn, wheat, and peanuts cannot be calculated so easily. The formula for calculating parity prices has been altered because costs of producing some farm products have changed relative to costs of producing other products. On the other hand, the index of prices paid, which is used in computing parity prices, is a composite for all commodities. For this reason, multiplying base prices by the index of prices paid tends to overestimate the value of some commodities relative to others. An attempt was made to remedy this difficulty by adjusting costs of production of farm commodities to a newer base period, 1935–1939. It also provided that base prices of individual commodities would be above or below the 1910–1914 average according to the relative prices prevailing in the 10-year period prior to the date for which parity is being calculated. Use of the adjusted parity formula resulted in parity prices for many agricultural commodities which were lower than when the old parity formula was used. In order that there would not be a sharp reduction in the parity price for any one commodity, effective parity prices were lowered by not more than 5 per cent per year in going from the old to the new parity price. For this reason, some commodities had transitional parity prices such as shown in Table 50.

Part **IV**

ECONOMIC PROGRESS

Technological improvements
increase food
and fiber supplies

Man is continuously looking for new and improved ways of producing goods and services. Changes in production methods that enable him to obtain larger quantities of product with the same or fewer inputs are called technological improvements.

Changes in the combination of inputs used in production may be caused by changes in input prices and by technological improvements. As was pointed out in Chapter 9, it is often possible to reduce the cost of production by changing the combination of inputs when the prices of inputs vary. A technological improvement, on the other hand, results from the fact that new and previously unknown methods of production are discovered. These new methods reduce per-unit costs in the ranges of output in which producers plan to operate.

The Rate of Technological Change Greatly Affects the Rate of Economic Progress

Economic progress is frequently referred to as an increase in the per capita quantity of goods and services available for consumption. Economic progress is accomplished by increasing the quantity of resources or the quantity of goods and services produced with a given amount of resources. Technological improvements represent one of the major ways of obtaining economic progress, since the discovery of new and improved methods of production allows more goods and services per capita to be produced.

It is particularly important that technological improvements be made in the production of food and fiber in order to obtain economic progress. In most low-income countries, a high proportion of the labor is devoted to the production of food and fiber. To free people for the production of other goods, such as television sets, automobiles, airplanes, houses, and schools, it is necessary to increase the productivity of labor in agriculture so that a smaller proportion of the population is needed to produce the food and fiber necessary for subsistence.

Technological improvements cannot be accomplished unless people are willing to change production methods. We know that all farmers do not employ the most modern technology at any point in time. This often results from the fact that farmers frequently associate an increase in risk with a change in technology. They have learned from past experience that it is possible to subsist with the methods of production they have used for many years. Furthermore, many farmers have very little wealth and low incomes. They are not willing to risk the loss of their wealth to try out new methods which have not proved superior to the ones previously used. For example, when a tractor is substituted for workstock on a farm, it is no longer necessary to produce feed and fiber for the workstock. Inputs formerly devoted to this purpose can be used for more productive employment. However, risk is increased because gasoline, oil, and repairs must be purchased where grain and hay for feeding the horses were formerly produced on the farm. Adoption of new methods of production frequently involves a complete change in farming systems or a complete change in plant layout in the processing industries. The risk associated with these changes often discourages producers from adopting new practices.

Technological Improvements Reduce Per-Unit Costs

A producer will not adopt a change in technology unless he expects that the adoption will lead to a reduction in per-unit costs at the output at which he expects to operate. Since most innovations involve additional expenditures, total costs are likely to be increased at lower levels of output as a result of technological changes. For example, purchase of a forage harvester increases total cost of harvesting forage if small volumes of forage are harvested. Likewise, the installation of vacuum-cooling equipment to cool lettuce greatly increases the investment capital in a small firm processing lettuce. In the lower

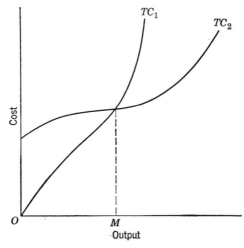

Figure 62. Effects of a change in technology on costs of production.

ranges of output, per-unit cost likely would be increased by additional investment. On the other hand, as the level of output increases, the additional investment required to use the new production practice is spread over a larger volume of output, and per-unit cost is reduced. Whether cost per unit of output is reduced depends upon the number of units that can be processed in a given time period.

A typical cost situation facing producers considering a change in production methods is presented in Figure 62. Suppose that a new item of equipment such as a mechanical tobacco harvester is developed. TC_1 represents the total cost with respect to output under the initial methods of production. Since the harvester has a cost, the total amount of investment on the farm would be increased with a zero level of output. Let TC_2 represent the total cost curve of the new method. The total cost with the harvester exceeds the total cost without the harvester until a level of production of OM is obtained. Beyond this point, the total cost with the harvester is less than the total cost without the harvester. Hence, whether an individual wants to adopt an innovation or new method of production depends on the level of output which he expects from his firm.

Technological Improvement in United States Agriculture

Technological improvements have been rapid in the production of farm commodities in the United States, and farm output has increased rapidly during the 20th century. Output of farm commodities in-

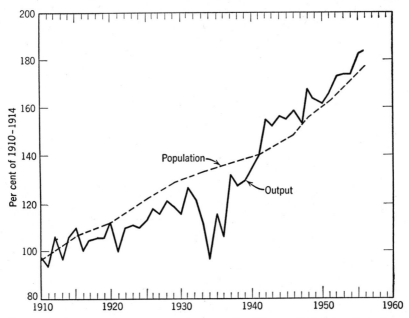

Figure 63. Farm output and population growth. (*Source:* U.S.D.A., *Agricultural Outlook Charts, 1957*, Washington, D. C., Nov. 1956, p. 14.)

creased about 75 per cent between 1910–1914 and 1952–1956. We can see from Figure 63 that farm output in the United States during recent years has been high relative to the population. This has been true in spite of the fact that the rate of increase in population in the United States has increased greatly during the last decade.

The increase in production of farm commodities has been accomplished with a decrease in number of farm workers and an increase in the output per farm worker. In Figure 64, we see that the number of persons supported per farm worker in the United States has increased from about 7 in 1900 to approximately 21 in 1957. The large increase in productivity per farm worker reflects both input substitution and technological improvements in production. The development of newer techniques of production has made it possible for each worker to increase his productivity, and for a smaller number of people to produce the food and fiber needed.

Output of agricultural products per man-hour increased greatly between 1910 and 1957, as shown in Figure 65. Since 1940, the increase has been taking place at an even more rapid rate, doubling between 1940 and 1957.

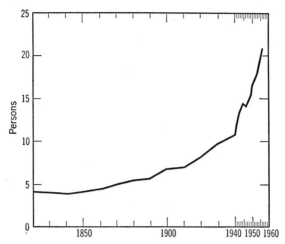

Figure 64. Persons supported by one farm worker. (*Source:* U.S.D.A., *Agricultural Outlook Charts, 1958,* Washington, D. C., Nov. 1957, p. 78.)

The increase in productivity per man-hour has been accomplished largely through mechanization of farm production. There has been a tremendous expansion in the number of tractors, combines, and numerous other machines in agricultural production. In fact, this increase in mechanization has been so large as to be almost unbelievable. Between 1945 and 1956, there was an increase of 89 per cent in the number of tractors, 167 per cent in the number of grain combines, and 317 per cent in the number of corn pickers. These ma-

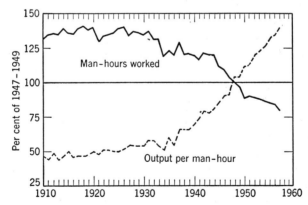

Figure 65. Inputs of labor and output per man-hour of labor in agriculture. (*Source:* U.S.D.A., *Agricultural Outlook Charts, 1958,* Washington, D. C., Nov. 1957, p. 70.)

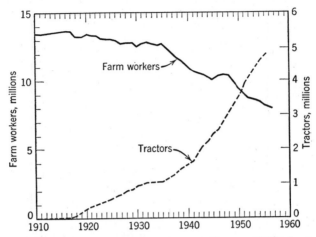

Figure 66. Farm workers and tractors on farms. (*Source:* U.S.D.A., *Agricultural Outlook Charts, 1957,* Washington, D. C., Nov. 1956.)

chines greatly decrease the labor required to produce given quantities of output and make it possible for fewer workers to produce food and fiber needed by the nation. It may be seen from Figure 66 that as the number of tractors on farms increased, the number of workers on farms decreased.

Perhaps the best way of indicating the effects of changes in technology on agricultural production is to hold the total quantity of inputs used in agricultural production constant over time and estimate the change in the quantity of product produced. Actually, the quantity of inputs used in agricultural production has increased substantially during the 20th century. This is in spite of the fact that the use of some inputs has greatly decreased. Professor Schultz has estimated that the total inputs used in agricultural production during the period 1910–1950 increased somewhere between 14 and 33 per cent, with the major increase being in use of land and capital, and that a decrease occurred in the quantity of labor used.[1] Farm output actually increased during this period about 75 per cent. Hence, had the total farm inputs remained constant, total farm output would have increased between 1910 and 1950 about one-third to one-half as a result of improvements in farm production technology and in farm management.

The rate of increase in production relative to the rate of increase

---

[1] T. W. Schultz, *The Economic Organization of Agriculture,* McGraw-Hill Book Company, New York, 1953, pp. 108–109.

in inputs has been much greater during the 1940's and 1950's than prior to World War II. During the 1940's, agriculture was relatively profitable and farmers were in a position to purchase the inputs needed to change technology. Technological improvements cannot be adopted unless producers can obtain capital to purchase the inputs. During the 1930's the low net revenue from farming and the shortage of capital for investment in agriculture impeded the adoption of many known technological improvements. During the 1940's, on the other hand, farm prices and profits from farm production rose relatively fast. This rise permitted farmers to obtain capital needed to adopt technological improvements. Also, rising prices and rising incomes provided them with an incentive to adopt technological improvements. This was particularly true because labor costs were rising relative to the costs of other inputs.

The contribution of technological improvement to agriculture has been emphasized by Professor Schultz.[1] He indicates that during the period 1930–1950 there was a 39 per cent increase in agricultural output in the United States with a 1 per cent increase in inputs. His study suggests that, at present, a 10 per cent increase in United States agricultural output can be obtained with no additional inputs. That is, by a recombination of the inputs currently used in agriculture, approximately a 10 per cent increase in output can be obtained through improvements in managerial and technological functions.

Most of the world is not so fortunate, however, and in some countries much of the additional output can be attributed to the use of additional inputs. In a good many of the so-called underdeveloped countries, such as in Latin America, about half of the additional output of agricultural products currently is accounted for by additional inputs. For example, in Brazil about 55 per cent of the additional output of agricultural products which occurred between 1925–1929 and 1945–1949 can be accounted for by the use of additional inputs. In Argentina, on the other hand, only about 22 per cent of the increase in output of agricultural commodities can be accounted for by additional inputs during the period 1920–1940.[2]

The major problem confronting many countries is to increase their production of food, fiber, and industrial goods. In many cases, it will be necessary to develop and adopt technological improvements in agriculture to increase levels of living. In this manner, these coun-

[1] T. W. Schultz, "Reflections on Agricultural Production, Output and Supply," *Journal of Farm Economics,* Vol. XXXVIII, Aug. 1956.

[2] Clarence A. Moore, "Agricultural Development in Mexico," *Journal of Farm Economics,* Vol. XXXVII, Feb. 1955.

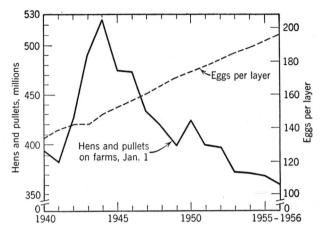

Figure 67. Chicken numbers and egg production. (*Source:* U.S.D.A., *The Poultry and Egg Situation,* Washington, D. C., Nov. 1957.)

tries will be able to increase food and fiber production and, at the same time, free inputs for use in production of nonagricultural commodities.

Technological Improvements Have Greatly Increased Productivity per Unit of Livestock and Poultry

Estimation of the extent to which technological improvement has increased the production of particular farm commodities is difficult because of changes in the proportions of inputs over time. However, a rough indication of the importance of technological improvement can be obtained by study of changes over time in the production per unit of farm products.

Egg production. Farmers now raise fewer layers and get more eggs than they did during the early 1940's. The rate of lay per layer in 1954 was 184 eggs compared with 160 in 1947.[1] Between 1947 and 1954, egg production per hen and pullet on farms, as of January 1, increased approximately 15 per cent. The progress made in increasing the number of eggs per layer is shown in Figure 67. The phenomenal increase in egg production per layer has been brought about by development of improved strains of layers and by better feeding, better management, and disease-control practices.

Broiler production. There has been a rapid expansion in broiler production in the United States since 1940. This expansion has been

[1] U.S.D.A., *Agricultural Outlook Charts, 1956,* Washington, D. C., Nov. 1955, p. 73.

brought about as a result of improvements in the production and marketing of broilers. One of the major improvements which permitted the large expansion in broiler production was an organizational change in the input markets, making it possible for farmers to obtain capital and know-how needed to produce broilers on a relatively large scale. Financial arrangements were worked out with feed dealers, processors, and hatcheries to supply farmers with the capital needed and to collect payment for the use of this capital when the broilers were sold. This change in the organization of the input markets made large quantities of capital available to farmers where it was limiting before.

Another improvement which greatly facilitated the production of broilers was in the breeding of meat-type birds. Still another improvement was in the kinds of feeds fed to broilers. Improvements in feeding and in management have greatly decreased the number of pounds of feed required to produce a pound of broiler meat. For example, in 1925 it took on the average about 3.5 pounds of feed to produce a pound of broiler meat. In contrast, many successful producers today obtain a pound of meat for less than 2.3 pounds of feed. Even more striking, the University of Maryland recently produced broilers on an experimental ration using 1.6 pounds of feed per pound of meat. Such improvements have greatly increased the supply of broilers produced on specialized farms. The proportion of broilers produced on

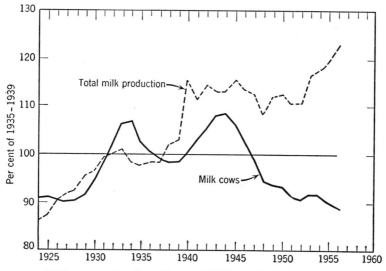

Figure 68. Milk cows and milk. (*Source:* U.S.D.A., *Agricultural Outlook Charts, 1955*, Washington, D. C., Oct. 1954; and *Agricultural Outlook Charts, 1957*, Washington, D. C., Nov. 1956.)

specialized farms in the United States increased from 24 per cent in 1947 to 60 per cent in 1955.[1]

Milk production. There have also been large improvements in milk production during the last two decades. From Figure 68, we see that milk production per cow has increased greatly since World War II. This increase in production has been brought about through improvements in feeding, breeding, and culling of cows. During the period 1946–1952, milk production remained fairly stable, while the number of cows kept for milk in the United States decreased approximately 8 per cent. The increase in productivity of milk cows also has been accomplished through such technological improvements as insect controls, improved rations, and artificial insemination, resulting in better and more productive livestock.

Gains from Technological Improvement in Agricultural Production are Divided Between Producers and Consumers

Consumers benefit from technological improvements in that they are provided with an abundant and stable food and fiber supply. Technological improvements also alter the relative prices of commodities and make products available to consumers which previously were not available or which could be had only at relatively high prices.

It is often assumed that technological improvements that enable farmers to produce a large volume of output with the same input will increase their net revenue. This is not necessarily the case. There are two sets of forces which must be considered in determining the effects of technological improvements on the incomes of farmers. Technological improvements decrease per-unit cost in the range of output in which producers adopting the improvement operate. As pointed out above, however, there usually is an incentive to increase output when a technological improvement is adopted. This increase in output causes downward pressure on prices. Therefore, whether the improvement in technology increases net revenue depends on the extent to which product prices decrease as production expands and on the extent to which per-unit costs are decreased by the technological improvement.

The demand for most agricultural commodities is inelastic. That is, the percentage increase in consumption is less than the percentage decrease in price. Under these conditions, an increase in output results in a decrease in total revenue from the sale of the product.

[1] U.S.D.A., *Agricultural Outlook Charts, 1956,* Washington, D. C., Nov. 1955, p. 72.

When demand is inelastic, the technological improvement must reduce total cost if net revenue is to increase. Furthermore, the decrease in total cost must be greater than the decrease in total revenue.

On the other hand, technological improvements adopted in the production of commodities for which the demand is elastic increase total revenue to farmers. Since the demand is elastic, the percentage decrease in price from the increased production is less than the percentage increase in production. Therefore, total revenue increases. If total cost decreases or remains constant as output increases, net revenue will increase. Even if total cost increases, net revenue will still increase as long as the increase in total cost is less than the increase in total revenue.

It should be emphasized that technological improvements may be adopted on individual farms even though aggregate net revenue from agriculture is decreased. In deciding whether to adopt a technological improvement, any individual farmer compares the expected cost of the improvement with the expected returns from adopting the improvement on his farm. He expects to lower his per-unit cost by adopting the improvement. He does not expect the increased production on his farm to be large enough to lower the price; that is, he views the demand for his product as being perfectly elastic. This provides an incentive to adopt the improvement and expand production.

But when many farmers increase their production, the price of the commodity falls. The reduction in price may be greater than the reduction in cost, thereby resulting in decreased net revenue. Even so, a farmer will still be better off to adopt the improvement as long as it reduces his per-unit cost. If he does not adopt the improvement, his price will be reduced anyhow as a result of increased production on other farms. By adopting the technological improvement and reducing his costs, his income is reduced less than if he continues to use old production methods.

Consumers gain from technological improvements insofar as these improvements lower prices of the products. The extent to which they gain, however, depends upon the elasticity of demand for the products and upon the amount of increase in output due to the technological improvements. For any given increase in output, the more inelastic the demand for a product, the greater will be the gain received by consumers. Likewise, for any given demand curve, the amount of the gain by consumers increases as the amount of the output resulting from the technological improvement increases. We know that the demand for most agricultural products is inelastic. Also we know that the growth in agricultural production resulting from adoption of technological improvements in agriculture has been very rapid. As a result, therefore, most of the gains from technological improvements have been passed on to consumers.

In summary, the possibility of receiving gains from the adoption of an improvement provides an incentive for its adoption. Most technological improvements increase output and reduce price. Producers who are first to adopt a technological improvement receive most of the benefits. After widespread adoption of a technological improvement in the production of a commodity for which the elasticity of demand is less than unity, there is a good chance that prices may decrease to such an extent that the last producers to adopt it will gain little by doing so.

We see that, when technological improvements are developed, an incentive of material gain is provided to adopt the improvement. In the mad scramble to get ahead, those who adopt first either gain from the improvement or lose if it proves to be unprofitable. As a result of falling prices for their products, those who adopt later gain little or nothing. However, they are forced to adopt the improvement, even though their net income may not be greater than it was before the improvement was first adopted by any producer. Since the improvement lowers per-unit costs, adoption would at least reduce the loss in net revenue which would result if they failed to adopt.

The effects of increased output on prices are often reduced by the fact that the demand is moving over time. Population and incomes are increasing, and we know that the demand for commodities is related to population and income. Incomes may actually rise, therefore, as a result of increases in demand when the adoption of a technological improvement otherwise would decrease income.

22 | Our population is changing

The rate at which an economy grows depends on the relative rates of growth of production and population. In a sense, economic progress is a race between two powers, the power to increase population and the power to increase production. Should the power of population exceed that of production, per capita production is lowered. Should production increase at a more rapid rate than population, we have economic progress.

Many writers have put forth ideas and theories concerning the eventual outcome of this race between population and production. One of the more pessimistic and famous of these writers was Sir Thomas Malthus, an English clergyman. In the latter part of the 18th century, Malthus predicted that, although food supply would continue to increase in the world, the faster growth of population would continually keep man's level of living at a subsistence level.

Our experience of today indicates that Malthus overlooked many things in his predictions. Malthus lived during a period of relatively slow technological change, and he based his conclusions on conditions as they existed in the 18th century. He was not able to foresee either the ability to control births or the large expenditures for research and the rapid changes in technology which characterize many nations in the 20th century. Even today, however, nearly 60 per cent of the world's population is living under conditions similar to those which

Malthus predicted for the world in general. In those countries of the world where present populations live at a near subsistence level, as well as in the more highly developed nations, a great deal of work is going on in an attempt to improve the levels of living of the people. Knowledge of the effects of population growth on economic progress is basic to this work.

Population and Economic Growth

Economic progress was defined in the last chapter as an increase in per capita production of goods. In discussing population and its effects, it must be recognized that people may be willing to give up some goods and services in order to have more children, and vice versa. Recognizing that having a larger family reduces per capita goods, many people still prefer the larger family. That is, people knowingly substitute children for goods up to a point. In general, however, those countries which have been successful in reducing the rate of growth of their population have more goods and services per capita.

Some controversy exists as to whether economic growth can be accomplished best under a growing or under a stationary population. Spengler[1] states that, "It is growth rather than nongrowth of population that is a major obstacle to man's economic betterment in all but a few countries." He feels that nations have learned how to maintain employment and increase productivity while maintaining a constant labor force. That is, Spengler maintains that, for most countries, the race between population and production will be won by population unless positive steps are taken to control the population.

On the other hand, it is apparent from observing the behavior of the American economy since World War II that economic growth has not been hurt by the rapidly increasing population. In fact, it may have been helped. It seems contradictory to note that a country like the United States can increase its level of living under conditions of rapidly growing population while, at the same time, many nations of the world are faced with a definite problem of overpopulation. Overpopulated countries with their continuing pressure of population on resources find that the population itself is one of their most serious obstacles to economic progress.

In looking for an explanation of this seemingly paradoxical situation, we should note that population influences both the demand for

[1] Joseph J. Spengler, "The Population Obstacle to Economic Betterment," *American Economic Review*, Vol. XLI, No. 2, May 1951, p. 347.

products and the supply of these same products. It is quite clear that as population increases, demand increases. That is, more products are desired for consumption at the same price. If population grows, but production does not, per capita consumption obviously decreases.

On the other hand, as population increases, more labor becomes available to produce additional goods and services. Whether this additional labor increases production more than it increases demand depends primarily upon the relationship that exists within the country between labor and other inputs. Our economic principles of Chapter 4 appear relevant here. The manner in which production increases as an input is added depends upon the proportions in which the various inputs are used. As more and more of any one input is added to a fixed amount of other inputs, the added return from using more of this input eventually declines. The United States economy is one in which the ratio of capital to labor is high, and additional labor has a relatively high productivity. That is, the marginal productivity of labor in the United States is high; in fact, it may actually be increasing as more labor is added. This same situation appears to exist for Canada, Australia, and New Zealand. After a period of time, population growth in these countries may cease, but present indications point to continued rapid growth. The inputs available are adequate to support a much larger population in all of these nations.

The Demographic Transition

Most demographers (students of population) believe that populations go through a more or less regular transition in moving to relatively high levels of living. Notestein[1], for example, has placed nations of the world into three categories according to their population growth characteristics. About 60 per cent of the world's population is found in the class which Notestein calls the nations of *high growth potential*. These are nations in which the people presently live at or near subsistence levels. Birth rates in these nations are extremely high, but, at the same time, death rates are very high because of poor hygienic conditions and lack of food. Life expectancy in these nations is short, and a large proportion of the population is young and, therefore, not in the income-generating class. As a result, per capita production increases slowly, food is scarce, and population in these nations is not growing at a very rapid rate. These nations are classed as having high growth potential because of the fact that,

[1] F. W. Notestein, "Population—The Long View," *Food for the World* (edited by T. W. Schultz), University of Chicago Press, Chicago, 1945, pp. 36–65.

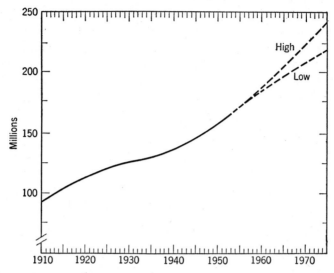

Figure 69. Growth of United States population, 1910–1950 and projected 1950–
1975. (*Source:* Rex F. Daly, "The Long-Run Demand for Farm Products,"
Agricultural Economics Research, Vol. VIII, No. 3, July 1, 1956, pp. 73–91.)

should they be able to bring their death rates under control, population would increase at a rapid rate, provided that the production of
goods and services increased. All but a small proportion of the nations which Notestein places in this group lie in the areas of southern
and eastern Asia.

The second group of nations in the Notestein classification includes
primarily those countries in southern and eastern Europe, Japan, and
some countries in South America. These countries are the nations of
rapid or *transitional growth* and comprise about 20 per cent of the
world's population. They have had some reduction in their death
rates, while birth rates have remained relatively high. As a consequence, population is increasing at a very rapid rate. These nations
possess sufficient natural resources and know-how to have been able
to keep production ahead of population growth during this transition.
Had they not been able to do so, the increased population growth
would have brought additional pressure on the food supply, and people would have starved. Thus, population growth would have been
limited by the food supply.

Another 20 per cent of the world's population is found in nations
where Notestein says population growth has abated to some degree.
These countries are classified as nations of *incipient decline*. The
power of producing food and fiber is so great in these countries that

this does not limit population growth. Rather, population growth has slowed as a result of planned reductions in birth rates. Population controls are brought about voluntarily as a result of people's knowledge of and desires for higher levels of living. Notestein includes such countries as the United States, Canada, countries of western Europe, Australia, and New Zealand in this group.

Experience of the last 15 years has shown that all nations which Notestein placed in this latter group, with the exception of western European countries, have recently experienced tremendous population growth. The United States, for example, appeared to be experiencing a leveling off in population during the 1930's, as shown in Figure 69. Many demographers had forecast a nearly stable population of about 140 million people for the United States by about 1960. It likely was on this basis that Notestein made his classification. This thinking has been radically revised because of recent experience, until present estimates call for over 200 million people by 1970. In fact, the 170-million mark was passed early in 1957. Few people, if any, are now forecasting a stationary population for the United States at any time in the near future.

Recent experience indicates that a new look at the whole idea of classing nations according to population growth may be necessary. The three broad classifications, although helpful in studying population growth and economic development, are too restricting to be universally correct. The factors affecting population growth are very complex. In general, of course, population growth is dependent upon both birth and death rates. Yet the factors determining these rates are not simple. Particularly, there appears to be no one acceptable

TABLE 51. Annual Birth and Death Rates
per 1000 Persons, 1950

Nation	Births	Deaths
United Kingdom	16.1	11.7
Italy	19.6	9.8
France	20.4	12.6
United States	23.4	9.6
Canada	26.6	9.0
Japan	28.4	11.0
Mexico	45.7	16.4

Source: W. S. Woytinsky and E. S. Woytinsky, *World Population and Production Trends and Outlook*, The Twentieth Century Fund, Inc., New York, 1953, pp. 140, 163.

explanation of the factors affecting the birth rate. Birth and death rates vary among nations as shown in Table 51. The differences between birth and death rates indicate the rate of population growth of a nation. The United Kingdom and France, for example, have a difference of less than 8 per 1000 between the birth and death rates. This is a growth rate of less than 1 per cent per year. The United States' growth rate is about 1.5 per cent per year, whereas, if we accept these figures, the Mexican population is growing at a rate of nearly 3 per cent each year.

Death rates in most countries have been greatly reduced in this century, largely because of a substantial reduction in infant deaths. Annual infant mortality rates for some representative countries are shown in Table 52. In all cases, the infant death rate is much lower

TABLE 52.   Annual Average Infant Mortality Rates,
1911–1919 and 1941–1949

| | Deaths Under 1 Year per 1000 Live Births | |
Nation	1911–1919	1941–1949
England and Wales	102	44
Italy	146	96
France	126	72
United States	97	37
Japan	165	76
Sweden	70	28

Source: W. S. Woytinsky and E. S. Woytinsky, *World Population and Production Trends and Outlook*, The Twentieth Century Fund, Inc., New York, 1953, p. 167.

than in the 1911–1919 period. Yet, Italy, France, and Japan apparently have a great opportunity to increase population growth by reducing infant deaths still further. In the United States and Sweden, on the other hand, infant deaths are quite low; decreases in death rates in these two countries are likely to come about primarily by reducing deaths in the older age groups.

In Figure 70, past growth of five nations is shown. A particularly interesting point is that British India (now Pakistan and India), Japan, and the United States are all now exhibiting nearly the same rate of growth; yet, all three nations are in different groupings in the Notestein classification—British India in the high growth potential class, Japan in the transitional growth class, and the United States among the nations of incipient decline. France and the United King-

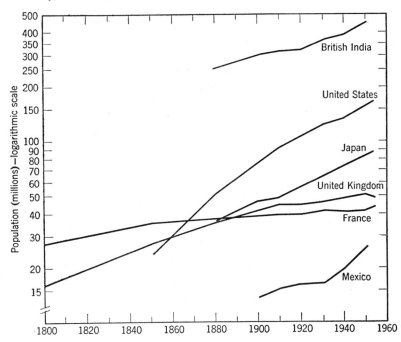

Figure 70. Population growth in six selected nations. (*Source:* Data to 1950 from W. S. Woytinsky and E. S. Woytinsky, *World Population and Production Trends and Outlook,* The Twentieth Century Fund, Inc., New York, 1953, p. 44. Data for 1954 from United Nations, *Demographic Yearbook,* 1955, pp. 118–124.)

dom, on the other hand, appear to have reached a plateau of population, or at least their population is only slowly rising.

Population Characteristics

Population growth of a nation does not proceed in a completely steady manner. We can expect waves or cycles of growth as population increases. When there is a rapid increase in the number of people in the child-bearing ages, a rapid increase in the number of births is ordinarily experienced. For this reason, another sharp upturn in the population of the United States may be expected in the 1960's, as the large number of children born during the war years and immediately afterward reach marriage and child-bearing age.

Figure 71 shows a breakdown by age and sex (population pyramid) of the United States population in 1955 and an estimate for 1975 based on a continued population increase like that of 1950–1953. Both the supply of and demand for products are affected differently by dif-

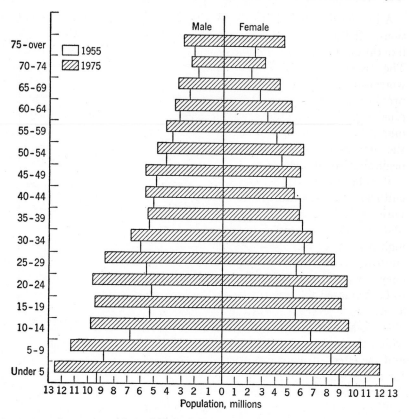

Figure 71. Age composition of United States population, 1955, and estimate for 1957. (*Source:* Bureau of the Census, "Current Population Reports, Population Estimates," p. 25, No. 123, Oct. 20, 1955, pp. 9, 10. Estimate for 1957 based on 1950–1953 population increase.)

ferent age groups. Therefore, a breakdown of future population by age groups is more useful than merely looking at total numbers of people if we are to gain insight into the economic effects of future populations. Two features of the 1975 population shown in Figure 71 are quite striking. They are the relative increases in the number of persons in the 60-year-old and over group and in the number of younger people, particularly those under 20. As more and more of our population comes into these very young and older age groups, a lower proportion of the total population is in the active labor force. This tends to have a dampening effect on per capita income; there are more people for whom goods need to be produced, but relatively fewer are actively engaged in production.

A population breakdown like that in Figure 71 permits other predictions. It takes little imagination to see what effect a 1975 population like that in Figure 71 will have on the demand for educational facilities. The crowded school conditions of the 1950's will be considerably worsened by 1975 unless steps are taken to train more teachers and provide more classroom space. Housing is another area in which a pinch may be felt as the large numbers in the 20–30 age group become married and set up new households. Still another observation is that the number of people entering the labor force will increase greatly, beginning about 1965.

Population growth affects the total demand for all products, agricultural and industrial. But the extent to which the demand for the various products is affected depends on the age composition of the population. For example, elderly people tend to eat smaller amounts of high-calorie foods. Therefore, though the total demand for agricultural products is increased by a larger population, there is a tendency for the demand for certain foods, such as vegetables and fruits, to be increased relative to the demands for cereal products and grains, as a larger proportion of the population is in the older age groups. The foods most in demand by elderly people are those same foods for which the income elasticity is relatively high. Both the income effect and the effect of older people's dietary preferences emphasize the need for a continuing shift toward relatively more agricultural inputs used in production of lean meat, fruits, and vegetables.

The outlook in the aggregate for the demand for agricultural products is not clear. Changes in nutritional knowledge cannot be predicted accurately, nor can we ever be certain as to the accuracy of population forecasts. Should the population continue to grow at its present pace or faster, however, the outlook from the demand side is bright for producers of agricultural products. A rapid population growth ensures a continuing growth in demand for food and fiber. In the next chapter, we shall see how certain population characteristics influence per capita incomes within various regions of the United States.

23

Economic progress alters the level and distribution of income

All nations are greatly concerned over poverty. Formation of United Nations organizations and the many programs developed since World War II by governments to export technology and to grant loans to nations in the development of their resources are evidence of the international concern over poverty. Intensive efforts are being made in all countries to develop resources and to increase resource productivity in an effort to raise levels of living.

Economic progress raises the level and alters the distribution of income by making it possible to increase the quantity of product produced in a nation. Changes in technology usually result in an increase in the productivity of labor. This increased productivity makes it possible to produce more food and fiber per worker and, consequently, to have more goods available for consumption per person.

The Concept of Poverty

From the standpoint of welfare of people, we are concerned with incomes as a measure of the amount of goods and services that can be purchased per capita or per family. Poverty is thought of in terms of goods and services consumed. Consumption of some minimum amount of goods and services is necessary for subsistence. Occasionally, some people are unable to obtain sufficient goods and services for subsistence, and death results from starvation or exposure. Famines, pestilence, and the aftermath of wars contribute to such occurrences. On the whole, however, few families in the United States control so little wealth as to be unable to obtain subsistence needs.

For the most part, poverty is thought of in relative rather than absolute terms. Whether a person is said to be poor depends upon the community in which he lives. The kinds and amounts of goods and services regarded as necessities and luxuries vary among nations and communities. A minimum level of living in some communities may consist of ownership of two cars, two television sets, and a house equipped with a bath for each household member. In another community, one car may be regarded as acceptable, a television set may not be thought necessary, and one bath per household may be acceptable. Therefore, a person who is considered poor in one community may be considered wealthy in another community.

Income is received as payment for use of inputs. Thus, income is related to the amount of property owned. Some people own too few resources to earn incomes high enough to support what is regarded as a minimum level of living in their community. The return which these people obtain from the use of their resources, even when they are employed in their most productive uses, does not provide them with sufficient income to sustain a level of living considered socially desirable.

The existence of poverty is a cause for concern in all nations. In order to combat poverty, individuals and charitable organizations frequently make donations to persons considered very poor. Likewise, governments concerned over the existence of poverty frequently make grants to individuals and families to improve their welfare. For example, payments are made to widows and orphans and to aged persons who own little wealth. Also, certain welfare payments are made to others in case of extreme poverty. In each case, society sets some minimum level of income and wealth considered necessary to meet basic subsistence needs, and those with less than this amount are provided with grants.

Measurement of Income

The measurement of income is a complex problem. Usually, we are inclined to view money income and wealth as an index of welfare. Not all people, however, are motivated to the same extent by money income. Some place a high value on things other than money. For example, some people prefer to farm and take a lower money income than can be obtained in nonfarm employment. Others prefer to work in nonfarm employment and to receive a lower money return than can be obtained from farm employment. These preferences of individuals cannot be ignored in income comparisons.

Payments to owners provide incentives for use of their resources. In comparing the alternative uses of their resources, the income values relevant to owners making decisions consist of estimates of the satisfaction to be derived from particular uses of their resources. These satisfactions, of course, must include such things as desire to be one's own boss, desire to live in a particular locality, desire to be near relatives, and a host of other nonmonetary considerations. These nonmonetary considerations in resource use vary from one person to another. Little information is available concerning the effects of nonmonetary returns on resource use. For lack of better information, therefore, we are forced to use money incomes in studying resource use, but we must keep in mind the limitations of doing so.

Incomes of Farm and Nonfarm Families

Several series of data are published containing information relative to the incomes of farm families. The United States Department of Agriculture publishes information on receipts from farm marketings and estimates of the value of farm products for home consumption. These data, however, do not contain estimates of the income received by farm families from nonfarm sources and do not make allowances for payments to nonfarm persons for use of their resources in agriculture. Many landlords do not farm but engage primarily in nonfarm occupations and live in urban residences. Payments for use of land, therefore, in many cases do not go to farm families. For example, persons not living on farms received about one-sixth of the net income from farming in 1954.

Farm families, on the other hand, receive a large proportion of their net income from nonagricultural sources. During the 1940's and 1950's, farm families received one-fifth or more of their net income from nonagricultural sources. During 1954, persons on farms received $5.7 billion from nonagricultural sources and $14 billion from farming. On a per capita basis, the net income to farm people was $860 with $276 received from nonagricultural sources and $584 received from farming. In comparison, the net income per capita of the nonfarm population was $1922.

The best information available on the number of families in various income groups is contained in the 1950 Census. The percentage distribution of farm-operator families and of nonfarm families by total money income in 1949 is shown in Table 53. We see that more fam-

TABLE 53. Distribution of Farm-Operator Families, and all Families by Total Money Income in 1949, United States

Item	Farm-Operator Families*	All Families
Total number of families, thousands	5,380	38,311
Number reporting income, thousands	4,856	36,440
Per cent distribution by total family income		
Total	100.0	100.0
Under $1,000	28.1	14.7
$ 1,000 to $1,999	24.8	14.6
$ 2,000 to $2,999	17.8	19.1
$ 3,000 to $3,999	11.8	19.4
$ 4,000 to $4,999	6.8	12.1
$ 5,000 to $5,999	3.5	7.8
$ 6,000 to $6,999	2.2	4.3
$ 7,000 to $9,999	2.8	4.9
$10,000 and over	2.2	3.1
Median income, dollars†	$1,867	$3,073

Source: 1950 Census of Population.
* Of which about 4 per cent were single-person families.
† Medians computed from $500 income intervals.

ilies have low incomes than high incomes; approximately one family in seven has an income of less than $1000. A higher proportion of these low income families live on farms. On the other hand, only 3 per cent of all families have incomes in excess of $10,000, and very few of these families live on farms.

In the comparison of incomes of families living under different conditions, we must keep in mind that the income data often are not comparable. For example, in the income distribution data given above, no allowance is made for the fact that farm families usually have greater nonmoney income than nonfarm families. Practically all farm families consume some of the products produced on their farms. In 1950, the average farm family consumed approximately $400 worth of home-produced products.

Also, we must give consideration to the amount of goods and services that a dollar of income will purchase in different regions. A given expenditure will purchase more farm products at the farm level than at the retail level. By the same token, the same amount of money will provide fewer nonfarm services at the farm level than in urban areas. It is difficult to know exactly how much more goods and services a dollar will purchase in a rural area than in an urban area. A study conducted by the United States Department of Agriculture in 1941 indicates that a dollar of income to the farm population had a purchasing power of about 25 per cent more than a dollar of income to a nonfarm family at that time.

Most estimates indicate that there are basic economic forces that tend to keep the incomes of nonfarm families relatively high. Several studies have concluded that the net income of persons on farms in the United States is approximately one-half that of persons not on farms. This situation of having nonfarm income greatly exceed farm incomes applies not only to the United States but is true of most countries throughout the world. In a recent book, Bellerby and others call attention to the fact that incomes of farm families in England, Canada, Australia, New Zealand, and in practically all the countries in the British Commonwealth are much less than incomes in nonagricultural occupations.[1]

As has been pointed out earlier, the income elasticity of demand for farm products is relatively low. Technological improvements in the production of agricultural products have been rapid, and the rate of increase in the supply of agricultural products has been greater than the rate of increase in the demand. Therefore, there is a tendency for income in nonagricultural sectors to rise relative to agricultural incomes as the result of a relatively faster expansion in demand for nonfarm products than for farm products. These conditions have enabled workers in most countries to transfer from farm to nonfarm occupations at relatively high rates. The fact that average farm incomes are low, however, should not be taken to mean that incomes of all farm families are low. By referring back to Table 53, we see that some farm families in the United States had net incomes in 1949 in excess of $10,000. Three per cent of the farms in the United States sold more than $25,000 of farm products in 1954; 12 per cent sold more than $10,000 of farm products. Since only some farmers have low incomes, we would like to know which ones have low incomes and what the causes are for the low incomes.

[1] J. R. Bellerby et al., *Agriculture and Industry Relative Income*, St. Martin's Press, New York, 1956.

The Geography of Low-Income Farm Families

Low-income families in agriculture tend to be concentrated in the southeastern part of the United States. In 1949, there were 51 areas in the United States where the median income of farm families was less than $1000.[1] Forty-seven of these areas were located in the southern states of Kentucky, Tennessee, Arkansas, Louisiana, Mississippi, Alabama, Georgia, Florida, North and South Carolina, Virginia, Oklahoma, and Texas. Two additional areas were located in southeastern Missouri, adjoining the Southeast. Hence, only two of the areas where farm families had median incomes of less than $1000 were located outside the South. Eighty-four economic areas had median farm family incomes of from $1000 to $1499, and 94 per cent of these areas were in the South or contiguous to it. Incomes of farm families in the Southeast were only about one-half as high as incomes of farm families in the Corn Belt.

The relation between incomes of farm and nonfarm families also varies among regions. A recent study indicates that in 1949 the incomes of farm families in the Corn Belt were approximately equal to those of nonfarm families in the United States.[2] Incomes of farm families in the Southeast, on the other hand, were only about one-half as high as the incomes of nonfarm families in the United States.

Causes of Low-Income Areas in Agriculture

Many programs have been developed to raise incomes of families in low-income areas. If we are to make progress in raising the incomes of low-income families, we need to know why their incomes are low. Some insight into causes of low incomes can be found by looking at combinations of resources used in various regions. First, there is a relatively large amount of labor in relation to the land in low-income areas. Second, the amount of capital invested on farms is low relative to the amount of labor in these areas. For example, the dollars invested per farm worker in the form of land, buildings, machinery, livestock, and operating expenses in the Southeast amount

[1] W. E. Hendrix and R. B. Glasgow, "Low-Income Areas in American Agriculture," *Farm Policy Forum,* Vol. 8, No. 4, 1956. The Iowa State College Press, Ames, Iowa, p. 9.

[2] C. E. Bishop, "Underemployment of Labor in Southeastern Agriculture," *Journal of Farm Economics,* Vol. XXXVI, May 1954.

to only about one-third the dollars invested per farm worker in the Corn Belt. We learned in previous chapters that the productivity of one input depends on the amount of other inputs combined with that input. We expect that, as the amounts of capital and land increase in combination with the labor input, the productivity of labor increases. When agricultural areas are classified by investment, earnings per worker tend to increase as investment increases.

Two other consequences of the high ratio of labor to land should be emphasized. In low-income areas, mechanization of production has not developed to the same extent as in high-income areas. Also, where there is a relatively large amount of labor in relation to cropland in an area, competition for land is intense, and the price of land is bid up relative to the price of land in other areas.

Many factors tend to perpetuate low-income areas. In such areas, families are inclined to be large, and the number of dependents per worker tends to be high. That is, the ratio of income-producers to nonproducers is low in low-income areas, and each dollar has to support more people. Therefore, there is less opportunity for accumulation of savings in low-income areas. This means that less money is available for increasing investment and providing for economic progress in agriculture.

Another factor which tends to perpetuate low-income areas is the fact that in such areas the tax base is low, and the quality and amount of public-supported services tend to be low. The number of physicians and dentists and the number of hospital beds are small in relation to the population in low-income areas. Educational facilities are inferior, and the amount of formal education of the people is low. There is a positive correlation between the amount of formal education and incomes of people in the United States. When education is low, incomes are low. It is difficult for people with little education to assimilate and analyze information relative to income-earning opportunities.

Adjustments of Farm Families to Raise Incomes

In view of the low incomes of farm families, we would expect to observe adjustments in resource use on farms over time. On the basis of the geographical differences in incomes of farm families, we might expect to find the farm population moving from one agricultural area to another if incomes would be increased. Actually, we observe little or no migration within agriculture from the low-income areas to high-income areas. For example, we find very little migration within agriculture from the Southeast to the Corn Belt.

Actually, farmers have responded quite sharply to differences in income opportunities. This response has taken three broad, general forms. First, there has been a substantial migration of farm people from farm to nonfarm work, especially from low-income areas. Second, there has been a rapid increase in part-time farming as industrial development has taken place in low-income areas. Third, there has been a change in the kinds of farm products produced and an increase in the efficiency of production of farm commodities. These changes have increased the productivity of farm labor.

The number of persons migrating from farms to nonfarm employment has been especially high during periods of expanding industrial employment. Since 1920, there has been a net migration from farm to nonfarm residences in each year except 1931 and 1932, and 1945 and 1946. In the latter two years, large numbers of personnel released from military service returned to farms. During the 1950's, the transfer of people from farm to nonfarm residences averaged about 1,200,000 persons per year.[1] Between April 1956 and April 1957 one person in nine moved from farm to nonfarm residences. Farmers have been converting themselves into nonfarmers at a much faster rate than nonfarm people have been converting themselves into farmers. Consequently, the farm population has declined sharply in the United States. Currently, farm population constitutes only about 12 per cent of the total population, contrasted with 23 per cent of the total population in 1940. Actual farm population declined from 30 million to approximately 20 million during this period.

Another adjustment that farm families have made in an effort to increase incomes is expansion in part-time farming. Industry has been attracted to low-income agricultural areas, providing an opportunity for farmers to combine farm and nonfarm employment. As was pointed out earlier in this chapter, farm families receive a high percentage of their incomes from nonfarm sources. Forty-five per cent of the farmers in the United States were employed in off-farm work at some time during 1954. Twenty-eight per cent worked in off-farm employment 100 days or more.

Farm families have also made numerous adjustments on their farms in an effort to raise their incomes. For example, the production of broilers and livestock in many low-income areas has increased the

[1] U.S.D.A., *Farm Population Migration to and from Farms, 1920–1954,* Washington, D. C., Dec. 1954.

productivity of labor in these areas. Also, there has been a rapid adoption of improved technology in the production of agricultural commodities. Machinery and equipment have been developed which reduce the amount of labor required in the production of many commodities. Improved varieties of farm products have been introduced, and new production practices have been developed which increase the product per unit of land and per unit of labor.

In spite of the adjustments that have been made in increasing the efficiency of production of farm commodities and in transferring labor out of agriculture, incomes in agriculture remain relatively low. It is likely that many more farm people will find it profitable to transfer to nonfarm employment, and that extensive changes in agricultural production will be necessary before average incomes of farm families will equal those of nonfarm families.

In summary, the rate of growth in demand for farm products is relatively low because of the low income elasticity of demand. Improvements in technology and reductions in cost have encouraged farmers to produce more commodities. That is, improvements have shifted the supply curve for agricultural commodities to the right at a fairly rapid rate. The low price elasticity of demand for farm commodities has resulted in relatively large decreases in price for small increases in supply. The relatively rapid rate of growth of supply has caused downward pressure on the prices of farm products. It has also placed small farms at a disadvantage in that the small farm frequently is not in position to adopt improvements in technology. Incomes of families on small farms likely will remain low. If the nonfarm sectors of the economy continue to expand at a rapid rate, part-time farming and nonfarm employment will continue to be profitable alternatives to families on small farms.

Index

Abshier, G. S., 88 n., 89
Agricultural Adjustment Act, 11
Agricultural ladder, 153
Agricultural production, 228
  variations in, 173 ff.
Ashton, Gordon, 106, 107, 107 n., 108
Atkinson, L. J., 64 n.
Average fixed cost, 73
Average product, 36
Average total cost, 75
Average variable cost, 75

Balance of trade, 200
Barter, 199
Baum, E. L., 84 n., 85, 86
Bellerby, J. R., 250, 250 n.
Birth rates, and economic growth, 241
  selected countries, 241
Bishop, C. E., 85 n., 251 n.
Bredo, William, 215
Budget, enterprise, 129
Budgeting, 129 ff.
  combination of enterprises, 133
  single enterprise, 129
Business, definition, 20

Capital, 8, 11
Catron, Damon V., 106, 107, 107 n., 108

Chamblee, D. S., 43, 56, 57
Chandler, W. B., 54 n.
Cobweb theorem, 169
Commercial farms, 17
Compensation, for unexhausted improvements, 161
Competitive products, 116
Complementary products, 118
Conservation of resources,147
Contant returns, 34
Consumer preference, 181
Contract farming, 150
Corporation, 18
  farms, 19
Cost, average fixed, 73
  average total, 75
  average variable, 75
  compounding, 144
  marginal, 75
Cost functions, fryer processing plants, 84
  grain drying and storage, 82
  harvesting cotton, 86
  hydrocooling peaches, 88
Cost of production, 68
Crop rotation, 119
Curtice, Harlow H., 17 n.
Cycles, price, 210

Daly, Rex F., 240
Davis, J. H., 15 n.
Death rates, and economic growth, 241
  selected countries, 241
Decision-making, framework for, 23
Decreasing returns to size, 81
Demand, changes in, 193
  consumer, 181 ff.
  for inputs, 51
  market, 188
Demand curve, 188
Demographic transition, 239
Depreciation, 146
  obsolescence, 146
  use, 146
Diminishing returns, 35
  law of, 35
Discounting, 142
Diversification, 125, 149
Donald, J. R., 85 n.

Economic problem, 23
Economic progress, 225 ff.
  definition, 225
Economy, free enterprise exchange, 5
Efficiency, 26
Elasticity of demand, arc, 189
  average, 189
  income, definition, 194
    for selected food products, 196
  price, definition, 188
    for selected food products, 193
    relation to total revenue, 190 ff.
Elasticity of supply, 164 ff.
  agricultural products, 170
  definition, 164
  short-run, 175
Employment, agricultural industries, 15
  nonagricultural industries, 15
Engel's law, 195
Enterprise budget, 129
Exports, 200
  major farm commodities, 207
  total agricultural, 206

Faris, J. E., 84 n., 85
Farm, assets, 16
  income, 14, 248 ff.
  numbers, 15
  owners, 154
  part-owners, 154

Farm, population, 14
  tenants, 155
  value of products sold, 17
  workers, 230
Farmer's Home Administration, 11
Farmer's share of consumer's dollar, 216
Federal Housing Authority, 11
Federal Land Bank, 11
Fellows, I. F., 63
Firm, definition, 6
Fixed cost, 70
Flexibility, 151
Food, expenditures for, 195
  per capita consumption of selected
    products, 197
Ford, J. E., 142 n.
Fox, K. A., 193, 196
Free enterprise exchange economy, 5
Functions of an economic system, 3 ff.

General Motors, 17
Goldberg, R. A., 15 n.
Glasgow, R. B., 251 n.

Hansen, P. L., 61 n.
Hatton, T. T., 88 n., 89
Heady, E. O., 64 n., 65, 67, 105, 106, 107,
  107 n., 108, 160 n.
Hendrix, W. E., 251 n.
Hildreth, R. J., 82 n.

Imports, 200
  major farm commodities, 207
  total agricultural, 206
Income, farmer's share of, 14
  low income areas, 251
    causes of, 251
  major industry groups, 17
  measurement of, 247
  of farm families, 248
  of nonfarm families, 249
Income changes, effects on consumption,
  185 ff.
Increasing returns, 34
  to size, 81
Index number, computation of, 218
Index, of prices paid, 219
  of prices received, 218
Indifference curve, 182
  properties of, 183

Individual proprietorship, 18
Industrial production
  variations in, 173
Industry, 7
Infant industry argument, 205
Inferior good, 185
Input combinations, constant rate of
    substitution, 94
  fixed proportions, 93
  varying rates of substitution, 95
Input substitution, in beef feeding, 101
    grain combinations, 101
    hay and grain, 105
  in cotton production, 109
  in dairy cow feeding, 103
  in hog feeding, 106
Inputs, 20 ff.
Insurance, 149
Interest, 8
International trade, 199 ff.
  gains from, 201 ff.
Irrational production, examples of, 41
Isocost line, 97
Isoproduct contour, 92

James, H. B., 86 n.
Jennings, R. D., 101 n., 102
Jensen, Einer, 59
Jensen, H. R., 119
Johnson, D. Gale, 176 n.
Johnson, P. R., 54 n.
Joint products, 115
Judge, G. G., 63

Kehrberg, E. W., 160 n.
Krantz, B. A., 54 n.

Labor force engaged in agriculture, for-
    estry, and fisheries, 13
Labor productivity, agriculture, 229
Leasing practices, 155 ff.
Least-cost production, 96
Linear programming, 137 n.
Liquidity, 152
Long run, 70
Long-run average cost curve, 81
Long-run marginal cost curve, 81

Malthus, Sir Thomas, 237
Marginal cost, 75

Marginal product, 36
Marginal rate of substitution, 94
  inputs, 94
  products, 114
McArthur, W. C., 103 n.
Migration, 253
Minimum cost production, 96
Monopoly, 11
Moore, C. A., 231 n.
Morrison, F. B., 58 n.

Nerlove, Marc, 170 n.
Net revenue, 24
  condition for maximum, 46, 78
Normal good, 185
Normal return, 166
Notestein, F. W., 239 n.

Olson, R. O., 105
Opportunity return, 69
Optimum output, of an industry, 166
Optimum product combination, 121 ff.
Outputs, 20 ff.

Parity prices, 217
  computation of, 218
  selected commodities, 220
  transitional, 220
Parity ratio, 219
Part-time farming, 253
Pierce, W. H., 142 n.
Plant, 6
Population, and economic growth, 238
  composition of, 243
    effects on consumption, 243
    effects on economic growth, 244
  demographic types, 239 ff.
  farms, 14
  growth in, 228, 240
  selected countries, 243
Poverty, 246
Price changes, and consumption, 186
  and inputs used, 98
  and production, 49
  income effect of, 185
  substitution effect of, 185
Prices, cycles in, 210
  long-term movements, 209
  nonfarm commodities, 210
  role of, 5 ff.
  variation for farm products, 173

Prices paid by farmers, index of, 219
Prices received by farmers, 210
  index of, 218
Price variation, and services, 216
  by grades, 214
  locational, 214
    milk, 215
  seasonal, 211
    hogs, 212
    eggs, 213
Production, definition, 29
  organization of, 6
Production function, broilers, 62
  corn, 53
  definition, 30
  eggs, 60
  fescue seed, 57
  hogs, 64
  linear, 32
  milk, 58
  regions of a, 39
  sudan grass, 55
Production possibilities function, 113
Profits, 8
Proprietorship, individual, 18

Rational action, 23
Rent, definition, 8
  fixed, 157
  share, 158
Resources, 20 ff.
Risk, 149
Rojko, A. S., 215

Schultz, T. W., 174 n., 230, 230 n., 231,
  231 n., 239 n.
Short run, 70
Slope, 34
Soil Bank, 11
Sorenson, J. W., Jr., 82 n.
Specialization, 125, 150
Spengler, J. J., 238 n.
Substitution, input, 93 ff.
  product, 114 ff.
Supplementary products, 120
Supply, 163
  aggregate farm product, 172 ff.
  changes in, 163, 168
  elasticity of, 164
  of individual farm products, 163 ff.
  total, 164

Supply curve, 80
Sutherland, J. G., 86 n., 131

Technological change, 42, 225 ff.
  and cost of production, 226
  and economic progress, 225
  effects on optimum input, 52
  gains from, 234 ff.
    broilers, 232
    eggs, 232
    milk, 234
  in U. S. agriculture, 227
Tenants, 155
Tenure, classes, 154
  land, 153
Total cost, 71
Total product, 36
Total revenue, 44
Toussaint, W. D., 88 n., 89
Tractors on farms, 230
Trade, balance, 200
  gains from, 201 ff.
  international, 199 ff.
Type-of-farming area, 126
  map of, 127

Uncertainty, 148
  price, 148
  yield, 148

Valuation, input, 145
Value of the average product, 45
Value of the marginal product, 45
Variable cost, 70
Variable proportions, 36
  law of, 36
Vertical integration, 151
Viner, J., 70 n.

Wages, 8
Walkup, H. G., 84 n., 85
Waugh, Fred V., 212, 213
Wiegmann, F. H., 217 n.
Williams, M. S., 142 n.
Woodhouse, W. W., 43, 56, 57
Woodworth, Roger, 106, 107, 107 n.,
  108
Woytinsky, E. S., 241, 242, 243
Woytinsky, W. S., 241, 242, 243